I0816934

LIGHTBULB MOMENTS *in* MARRIAGE

LIGHTBULB MOMENTS *in* MARRIAGE

12 BIBLICAL PERSPECTIVES FOR SUCCESSFUL AND SATISFIED COUPLES

EMERSON EGGERICHS PHD

W Publishing Group
An Imprint of Thomas Nelson

Lightbulb Moments in Marriage

Published by W Publishing, an imprint of Thomas Nelson, 501 Nelson Place, Nashville, TN 37214, USA.

Published in association with Punchline Agency.

Thomas Nelson titles may be purchased in bulk for educational, business, fundraising, or sales promotional use. For information, please email SpecialMarkets@ThomasNelson.com.

ISBN 978-1-4003-5219-7 (audiobook)
ISBN 978-1-4003-5218-0 (ePub)
ISBN 978-1-4003-5216-6 (HC)

HarperCollins Publishers, Macken House, 39/40 Mayor Street Upper, Dublin 1, D01 C9W8, Ireland (https://www.harpercollins.com)

Library of Congress Control Number: 2025942756

Art direction: Meg Schmidt
Cover Design: Meg Schmidt
Interior Design: Mallory Collins

Printed in the United States of America

25 26 27 28 29 LBC 5 4 3 2 1

Dedicated to my three children—Jonathan, David, and Joy—and to their spouses, Sarah, Krista, and Matt.

Every marriage has its highs and lows—seasons of blessing and seasons of testing, times of laughter and times of tears. My prayer is that each challenge you face will become a lightbulb moment of growth, drawing you nearer to each other and nearer to Christ. May these pages remind you again and again that God is faithful, His light is enough, and His wisdom shines through the twelve "Aha!" insights you'll discover here—not just as discoveries, but as reminders of what your heart most needs to remember.

Join "Mimi" and me on the journey.

"Poppi," 2026

CONTENTS

PART B: ENHANCING SKILL—OUR EFFECTIVE INTERACTIONS

PART C: CULTIVATING WISDOM—OUR INNER COMPETENCIES

INTRODUCTION

THE LIGHTBULB MOMENTS THAT CHANGE EVERYTHING

One lightbulb moment can change everything about your marriage.

Whether it's a moment of sudden clarity or a hard-won realization etched through experience, insight has the power to reshape everything we thought we knew. In this book, you're invited into that kind of awakening—not just once, but again and again.

You'll notice a natural journey unfolding as you go—upward, outward, inward.

First, we look upward—strengthening our faith by seeing our worth in Christ, responding to Him through how we treat our spouse, embracing the eternal significance of our marriage, and grounding our view of marriage in God's Word rather than Hollywood scripts.

Then, we turn outward—learning to handle the day-to-day challenges of marriage by seeking mutual understanding (not just communication), embracing our differences to discover creative alternatives, honoring each other's perspectives, and focusing on the 80 percent of goodwill rather than magnifying the 20 percent of frustrations.

Finally, we look inward—cultivating wisdom by recognizing our defensive tendencies, learning to motivate with love and respect (not control or fear), understanding the healing power of forgiveness when misunderstandings wound us, and owning our responses that enable spiritual strength and freedom.

Each lightbulb moment you encounter is meant to bring clarity and hope at exactly the point you need it most, whether in your view of God, your daily interactions, or your personal growth. Together, these sudden insights can change everything.

The Lightbulb Moments That Shape Our Lives

From adolescence to adulthood, we all experience defining moments of clarity—those sudden, eye-opening realizations that forever change how we see the world. These insights don't just shift our perspective; they redefine how we navigate life. They're the kind of truths that, once grasped, we can't unsee:

- My parents are human too.
- Failure isn't the end; it's the beginning of growth.
- Happiness isn't found—it's built from within.
- The people I surround myself with shape my future.
- Health is a daily choice, not a onetime fix.

Do you remember the moment one of these truths first hit you? These aha moments don't just inform our choices—they separate wisdom from folly and set the course for a life of fulfillment or a path of regret.

Proverbs: The Fields Preached a Sermon

Scripture gives us a striking example of an aha moment—one that didn't come from a lecture or a teacher but from a simple observation of life.

In Proverbs 24:30–34 (MSG), Solomon reflected on what he saw as he passed by a neglected field:

> One day I walked by the field of an old lazybones, and then passed the vineyard of a slob; they were overgrown with weeds, thick with thistles, all the fences broken down. I took a long look and pondered what I saw; the fields preached me a sermon, and I listened: "A nap here, a nap there, a day off here, a day off there, sit back, take it easy—do you know what comes next? Just this: You can look forward to a dirt-poor life, with poverty as your permanent houseguest!"

The fields preached a sermon: Neglect leads to ruin, but diligence leads to abundance. Solomon had an aha moment, one that revealed a truth many miss: Success isn't a mystery; it's the fruit of consistent effort.

NEGLECT LEADS TO RUIN, BUT DILIGENCE LEADS TO ABUNDANCE.

At this point, someone might say, "But Emerson, that's just common sense."

If common sense were truly as common as we assume, we wouldn't have to keep explaining things that should already be obvious. It turns out, common sense is neither as common nor as full of sense as we'd like to believe.

I've seen this same kind of wisdom unfold in my own life—not from a field but from a kennel. I remember as a boy, maybe nine or ten, a man named Mr. Ganson raised boxer dogs, which I loved. I'd visit his kennel, feeding and playing with the pups, and one day I asked if I could have one. He agreed, under the condition that I come regularly and help feed the dogs. I was thrilled and said yes immediately.

He handed me the pup. And I still remember that joyful moment. Indeed I do.

What I also remember, just as vividly, is how I showed up only once or twice after that. I failed to follow through on my commitment. I began avoiding riding my bike past his house because of the guilt and fear that flooded my young soul. I had made a promise, and I broke it.

To this day, I feel regret and even shame when I think about it. But something redemptive came from that memory. It became an internal teacher. As I grew older, I would find myself in moments of decision—moments when keeping a commitment was hard or inconvenient—and I would say to myself, *Don't do what you did with Mr. Ganson.*

That was my aha moment. Not one that came through a sermon or a parent's correction, but one that was etched into my heart by experience and illuminated by the conscience God placed in me. It was as though the fields of my own young choices preached a sermon, just like Solomon described in Proverbs 24.

We often talk about "lightbulb moments" as if they're random sparks of brilliance, and they can be. But more often, they come from something far deeper. They are born from real-life collisions between our conscience and values and our poor choices and missteps. For example, the first time we lie and can't sleep that night. The first time we quit something and feel the sting of knowing we could have pushed through. The first time we let someone down—and remember how we never want to feel that way again.

These moments don't just teach us—they shape us. They become a kind of internal compass, often more lasting than any lesson someone else could have given us.

The Breakthrough Moments: What to Expect in These Pages

Marriage, like life, has its lightbulb moments—when, after struggling for so long, we suddenly realize something fundamental that changes everything.

In this book, just as Solomon walked by an open field and gained wisdom, we will walk by the homes of the married—those who are thriving and those who are struggling. We will look, we will ponder, and we will listen. As we do, we will hear sermons preached not from pulpits but from real-life marriages.

This book is a journey into moments of marital discovery—those sudden flashes of insight, the breakthroughs that change everything. Like a light turning on in a dark room, these aha moments illuminate truths that can profoundly change our marriages in three key areas:

1. **Faith.** We uncover the foundational beliefs that anchor and strengthen our marriage in God's truth, love, and glory. We learn to see our value as God-given, not spouse-driven, and we realign our perspective with the timeless wisdom of God's Word rather than fleeting cultural misconceptions.
2. **Skills.** Our eyes are opened to practical tools that empower us to interact successfully with our spouse, helping us navigate differences with understanding and strengthening our friendship. We shift our focus to what's working, embrace each other's unique approaches, and discover the joy of collaboration over the exhaustion of conflict.
3. **Wisdom.** We awaken to the power of self-awareness and authenticity in increasing trust and respect, both emotionally and sexually. We grasp the why and how of forgiveness, and we take ownership of our responses, realizing that true empowerment comes not from controlling our spouse but from aligning ourselves with God's design for marriage.

Each breakthrough in these areas has the potential to reshape the way we see and do marriage. One day, we didn't see it. The next day, we did. These eureka moments deepen our faith, enhance our skills, and cultivate wisdom that leads us toward a healthier, more God-centered relationship. Because of the twelve biblical lights "flipped on" in each chapter, we will be strengthened and successful as a couple.

At the same time, each part and chapter invites you to see what you might have missed. Just as the revelations of youth awakened you to truths about life, let this book spark fresh realizations in your marriage—causing you to exclaim, "I had no idea what I was missing! Now that I see it, I can't unsee it—and I'll never be the same again."

The Problem We Never Expected

Some couples reach a point where they feel they are in the dark about their marriage. Confusion sets in, and the relationship they once envisioned as joyful and fulfilling seems to have shifted into a fog of misunderstanding and disconnection. Never, when first meeting, dating, and marrying, did they anticipate this bewilderment.

Here's how real couples describe this stage:

- Speaking different languages: "We thought we had a strong marriage, but it felt like we were suddenly speaking different languages. The confusion scared me."
- Living like roommates: "I realized we were living like roommates, not partners. It wasn't what I imagined, and I didn't know how to fix it."
- Something isn't right: "What went wrong? I used to believe love was enough, but after all the arguments, I felt lost, wondering if we made a mistake in marrying each other."

These moments of darkness can leave couples questioning their relationship. They may sense a growing gap but not understand why. At first, the instinct is often to blame the other person. Over time, though, many begin to wonder, Are we missing something? Could it be that we don't know what we don't know?

This is where *lightbulb moments* come in. These profound realizations—what some call "aha" or "eureka" moments—can illuminate the path forward. They reveal what was previously unseen and provide clarity to navigate the challenges of marriage.

They are breakthroughs.

This book is a collection of such moments—twelve pivotal insights grounded in Scripture and designed to deepen your faith, improve your interactions, and strengthen your inner competencies. Through real-life stories and practical applications, you'll see how small but significant changes can bring satisfaction to your marriage. You won't be problem-free, but you will have the knowledge and skill to resolve the tension.

Examples of Lightbulb Moments

- Living marriage backward: "I realized that my attempts to gain respect often came across as unloving, while my spouse's desire for love often felt disrespectful to me."
- Misunderstanding good intentions: "I thought I was being helpful with suggestions, but my spouse saw it as criticism. We learned to recognize and appreciate each other's intentions."
- Inviting God into the center of marriage: "When we sought God's guidance together, everything started to change. We realized we had been trying to fix things on our own strength."

A Guide to Lasting Change

This book is not a quick fix but rather a guide to understanding oneself, each other, and God's purpose and plan. By focusing on *core beliefs* (faith), *successful interactions* (skills), and *inner competencies* (wisdom), it offers the tools to build a stronger, more godly marriage. As you turn the pages, you'll see what you may not have seen before and gain confidence in doing marriage God's way.

SMALL BUT SIGNIFICANT CHANGES CAN BRING SATISFACTION TO YOUR MARRIAGE.

Let this be the beginning of a new chapter—a brighter, more hopeful chapter for your marriage.

Good intentions can get you only so far, because no matter how well-meaning you are, it's the know-how that makes the real difference—and what you don't know can't be fixed by just meaning well.

PART A

DEEPENING FAITH—OUR CORE BELIEFS

As you reflect on the main headings in part A, I invite you to pray in the spirit of the individuals whose stories follow—people who sought the Lord about their worth, longed to see Jesus more clearly, hoped to hear "Well done," and desired to walk in God's revelation for marriage. While their words are summarized and shaped for clarity, their journeys are real, their prayers sincere.

1. Our Value: God-Given, Not Spouse-Driven
   Identity awakening: They were a couple caught in the cycle so many find themselves in—looking to each other for value and affirmation. The breakthrough came when one of them, in a moment of deep spiritual clarity, stopped depending on their spouse for identity. "I had always looked to my spouse to feel valued," they admitted. "But when I prayed and asked God to show me how He truly sees me, it was like a lightbulb went off. I realized my worth is secure in Him." That revelation changed everything. The peace and inner strength that followed freed them from the pressure to extract constant validation from the other. Ironically—and beautifully—their

marriage improved. They still needed and cherished each other's affirmation, but now it flowed from grace, not desperation.

2. Our Intent: Seeing Jesus Beyond the Shoulder of Our Spouse
   Sacred shift: Another couple experienced a profound shift not through a change in their circumstances but through a change in spiritual perspective. One of them shared, "It wasn't until I asked God to help me see Jesus standing beyond my spouse's shoulder that a new energy and wisdom came to me." That vision reframed everything. No longer dependent on their spouse's consistency, they found fresh hope and motivation in doing marriage God's way—even when their spouse struggled. "Everything I did mattered to Jesus, who was very much present." For the first time, they connected Christ directly with their marriage—and that realization transformed their heart. It was, without question, a game changer.
3. Our Eternity: Living with "Well Done!" in Mind
   Forever spark: Another couple's transformation came when one of them began to view marriage through the lens of eternity. "When I prayed for guidance on how to approach my marriage with an eternal perspective," they recalled, "God opened my eyes to the bigger picture." No longer fixated on immediate responses or recognition from their spouse, they were captured by the vision of standing before Christ. Suddenly, every act of love—unnoticed or unreciprocated—mattered deeply to God. "Nothing I did in the marriage toward and for Christ was wasted." That thought brought new energy and purpose. They lived for the day they would hear, "Well done . . . you did marriage My way, even when your spouse did not fully value your efforts. I will put you in charge of many things. Enter the joy of your Master!" It was the eternal reward that gave their marriage new meaning.
4. Our Worldview: The Holy Word, Not Hollywood
   Reality reset: Another couple entered marriage shaped by culture's expectations—chasing the Hollywood ideal of endless romance and picture-perfect moments. But one of them reached a turning point.

"I used to believe what the world told me marriage should be," they said, "but after seeking God's guidance, He illuminated the truth in His Word." That clarity changed everything. The biblical vision for marriage revealed something far deeper and more enduring than media portrayals ever could. "Sure, Hollywood portrays the romance," they admitted, "but God's Word shows us how to be close, understanding, at peace, honoring, intimate, friendly, and—most importantly—vessels for His kingdom." That realization gave them the direction they had long been searching for, grounding their marriage in eternal purpose.

ONE

OUR VALUE: GOD-GIVEN, NOT SPOUSE-DRIVEN

Identity awakening: Your worth doesn't rise or fall with your spouse's moods, opinions, or actions—God gave you value because of Jesus. That settles it.

Marriage, at its best, can be a place of affirmation, joy, and purpose. But when it breaks down, it can cut deeper than almost any other wound. I have walked with husbands who feel belittled and insignificant in their own homes, and wives who feel dismissed or invisible.

The ache of rejection. The silence of disconnection. The sting of contempt. These are not small struggles. They can leave people gasping for air, desperate for some assurance that they matter.

As a pastor, I have carried these stories with me. And when one of those stories ended in the unthinkable—a spouse taking their own life—I found myself undone. I wept, and I cried out to the Lord:

Lord, this cannot be what You intended for marriage. Help me speak to the pain so many are carrying. Help me help them see You and Your love and purpose for them in this place of heartbreak, despair, and despondency.

That cry has shaped this chapter—and this entire message. Because I believe God wants to meet every hurting spouse right where they are. He does not shame our pain. He does not minimize it. He does not say, "Just get over it."

But He also does not want our sense of value to rise and fall with how we are treated in marriage. That path leads only to despair.

Here is the sobering truth we must face: When our sense of worth becomes dependent on another person's treatment of us, we are profoundly vulnerable.

There is a better way. A way of dignity, identity, and hope—not because of what a spouse does or does not give, but because of who we already are in Christ.

Each of us must come to a point where we recognize that no human being can define our worth—not our spouse, not our parents, not our friends, not our coworkers.

Our worth must be rooted in Christ.

This isn't just an abstract theological concept—it is a lifesaving truth that redefines how we navigate life and marriage. If we rely on another person to determine our value, we will constantly be at their mercy. But if we root our identity in Jesus, no person, no rejection, and no failure can shake our sense of worth.

I know this firsthand, though on a lighter scale, but it was my aha moment.

My Lightbulb Moment: Meeting Evan Welsh

My confidence was shaken when I entered Wheaton College as a freshman in 1969. I had thrived in military school, where I felt like a big fish in a small pond. But at Wheaton, I suddenly found myself surrounded by incredibly talented students—a radio host, a concert pianist who had played at Carnegie Hall, a high school all-American who looked like Atlas, the mythological and muscular figure carrying the heavens on his shoulders.

I felt small. *Who am I? Do I matter to God?*

During this time, I met Dr. Evan Welsh, the campus chaplain. Years earlier, he had suffered a devastating tragedy, losing both his wife and daughter in a car accident. And yet he radiated love and empathy in a way I had never experienced before.

At a freshman retreat, I playfully teased him in front of others: "Dr. Welsh, you are better than me in everything. You do more push-ups. You are smarter, better looking, and more loving."

Immediately, tears filled his eyes. He grabbed my shoulders, looked at me with compassion, and said, "Don't you ever say I love people more than you do. You will love people far more than I will ever love them."

I was stunned. His words felt like a holy rebuke—frightening yet filled with warmth and calling. Overwhelmed, I walked away on the verge of tears. Something good exploded in me, but I was uncertain exactly what went off.

After that retreat, I continued meeting with Dr. Welsh. What I experienced in those moments with him was something new—something sacred. His love for me as a person was not surface-level encouragement; it was deep, consistent, and holy. He saw me. He cared for me. He carried a compassion that reached past my insecurities and touched something eternal in me. Never before had I encountered anything like this.

During this period of time, as I wrestled with God's view of me, early one morning as I lay in bed convinced that my many shortcomings as a new believer made me unworthy of His love, He brought Evan Welsh to mind. It was as if He gently asked, *If Evan Welsh, a mere man, could love you that much, would I—your Creator and Redeemer—love you any less?*

The answer was undeniable: Of course not.

Of course You love me more than Evan Welsh loves me. You are God. Evan is a mere man. You love me far more, light-years more, infinitely more!

To this day, every time I recall this story, tears come to my eyes. It was indeed a life-changing moment for me.

My Second Lightbulb Moment: Forgiveness I Couldn't Comprehend

Again, early in my journey with Christ, I eagerly attended a collegiate New Testament class. One day, my professor acted out a conversation to illustrate Christ's forgiveness.

Bowing his head, he said, "Lord, I've sinned again. Please forgive me—again."

Then, portraying Jesus, he smiled and replied, "Again? Forgive you again? I don't remember the last time."

I froze. A lump formed in my throat.

Could it truly be that God not only forgives but also forgets?

Though omniscient, He chooses not to remember our sins. This is not divine dementia but divine mercy. There is no ledger of wrongdoing—no record kept in the archives of heaven. He deliberately and permanently erases iniquity. His forgiveness is not partial or temporary; it is final, complete, and absolute—forever.

The sins I kept begging forgiveness for were gone, separated from me as far as the east is from the west (Psalm 103:12).

This truth changed everything. No longer did I see myself as a sinner groveling for mercy. I was a child of God, fully forgiven and eternally loved.

How This Truth Transformed My Marriage

When Sarah and I married in 1973, I entered marriage with good intentions but faulty assumptions—one of the most prominent being that my value as a husband could quickly depend on Sarah's perception of me. I didn't realize it then, but my sense of worth was subtly tied to her approval, encouragement, and opinion of me as a husband and a man.

At first, this didn't seem like a problem. We were in love, and in the early years, there were plenty of moments when I felt appreciated and valued. But over time, as challenges surfaced—as they do in every marriage—I started to notice something. Whenever Sarah critiqued me, even in small ways, it didn't just sting. It unsettled me.

Once a month, we had what I called "The Talk." Sarah would say, "We need to talk."

- If she pointed out that I had handled a situation poorly *again*, I questioned my competence.
- If she was frustrated with something I did or didn't do *again*, I

wondered whether I was fooling myself—maybe I was far more of a failure than I had imagined.

- If she was upset *again*, I took it as a reflection of my inadequacy—not just as a husband but as a person.

Sarah's opinion of me mattered. In fact, it had a level of power over my sense of self-worth that I hadn't fully recognized.

One day, after a disagreement, I found myself asking, *Does this define me? Am I only as valuable as Sarah's opinion of me?*

It was a moment of deep realization. If I wasn't careful, I was going to ride a never-ending emotional roller coaster, feeling "good enough" when she praised me and completely deflated when she didn't. Sarah was never meant to sit in God's seat—and she didn't want to. My worth had to come from Him, not her.

The Struggle Between Teachability and Identity

As Sarah and I had those monthly talks, where she could share her concerns openly, I knew I needed to be teachable in our marriage, so I genuinely sought to listen to her, to take in what she was saying, and to reflect on my shortcomings.

I didn't want to be defensive. I didn't want to blame her. And I didn't want to justify myself.

But these talks weren't always easy.

MY WORTH HAD TO COME FROM HIM, NOT HER.

Sarah would express her frustrations strongly, sometimes using words like "You always" and "You never." These kinds of sweeping statements made me wonder, *Am I completely self-deceived?*

When you love someone deeply and they voice strong concerns about you, it's natural to question yourself. Was I as flawed as she was saying? Was I completely unaware of my own faults?

I wanted to remain teachable, but I also had to remember God's view of me. If I wasn't careful, I would let Sarah's words override God's truth about me.

This was a delicate balance—to listen well, to grow, to change where needed but not to let her perception of me become my identity.

As I stated earlier, over the decades of pastoral ministry, I have known several spouses who have taken their own lives on the heels of feeling rejected, unloved, and disrespected. Though few of us are suicidal, many can testify to moments of significant discouragement over feeling unseen or unappreciated, or as though their best efforts in marriage are never enough.

They may not act on those dark thoughts, but the weight of rejection and discouragement can settle deep into their hearts, leading to emotional withdrawal, bitterness, and even despair. Some have given up on marriage and pursue adulterous relationships with the hope that they will find their true worth in a soulmate. Others medicate.

I have seen husbands who have silently carried years of feeling unwanted or inadequate, and wives who have lived under a constant cloud of feeling unworthy or unseen. And while these emotions alone don't always lead to tragedy, they can erode the soul of a person and a marriage if left unchecked.

This is why what we believe about our worth is so crucial. Suppose we let our spouse's words, moods, or treatment define our identity. In that case, we risk placing our self-worth in the hands of another, making us vulnerable to insecurities, resentment, or temptation. We allow our worth to be spouse-driven.

IF WE DO NOT ROOT OUR WORTH IN CHRIST, WE WILL SUBCONSCIOUSLY DEMAND THAT OUR SPOUSE PROVIDE WHAT ONLY GOD CAN GIVE.

This isn't about ignoring our spouse's concerns. It's about being teachable without being tossed about by every criticism. It's about receiving feedback with humility and discernment. This is an exchange to refine us, not redefine us. We need to be led but not misled by the critique.

If we do not root our worth in Christ, we will subconsciously demand that our spouse provide what only God can give—and that expectation will eventually break both of us.

The only way to love and respect freely,

listen humbly, and stand confidently in marriage is to find our ultimate identity in the One who never wavers, never rejects, never stops loving us perfectly, and never threatens to remove our future glory with Him.

The Lightbulb Moment: Who Defines Me?

At some point, every spouse must face a pivotal question: Who gets to define my worth?

- **My spouse?** If so, I will be at the mercy of their emotions, words, and even their own struggles.
- **Me?** If so, my worth will be based on my ever-changing feelings and performance.
- **God?** If so, I can rest in a truth that never changes, diminishes, or fails.

I realized, and so must you, that my worth isn't based on Sarah's words, positive or negative.

Even when Sarah was encouraging and affirming, I couldn't let her praise become the foundation of my identity. Being an affirmation junkie is not healthy. And when she was frustrated or disappointed, I couldn't let that become my identity either.

I had to return to what I already knew from Scripture but had not fully applied to my marriage: God had already spoken the ultimate word about me. My value must be God-given, not Sarah-driven.

I was loved, redeemed, chosen, and complete in Christ. Sarah's feedback—whether good or bad—could refine me, but it could never define me.

Testimonies: Learning to Root Our Worth in Christ

Over the years, I have heard from countless husbands and wives who wrestle with the same battle of seeking validation in their spouse rather than in Christ.

Wives' stories:

- "I blamed my husband for my unhappiness, but I had been trying to make him my savior."
- "I had a deep bitterness after my husband's affair. I felt he owed me my worth back."
- "I kept seeking my husband's validation to heal my heart, but only God could fill that space."

Husbands' stories:

- "When my wife criticized me, I withdrew—because I felt like I wasn't enough."
- "I worked long hours to provide, but she didn't appreciate it. I felt unvalued."
- "After my wife's affair, I felt humiliated and inadequate. I wanted her to prove I was still worth choosing—but comparing myself to the other man was eating me alive."

The Consequences of Basing Our Worth on Another Person

When our sense of worth is based on another person, we are always left vulnerable.

- We are insecure—always needing approval.
  - "I found myself constantly checking my husband's mood to see if I was 'good enough' that day. If he was happy, I felt worthy. If he was distant, I felt like a failure. My self-worth was entirely tied to his approval, and it exhausted me."
- We are reactive—easily wounded by words.
  - "When my wife critiqued me, even gently, I took it as a personal attack. If she said I forgot something, I heard, 'You're

irresponsible.' If she was frustrated, I felt like I was failing as a husband. I was on edge all the time, afraid of disappointing her."

- We are controlled—letting another person's attitude determine our emotional state.
  - "I could feel great about myself in the morning, but if my husband came home grumpy and grouchy, my confidence would disappear. His attitude dictated how I felt about myself."

The Freedom of Anchoring Our Worth in Christ

But when we anchor our worth in Christ, everything changes.

- We are secure—resting in His love.
  - "When I finally realized that I was fully loved by God—regardless of my spouse's opinions—I stopped striving for constant affirmation. I could show love freely, without needing it in return to feel whole."
- We are stable—not tossed by emotions.
  - "My wife still gets frustrated with me sometimes, but now I don't crumble when she does. I listen, I process, I adjust—but I don't spiral into self-doubt, because my foundation is in Christ, not her criticism."
- We are free—able to love without fear.
  - "For years, I withheld love from my husband when I felt unappreciated. Now, I love him from the overflow of God's love for me. I don't wait for him to 'deserve' it—I love because I am already fully loved by Christ."

BASING OUR WORTH IN OUR SPOUSE	BASING OUR WORTH IN CHRIST
We are insecure.	We are secure.
We are reactive.	We are stable.
We are controlled.	We are free.

The Centrality of Scripture in Our Worth

This is not just an idea; it is God's truth.

Many people hear the message that our worth comes from Christ alone, but they struggle to believe it in the deepest places of their heart. Why? Because feelings of unworthiness are deeply ingrained, often from years of hearing messages—spoken or unspoken—that tell us we must prove our value.

But our feelings do not define us. Our spouse's opinions do not define us. Our mistakes do not define us.

ONLY GOD'S WORD HAS THE FINAL SAY ABOUT WHO WE ARE.

Only God's Word has the final say about who we are.

If we do not anchor ourselves in God's revelation (what He has revealed as truth), we will drift back into seeking worth in our spouse, our performance, or our emotions. That's why we must know what God says—because His truth never changes.

What Scripture Declares About Your Worth

Each of the following verses reveals a life-changing reality about our identity in Christ. Let's take a closer look.

You Are Not Condemned—You Are Set Free

"Therefore, there is now no condemnation for those who are in Christ Jesus" (Romans 8:1).

Many of us live as though we are on trial every day, waiting for our spouse's verdict on our worth. If they approve of us, we feel good. If they criticize us, we feel condemned.

But God has already ruled on this case, and His ruling is final.

- If you are in Christ, you are not condemned.
- Your spouse's disappointment does not place you under divine judgment.

Jesus took your condemnation on Himself. You are free to live in the security of His love—without fear, without shame, without constant self-doubt.

Remember my aha moment in Bible class?

"Lord, I've sinned again. Please forgive me—again."

"Again? Forgive you again? I don't remember the last time."

You Are Holy, Blameless, and Free from Accusation

"But now he has reconciled you . . . to present you holy in his sight, without blemish and free from accusation" (Colossians 1:22).

Let that sink in: holy, without blemish, free from accusation.

This is how God sees you.

The Enemy wants you to believe the opposite:

- That you are flawed beyond repair
- That you are permanently guilty
- That you must earn your worth every day

But God has already made His declaration. Because of Christ, you are fully reconciled, fully clean, fully accepted.

So when your spouse sees your flaws, you don't have to crumble. You can admit your mistakes, but you don't have to wear them as your identity.

God says you are blameless in His sight—not because on earth you are perfect but because Jesus has covered you with and imputed to you His righteousness. This is how God sees you! Each of us must believe what feels so unbelievable!

You Are Fully Loved—Not Just Tolerated

"See what great love the Father has lavished on us, that we should be called children of God!" (1 John 3:1).

God does not begrudgingly accept you. He is not disappointed that you belong to Him.

He has lavished His love on you.

The word *lavish* means "overflowing, abundant, extravagant."

God's love for you is not a bare-minimum requirement—it is overflowing beyond measure.

And this love does *not* change based on

- how well you perform,
- how much your spouse appreciates you, or
- whether you "feel" valuable on any given day.

You are His child. He chose you. And He is never letting you go.

The Choice: Will You Believe It?

These verses aren't just nice words. They are the foundation for how we must live.

But here's the reality: Just because something is true doesn't mean we live like it's true.

- We can read Romans 8:1 and still live as if we are condemned.
- We can memorize Colossians 1:22 and still act like we are defined by our failures.
- We can quote 1 John 3:1 and still feel desperate for human validation.

The question is, will we believe God's truth more than we believe our feelings? If we do, it will change everything.

- We will stop being controlled by our spouse's moods, words, or disappointments.
- We will stop demanding validation from them that only God can give.
- We will start loving them freely—without fear, without resentment, without conditions.

This is the lightbulb moment that changes everything. We can no longer unsee it!

So next time we are in the car en route to some social gathering and our spouse confronts us about something we failed to do or who we failed to be, we won't enjoy the sting of feeling critiqued, but we will receive it with humility, knowing our worth isn't on the line. Instead of reacting defensively or crumbling in shame, we will listen, reflect, and respond in love and with respect—secure in who we are in Christ.

WILL WE BELIEVE GOD'S TRUTH MORE THAN WE BELIEVE OUR FEELINGS?

The only way to have a secure, unshakable identity is to stand on what God has already declared:

You are not condemned.

You are blameless in His sight.

You are fully loved and accepted.

Will you take Him at His word? When you do, I predict you will feel that you are succeeding at marriage as God intended, and you will feel satisfied.

TWO

OUR INTENT: SEEING JESUS BEYOND THE SHOULDER OF OUR SPOUSE

Sacred shift: How you treat your spouse moves the heart of Christ. He invites you to look beyond them to Him—loving and reverencing Him in a way that naturally overflows onto your spouse.

A husband sat across from me, his shoulders slumped, voice filled with quiet exhaustion.

"For years I struggled with frustration in my marriage. I kept thinking, *Why should I keep trying when my wife doesn't respond the way I want?* I felt unappreciated and discouraged, and honestly, I started pulling back."

I've heard variations of his story so many times—spouses who seek to love and respect yet feel disconnected, unseen, unappreciated, and stuck in an endless cycle of unmet expectations.

Then his voice changed.

"At your Love and Respect Conference, I heard something that stopped me in my tracks: 'Marriage is a tool and a test to deepen and demonstrate my love and reverence for Christ.' That thought hit me like a ton of bricks. I had been looking at my wife, measuring her responses, when all along, my love for her was supposed to be an act of love for Christ."

What he said next was his lightbulb moment.

"I started picturing Jesus standing beyond her shoulder, as you said, watching how I treated her—not to condemn me but to call me to something greater. It wasn't about whether she changed. It wasn't even about whether she noticed. It was about Him. That changed everything. I always thought marriage was about my spouse and me, but it is about Christ and me. I had never, ever thought about that, and I have known the Lord for years."

Twenty-Five Thousand People Surveyed

He wasn't alone in making this discovery. I know of thousands of men and women who grasp this truth. Our survey of twenty-five thousand people before and after a Love and Respect Marriage Conference revealed a statistically significant finding: Spiritual satisfaction consistently increased and remained high even after the two-day event. At the conference's conclusion, individuals were challenged to love and respect their spouse "unto" Jesus Christ, regardless of their spouse's response, and many embraced this mindset. Often I call men and women forward to put a stake in the ground as the day and hour they decided to do marriage unto Jesus first and foremost. This concept served as the basis for the spiritual satisfaction scale.

In contrast, while positive feelings rose on the marital satisfaction scale immediately after the conference, some later experienced a decline in satisfaction when their spouse did not reciprocate the change. However, for those who committed to displaying a loving and respectful demeanor no matter what as an act of loving and reverencing Jesus, this spiritual scale stayed remarkably high no matter the sad state of the marriage. As we teach, marriage is both *a tool* and *a test* to deepen and demonstrate our love and reverence for Christ, and many couples powerfully comprehended this truth. Praise God!

What If Your Audience Is Christ?

A wife shared her own journey:

> For years, I felt stuck. Holding my tongue and having self-control—it all felt like an exhausting effort to respect a husband who didn't always show me love in return. I kept waiting for him to change, and my heart grew more bitter with every disappointment.
>
> Then I learned something at the Love and Respect Conference I had never considered before: "Your true audience is Christ." I began picturing Jesus standing beyond my husband's shoulder, as Emerson taught. Not only did the Lord call me to do what I did unto Him, but He watched how I responded to my husband as an indication of my faith in Him.
>
> It wasn't just about respecting my husband anymore; it was about obeying and reverencing God. Slowly, my perspective shifted. I stepped outside my own hurt, frustration, and unmet expectations, and I saw the Lord's presence in my marriage. It gave me a strength and perspective I didn't know would be available to me.

This is not an easy mindset shift, but it is powerful and truthful. Jesus is present in your marriage—the Invisible Listener and the True Witness to every word, tone, and motive. And how you respond to your spouse reflects your communion and walk with Christ.

Marriage Is Not Just Between Two—It's Before the One

When we react negatively toward our spouse in unloving or disrespectful ways, we tend to justify ourselves:

"They disrespected me first!"

"They don't love me the way I need them to!"

"Why should I be the one to change when they don't?"

But let me ask you a challenging question: Will you love and reverence

Christ in those moments of marital conflict? Will you put a stake in the ground from this day forward?

It's easy to focus on our spouse's faults. It's much harder to focus on the Faultless One watching beyond their shoulder—not to shame us but to remind us that we are ultimately responding to Him.

When I get frustrated with Sarah, Jesus gently reminds me: "Emerson, look at Me. This isn't about Sarah. She may be unlovable and disrespectful—that's not the point. You show love to Sarah to show Me that you love Me. Withdrawing and stonewalling her isn't loving her or Me."

And He says to Sarah, "Look at Me. This isn't about Emerson. Yes, he needs to change—without question he needs to be more loving and respectable, but this is about you coming across respectfully when talking to him about his many shortcomings as your way of showing your reverence for Me."

This is a radical shift. Jesus is not uninvolved in your marriage. He sees every moment.

Who Are You Watching, and More Importantly, Who Is Watching You?

Ask yourself these questions:

- Do you believe your obedience to Christ is required only when your spouse behaves perfectly?
- Do you make the case that your spouse deserves your negative reaction?
- Do you believe Christ would expect nothing different from you?

Each of these questions points to a powerful realm beyond our human seeing.

We fall into a dangerous mindset when we begin justifying our disobedience to the Lord based on our spouse's shortcomings and short temper. Who among us dare declare, "I cannot love and reverence Jesus beyond the shoulder of my spouse since my spouse makes that impossible for me"?

Do You Believe Your Obedience to Christ Is Required Only When Your Spouse Behaves Perfectly?

One person shared a sobering realization with me, something that forever changed how they viewed their role in the marriage. For years, they believed their spouse was the barrier to their spiritual growth. "I convinced myself," they said, "that I couldn't fully follow Jesus with a good attitude in the home because my spouse kept failing me." Every attempt to walk in faith felt knocked down by harsh words, apathy, or unloving actions. Their prayers echoed the same desperate theme: *Lord, how can I be who You want me to be when I'm stuck in a marriage like this?*

JESUS IS NOT UNINVOLVED IN YOUR MARRIAGE. HE SEES EVERY MOMENT.

But then they came across Romans 14:12: "So then, each of us will give an account of ourselves to God." That verse sharply affected them. "God won't ask me if my spouse made it easy to follow Him," they realized. "He'll ask if I followed Him—if I looked to Him daily and if I imitated Him in my own walk."

They saw how they had allowed their spouse's shortcomings to become their own spiritual justification for withholding love and respect—not just from their spouse but from Jesus Himself. "Without realizing it," they confessed, "I had bought into the lie that I was a powerless victim. But I'm not. I have a choice."

That wake-up call reframed their entire journey, and now it's a truth they humbly share with others.

Do You Make the Case That Your Spouse Deserves Your Negative Reaction?

One individual opened up about a pattern that had consumed their marriage for years. They had been convinced their spouse was to blame for every negative emotion. "If I was disgruntled, it was because of their attitude. If I was critical, it was because they provoked me. If I withdrew, it was their fault."

Every reaction felt justified. In their mind, retaliation was the only way to make their spouse "feel what they were putting me through."

But that strategy wasn't working; it was poisoning their peace. Even when they got what they wanted—an apology, an admission—they felt empty. The bitterness wasn't going away. Then they read 1 Peter 3:9: "Do not repay evil with evil or insult with insult. On the contrary, repay evil with blessing."

That verse pierced through the fog of self-justification. "It was God Himself telling me I was wrong," they admitted. They had been resisting the Holy Spirit and calling it fairness. But now they saw a higher calling: to respond in obedience, not just reaction.

"It felt unfair," they said. "But not as unfair as carrying around all that resentment and vindictiveness." In time, they discovered something surprising. It wasn't their spouse's behavior that was imprisoning them; it was their own reaction to it. Retaliation hadn't been power—it had been bondage. They came to realize they hadn't been voiceless. They had just been shouting from the wrong place. Now, they were speaking from a different center. Their voice became calmer, no longer driven by the need to punish.

Do You Believe Christ Would Expect Nothing Different from You?

People have said things like "Surely Jesus couldn't expect me to love and respect my spouse unconditionally—not with how difficult things are. Maybe that rule applies to other couples, the ones who at least try to get along. But not us."

Such folks had convinced themselves that their spouse's behavior was so problematic, so overwhelming, that personal change was impossible. They even justified disobedience with reasoning like "I'd respect them if they were more respectful and respectable" or "I'd love them if they were more loving and lovable."

But I have found the Lord speaking to them. He will often use His Word, like Luke 6:32–33: "If you love those who love you, what credit is that to you? Even sinners love those who love them. And if you do good to those who are good to you, what credit is that to you?"

That Scripture awakened them. God calls for the unconditional. Jesus never said to love only when it was easy or to respect only when it was earned. Many realized they have no excuse. They were not the exception.

This wasn't denial or pretending their pain didn't matter. It was about letting go of the lie that obedience to God was conditional. They discovered a deeper truth: Their spouse could not stop them from loving Jesus. While some pain remained, their heart changed. "I found peace—not always in my marriage, but in Jesus," they said. "My conscience was clear from doing the right thing even though I did not feel my spouse deserved it. Yes, I still lose focus at times and feel no one could live with my spouse. But now, I know the way back."

The Scriptural Basis: Doing Marriage "As Unto Christ"

This concept of doing what we do "as unto the Lord" is deeply rooted in Scripture.

Most of us know the words of Jesus in Matthew 25:40: "And the King shall answer and say unto them, 'Verily I say unto you, Inasmuch as ye have done it unto one of the least of these my brethren, ye have done it unto me'" (KJV).

This verse is often applied to acts of service toward the needy. Jesus is saying that when we serve others—even in the smallest ways—we are actually serving Him. This means that every time we do an act of kindness, even when others don't appreciate it, Christ sees it as doing it unto Him.

Paul developed this theme by directly applying it to marriage. In Ephesians 5:21, a husband and wife are to "submit to one another out of reverence for Christ." Their submission to each other is not just about a spouse—it's about being Christ-conscious and reverential. This is *unto Jesus.*

At our Love and Respect Conference, I share that there is no footnote in Ephesians 5:21 that reads, "Emerson is an exception to this divine command. He is not required to demonstrate his love and reverence for Christ by loving and honoring Sarah. Emerson doesn't need to look at Jesus beyond Sarah's shoulder. Sarah is so unlovable and disrespectful that obeying this command is impossible for Emerson. Therefore, he gets a pass. Duly noted."

Of course no such footnote exists. The command stands—for all of us. No exceptions.

Paul provides us with both the motivation and the method for doing marriage God's way, even when a spouse is unresponsive. Ephesians 5:33 makes it clear: A husband is commanded to love, and a wife is commanded to respect—not based on their spouse's behavior but as an act of obedience unto Christ in response to a divine imperative.

What This Looks Like in Real Life

Let's begin with the husband. When a wife is upset, critical, or distant, a husband feels dismissed. His impulse may be to withdraw or defend. But God calls him to love anyway. This doesn't mean ignoring pain; it means staying engaged because Jesus is present. This is to be the husband's ultimate intent.

Now the wife. When her husband is emotionally absent or withdrawn, she feels unseen. But in that moment, her respectful posture can become a bridge—not because he deserves it but because she honors the Lord. Respect sounds like "I know you don't mean to hurt me, but when I feel shut out, I start to feel invisible. I'm not criticizing. I just miss you." Why would she talk this way? Because Jesus stands beyond the shoulder of her husband. She speaks to the Invisible Listener. This is to be the wife's ultimate intent.

These moments don't require perfection. They require humility. They require faith in Jesus. Without that, couples fall into the Crazy Cycle I described in *Love and Respect*: without love, she reacts without respect, and without respect, he reacts without love. They keep spinning.

Both Love and Respect

Ephesians 5:33 doesn't simply say, "Love one another." It says, "Each one of you also must love his wife as he loves himself, and the wife must respect her husband."

Though our culture fixates on love, Scripture does not. Respect and honor emerge as equally central. It's biblical instruction.

Honor one another above yourselves. (Romans 12:10)
Show proper respect to everyone. (1 Peter 2:17)
Submit to one another out of reverence for Christ. (Ephesians 5:21)
They observe your chaste and respectful behavior. (1 Peter 3:2 NASB1995)
Treat [your wife] with respect. (1 Peter 3:7)

So why does Paul focus in Ephesians 5:21–33 on love for husbands and respect for wives? Because God is addressing each spouse's deepest need, especially in conflict. But even more profoundly, we obey this not based on how our spouse responds but out of trust and obedience unto Jesus. As an honorable man, he seeks to love Jesus beyond his wife's shoulder. As a loving woman, she intends to reverence Jesus standing behind her husband.

To the husband, God calls, "Love her as My Son loved the church, even when she's reacting. Why? Jesus is the Ever-Present Audience." To the wife, God calls, "Put on a respectful demeanor—unconditional positive regard—unto Jesus, even when your husband disappoints. He is the Over-the-Shoulder Savior."

Jesus is the unseen Recipient of every respectful tone, every loving gesture. We do it not merely for our spouse but for the Heavenly Observer.

A Second Biblical Cycle

While this "love and respect" dynamic is the foundational cycle, Scripture also gives hints of another pattern woven through 1 Peter 3:7 and Titus 2:4: Without warm affection and friendship (*phílandros*) from her, he may react without understanding (*súnēsis*) and honor (*timḗ*); without understanding and honor from him, she may react without warm affection and friendship.

I surface this other cycle for two reasons. First, it is biblical. Second, nearly every woman, when hearing of the first Crazy Cycle, immediately says,

"Women need respect too." Peter agrees. In fact, when Peter addresses marriage in 1 Peter 3, he says nothing about love. Instead, the Lord reveals through this apostle that it is all about respect and honor: Wives, win your husband's heart through respectful conduct (3:1); husbands, honor your wives so that your prayers will not be hindered (3:7). Yes, God commands husbands to treat their wives respectfully and wives to treat their husbands respectfully. No person has the right to say, "Treat me with respect, but I reserve the right to treat you disrespectfully when I feel you have not earned or deserved my respect." Respect and honor are not rewards for good behavior; they are commands from God, given to every husband and wife who follow Christ.

Intending to Be Unconditional Unto Jesus

As for my traditional Crazy Cycle, let me clarify something that often causes confusion. When we talk about unconditional love, we mean that a husband chooses to be a loving man unto Jesus, even while addressing behavior in his wife that feels disrespectful. He doesn't become unloving to motivate her to be respectful. That would violate the very meaning of unconditional love.

Likewise, unconditional respect means, as I just mentioned, showing positive regard for a husband's spirit—not because he's earned it but because the wife is ultimately reverencing Christ. She doesn't become disrespectful to provoke her husband into loving her more. That, too, would violate the very meaning of unconditional respect.

Unconditional means there is no condition, circumstance, or situation with my spouse that can prevent me from being a loving and respectful human being who loves and reverences Christ during marital conflict.

Unconditional does not mean unwise, nor does it mean enabling sin. Loving and respecting our spouse unconditionally is not a license to compromise truth or participate in wrongdoing. We must never lay aside our convictions or ignore the boundaries of righteousness in the name of "peace." If there is abuse, deception, or danger, we are responsible to act—especially to ensure that children are safe, protected, and not exposed to harm. As Paul wrote in Ephesians 5:11, "Do not participate in the unfruitful deeds of darkness, but instead even expose them" (NASB1995).

Unconditional love and respect is never silent in the face of sin. It speaks what is true, kind, necessary, and clear (Ephesians 4:15). It calls a lie a lie, but it does so with a heart that seeks redemption, not revenge.

Consider Acts 5, where a sobering story unfolds. A husband and wife, Ananias and Sapphira, conspired together to lie to the apostles (Peter in particular) and to the Holy Spirit about the money they gave. Sapphira may not have initiated the deception, but she was complicit. And because she participated in the lie, she suffered the same judgment as her husband. Her story reminds us: Agreement with sin, even under the guise of loyalty, can have grave consequences—literally!

By the way, Peter, the very apostle who later called a wife to win her husband with her respectful behavior (1 Peter 3:1–2), also witnessed the tragic death of Sapphira, who chose to respect her husband's ungodly scheme more than she reverenced the Lord. She gave her husband her agreement but withheld her obedience from God. The lesson is clear: Peter never, ever expects a wife to respect sinful choices. Respectful conduct in marriage is never a license to participate in deception or wrongdoing. That's why 1 Peter 3:1–2, Peter's exposition, must always be read in light of Acts 5, Peter's experience. Respect does not mean complicity in sin, for our highest reverence is owed to Christ.

Scripture calls us to shift from horizontal thinking (focused on our spouse's response) to vertical thinking (focused on Christ). Even when the spouse before us does not acknowledge our effort, Jesus above us sees what we do as unto Him (Colossians 3:23).

A husband once asked me, "Why should I keep trying when my wife doesn't notice or appreciate my effort?" I shared with him that you do this toward Jesus beyond your spouse's shoulder—because the Lord notices. Everything you do toward Him matters to Him. If we love and respect our spouses only when they deserve it, then our marriage is just a human transaction. But when we do it unto Christ, it becomes an act of worship.

A wife once shared with me a quiet but powerful turning point in her marriage. "For years," she said, "I felt invisible. I poured myself into our relationship, trying to make things better, but my husband barely acknowledged it." Over time, her heart grew bitter. The weight of unreciprocated effort left her drained and resentful. Then one day, while reading *Love & Respect*, a truth struck her in a way it never had before: Her love for her husband wasn't ultimately about his response—it was about her love for Jesus.

"Even if my husband didn't see what I was doing," she told me, "Jesus did." That realization shifted everything. It didn't erase the pain, but it reframed it. Her bitterness gave way to peace, and she began to serve in the marriage not from desperation but from devotion.

"There's a parallel universe now," she said. "Even in the heartbreak, I'm keeping my eyes fixed on Jesus."

Her words capture a profound shift, from feeling unseen in her marriage to being fully seen by Christ. Even in the heartbreak, she discovered a deeper reality—a "parallel universe," as she put it—where her focus was no longer on what was absent in her marriage but on who was always present. In this new perspective, her sense of invisibility faded, not because her husband suddenly saw her but because she realized Jesus had seen her all along.

In this regard, "unconditional" means this is the person I will be before the Lord, regardless of who my spouse is.

A Major Biblical Theme

Paul carries this theme of "unto Jesus" throughout his epistles. In Ephesians 6:7–8 we read,

> Serve wholeheartedly, as if you were serving the Lord, not people, because you know that the Lord will reward each one for whatever good they do.

This passage was originally written to slaves and servants, instructing them to work not just for their earthly masters but for the Master, with their hearts set on God.

He does not stop with slaves. Paul develops the "unto Jesus" revelation and applies it to everyone. We read in Ephesians 6:9 (NASB1995),

> And masters, do the same things to them, and give up threatening, knowing that both their Master and yours is in heaven, and there is no partiality with Him.

Paul might say to the married, "You are serving the Lord, not your spouse. This is unconditional. This is unto Jesus."

A wife once pushed back during a conversation. "I don't feel like respecting my husband when he doesn't deserve it—even if Jesus is there," she said honestly. Her frustration was real, and her objection heartfelt. But I gently reminded her of something simple yet profound: She stood at a crossroads—feelings versus faith.

This wasn't about her husband's worthiness. It was about her identity in Christ and the calling placed on her, even when her spouse fell short. At that moment, she didn't feel any desire to follow through, and I understood. But I also knew she loved Jesus.

So I said, "By faith, you can do this. Don't let your negative feelings toward your husband weaken your faith in Jesus. You have two relationships in this marriage: one with your husband, the other with Christ. Which is most important?"

Her answer revealed her maturity. She chose Jesus.

Another individual shared a common misconception: "I used to think marriage was about making my spouse happy. But no matter how much I did, it never seemed enough. I grew bitter."

Then, one day, a breakthrough came like a lightning bolt: "My job was to serve Christ in my marriage—not just my spouse." That simple truth set them free from the exhausting chase for constant validation. They no longer served just to be seen but out of reverence for Christ.

"Now," they said, "even when my spouse overlooks my efforts, I have peace—because God sees them. And He will reward me."

This echoes the truth in Colossians 3:23–24:

> Whatever you do, work at it with all your heart, as working for the Lord, not for human masters, since you know that you will receive an inheritance from the Lord as a reward. It is the Lord Christ you are serving.

Someone told me, "I poured my heart into my marriage for years without seeing much change. It was discouraging." But then came a new understanding: "My work wasn't just for my spouse—it was for Christ."

Their circumstances didn't shift overnight, but their heart did. That inner change, anchored in serving Christ, eventually softened their spouse's heart as well. The healing didn't start from the outside in but from the inside out.

As Colossians 3:23 reminds us, "whatever you do," God sees it. And He rewards it. Life isn't lived merely on the horizontal plane between two people—it's lived vertically, before God.

Intent may be invisible, but it is never unnoticed by God. When your heart's aim is to love and reverence Jesus, even the smallest act becomes sacred.

THREE

OUR ETERNITY: LIVING WITH "WELL DONE!" IN MIND

Forever spark: Your marriage carries eternal significance in God's story—every act of love and respect matters to Him and will not go unrewarded.

A few days before she passed in 2001, my mother wrote a simple poem—words that, at the time, seemed like just another reflection of her deep faith expressed in another rhyme among the hundreds she penned. But in hindsight, she had no idea her time on earth would end so soon. Neither did we.

And yet, as if heaven had already begun calling her home, she expressed these words with a heart full of faith, unaware that her own journey days later was reaching its final steps.

> There's a brand-new year 2001
> Waiting for you and me—
> It has twelve great months for each of us
> To be what God wants us to be.
> Faith, Hope, and Love are the Stairsteps to Heaven—
> Stairsteps we climb every day—

Let 2001 be your very best year—
Go with JESUS—He's the only way!

I read those lines now knowing she never made it past February of that year. And it undoes me.

She captures the kind of wisdom that only those walking closely with Jesus carry—always ready, always surrendered.

This would be her last poem, and God knew. He let her share her heart and put ink to paper so that, in the quiet of our grief, we could still hear her voice pointing us toward our eternal home.

She is gone now. But her words remain. Go with Jesus—He's the only way. Indeed, heaven awaits us.

What a perspective. She knew this life was temporary—but eternity is forever.

Eternalization

Eternalization refers to the process of reevaluating, reorienting, and redirecting our thoughts, priorities, and actions toward what has eternal significance. It is the intentional shift from a temporary, earthly mindset to a kingdom-focused perspective, where decisions are made not just for present comfort or success but for God's greater purpose. As Jesus prayed, "Not my will, but yours be done" (Luke 22:42).

We sometimes hear, "They are so heavenly minded, they are no earthly good." Maybe. But Jesus said, "Seek first the kingdom of God and His righteousness, and all these things shall be added to you" (Matthew 6:33 NKJV).

True heavenly mindedness doesn't remove us from earthly responsibilities—it refocuses them. It calls us to live with purpose, love, and reverence unto Jesus and to serve Him faithfully, knowing that what we do now has eternal significance. Life is lived with the grand finale in mind when we stand before Jesus and hear, "Well done, good and faithful servant."

I know of two men who were accepted into prestigious medical schools but chose full-time ministry instead. For them, ministry was the most straightforward way to live out their eternal perspective. One of these men first introduced me to the language of "having an eternal perspective."

The other knew that medicine could have been a powerful avenue for kingdom work—so much so that a pastor once advised him to pursue it for that very reason. (I have another friend who served as a medical missionary for forty years, using his profession to spread the gospel.) Yet this man—the one encouraged to choose medicine—became a pastor instead, and he has no regrets. I recently spoke with his wife, who shared how deeply fulfilling their life in ministry has been. Their choice wasn't about what career path was "better," it was about obedience to God's calling.

TRUE HEAVENLY MINDEDNESS DOESN'T REMOVE US FROM EARTHLY RESPONSIBILITIES—IT REFOCUSES THEM.

Each of us must ask, "Am I eternalizing my life?" The answer may lead us down different paths—some to medicine, some to missions, some to ministry, and others to music, marketing, or mechanics—but what does not vary is this: We must intentionally choose to live with eternity in mind, no matter our calling.

When we seek first the kingdom, we don't escape from the world. We engage it with a different perspective. We work, build, and steward our lives not for temporary gain but for God's greater purpose.

To be truly heavenly minded is to be the most earthly good, because those who live for eternity live differently today.

We can know when we are eternalizing. We will

- make decisions with a kingdom mindset, asking, *Does this have eternal value?*
- prioritize spiritual investments over material ones (mentoring, discipleship, giving, and serving above just accumulating wealth, seeking pleasure, or chasing recognition);

- measure success by faithfulness to God rather than financial security, status, or worldly accolades;
- view trials as refining tools rather than meaningless hardships.

What Does the Bible Say About Rewards?

For many of us, we go about life as if we have all the time in the world. We get frustrated with our spouse, hold on to resentments, and think, *I'll deal with it later.* But what if we don't have later? My mom did not have later.

Paul gave a sobering warning to those who will not hear "well done." We read in 1 Corinthians 3:13–15, "[Each one's] work will be shown for what it is, because the Day will bring it to light. It will be revealed with fire, and the fire will test the quality of each person's work. If what has been built survives, the builder will receive a reward. If it is burned up, the builder will suffer loss but yet will be saved—even though only as one escaping through the flames."

This means that not all our works will survive the refining fire of Christ's judgment. Some will burn away, leaving the believer saved but unrewarded, because those works were not done for the right reasons, with the right heart, or for Christ's honor.

Saved by Grace, Rewarded by Works

Salvation is always and only a gift. We do not earn eternal life; Christ purchased it for us by His blood. As Paul made clear, "It is by grace you have been saved, through faith . . . not by works" (Ephesians 2:8–9).

God saves us apart from works, but He takes our works seriously.

- Salvation is free; faithfulness is rewarded.
- Salvation is God's gift; rewards are His recognition.
- Salvation is given; rewards are gained.

Eternal life is unearned, a gift of grace. Eternal rewards are the gracious acknowledgment of lives lived in obedience and perseverance. Both truths matter, and both are meant to move us.

Yet, while all believers are saved by grace, secure in Christ, some may find their life's work lacking eternal significance. Their efforts, shaped by carnal self-interest rather than Christ's glory, will be exposed as fleeting and fruitless. The weight of that realization will be sobering as they grasp what could have been if they had lived with an eternal perspective. They gain heaven as a gift but lose the reward Jesus intends to give to them for godly, wise work.

> "Be [very] careful not to do your good deeds publicly, to be seen by men; otherwise you will have no reward [prepared and awaiting you] with your Father who is in heaven." (Matthew 6:1 AMP)

We can, by our choices, undo what others have faithfully poured into our walk with Christ—through their teaching, correction, and discipleship. And when we drift from the truth or fail to remain faithful, whether leader or laity, we risk losing the reward God intended to give us—not salvation itself, which is a gift, but the eternal rewards tied to our faithfulness. Rewards can be forfeited.

> Watch yourselves, so that you do not lose what we have accomplished together, but that you may receive a full *and* perfect reward [when He grants rewards to faithful believers]. (2 John v. 8 AMP)

> "I am coming soon. Hold on to what you have, so that no one will take your crown." (Revelation 3:11)

What does God reward? Here are the commonly understood eternal rewards/crowns mentioned in Scripture, and the authors expect us to live in light of these honors.

- Different levels of glory in heaven. Based on faithfulness (Daniel 12:3; 1 Corinthians 15:41–42).

- Crown of life. For enduring trials and remaining faithful unto death (James 1:12; Revelation 2:10).
- Crown of righteousness. For those who eagerly await Christ's return (2 Timothy 4:8).
- Crown of glory. For faithful shepherds and leaders of God's people (1 Peter 5:4).
- Crown of rejoicing. For those who lead others to Christ (soul-winner's crown) (1 Thessalonians 2:19–20).
- Gold, silver, precious stones. For those who build their life on Christ with eternal significance (1 Corinthians 3:12–14).
- Authority in the millennial kingdom. For faithful service and stewardship (Luke 19:17; Revelation 2:26–27).
- Right to sit with Christ on His throne. For those who overcome (Revelation 3:21).
- Hidden manna and white stone. A special reward for overcomers (Revelation 2:17).
- The incorruptible crown. For self-discipline and perseverance (1 Corinthians 9:25).
- Greater joy and rejoicing in heaven. For those who served faithfully (Matthew 25:21).
- Special access to Christ's presence. For those who remain devoted (Revelation 3:12).

Though many of us have not studied these, there is a sense that something glorious awaits those who trust and obey the Lord. Many husbands and wives have impressed me as individuals who live in light of God's honor of them.

What About Us and Our Marriages?

Why do I connect the rewards with marriage?

Picture Paul writing to the believers in Ephesus and Colossae. He has already spent the first half of each letter (Ephesians 1–3; Colossians 1–2) proclaiming doctrine: the unshakable truth that they have been saved by grace through faith, apart from works. Their eternal life is secure because of Christ's finished work, not because of anything they have done or will do. That's the gift.

Then Paul pivots. In Ephesians 4–6 and Colossians 3–4, he moves to application—what it looks like to live out that salvation. And where does he begin? Not with lofty public ministry but with the most ordinary and intimate places:

Husbands and wives
Parents and children
Slaves and masters (work relationships)

Paul is saying, "Here is where your theology gets tested. Here, in the daily grind of relationships, is where Christ's life in you shows up—or doesn't."

And then, right in the middle of these household instructions, he drops a staggering truth:

> Because you know that the Lord will reward each one for whatever good they do. (Ephesians 6:8)

> From the Lord you will receive the reward of the inheritance. It is the Lord Christ whom you serve. (Colossians 3:24 NASB1995)

These are not salvation verses. Paul isn't telling them how to gain eternal life. He already settled that earlier: It's a gift, "not a result of works, so that no one may boast" (Ephesians 2:8–9 NASB).

Here, he is speaking to those who already have eternal life, urging them to live faithfully because God is watching and will reward them. These rewards are given according to the believer's faithfulness, trust, and obedience after salvation. The Greek grammar matches other "according to works" reward passages (1 Corinthians 3:8, 14; 2 Corinthians 5:10).

This is why I point out that the husband-wife relationship is first and foremost in God's application section, not because it earns salvation but because it's the proving ground for obedience that God will reward. On that day, the Lord may say, "I observed you love and respect your spouse unto Me. You were loving and reverencing Me. Well done."

The Lord's "well done" is for a life of faithful obedience in the very relationships where grace was meant to shine most brightly.

The Lord's Grand Finale: Entering the Joy of Our Master

Jesus is clear: Death is coming, and, after death, the judgment. For some believers in Jesus, this will be a moment of fear, regret, and sorrow. How that plays out in eternity, I don't know. Some suggest it could involve a profound awareness of opportunities missed, rewards forfeited, and the sobering realization that we lived for ourselves more than for Him. But this does not last forever, for here the Lord "will wipe away every tear," which some believe are the tears of regret (Revelation 21:4 ESV).

However, to use that promise as a license for careless, carnal living is to misunderstand the heart of the One who will wipe those tears. Yes, He will comfort, but first He will evaluate. The wiping away of tears does not erase the reality of loss; it only ends the sorrow over it. Those moments before His throne will be real. To gamble that away because "it will all be hunky-dory in glory" is to trade the Lord's "well done" for an eternity remembering that you could have heard it but didn't.

Others will hear these stunning words from the Lord Himself: "Well done, good and faithful servant. . . . Enter into the joy of your master" (Matthew 25:21 ESV). That one sentence, spoken by Jesus, will outweigh every earthly joy you've ever known. Imagine this: Take the most celebrated moments of your life—

- your graduation,
- your wedding,
- the birth of your child,
- summer vacations,
- a long-awaited promotion,
- an unexpected gift,

- your father's proud words,
- the salvation of a loved one.

Now add in *any dream* you've ever cherished and multiply it *beyond imagination*. That is the kind of joy Jesus is talking about. His joy becomes your joy—fully and forever.

And in that moment, every heartache, betrayal, and disappointment you've ever carried, especially in marriage, vanishes into eternity.

Can You Imagine the Joy?

Try to picture it . . .

A ten-year-old boy dreams for months about a new bike. Christmas morning comes. He runs to the tree—and there it is: the exact bike he'd prayed for. His heart explodes with joy.

A woman sits across from the man she loves. He kneels down, opens a small box, and reveals a sparkling diamond. She gasps. Her hands fly to her mouth. *Pure joy.*

A man casually checks a lottery ticket—no expectations. But then . . . the numbers match. All of them. His hands shake. His knees buckle. His life has just changed forever.

These are glimpses. Earthly echoes. Foretastes.

And yet *none* of them compare to the joy you'll feel when Christ looks you in the eye and says, "Well done. Enter into My joy."

That is the Lord's grand finale—and it will be just the beginning of a joy beyond comprehension.

The Eternal Reward: A Glorious Governance

And, beyond the joy, few believers in Christ spend much time thinking about their glorious and meaningful work in heaven. Perhaps this is because the Lord has given us only hints; our knowledge is limited. Yet even with the glimpses He provides, we can lean into the truth that eternity is not about passive existence but about purposeful participation in His kingdom.

Jesus Himself tells us that faithful believers will be entrusted with greater responsibilities in eternity:

> Well done, good and faithful servant. You have been faithful over a little; I will set you over much. Enter into the joy of your master. (Matthew 25:21 ESV)

Paul echoed this promise:

> If we endure, we will also reign with him. (2 Timothy 2:12)

But what does this reigning involve? As those who co-reign with Christ, we will step into a holy governance beyond our current comprehension, overseeing aspects of His eternal kingdom. This privileged role—granted to us by His grace—reflects our deep, intimate relationship with the Lord, and it highlights the exalted position He has prepared for us. No matter what we imagine, eternity will far exceed it. We ain't seen nothin' yet.

God reveals these truths not just for the future but to bring us peace and hope today. Knowing what awaits us inspires perseverance, even when our earthly roles feel small or insignificant. Because one day, those hidden acts of faithfulness will be seen.

Live for That Day

Jesus is preparing us to hear "well done." The question is not whether He wants to say it—the question is whether we will live in such a way that we warrant hearing it.

The reward is coming. The joy is real. The work in eternity is glorious. And the time to eternalize our lives is now.

Every little act of unseen kindness, every little unassuming moment of perseverance, and every little sacrifice made for Christ's sake will be rewarded beyond anything we could imagine.

NO MATTER WHAT WE IMAGINE, ETERNITY WILL FAR EXCEED IT.

The joy of a child, the love of a bride-to-be, the shock of sudden wealth—all of it will pale in comparison to standing in His presence, being set over much, and entering into His eternal joy.

Are You Ready for That Day?

Jesus asks, "I am the resurrection and the life; he who believes in Me will live even if he dies. . . . Do you believe this?" (John 11:25–26 NASB1995).

The apostle Paul believed this: "For to me, to live is Christ and to die is gain" (Philippians 1:21).

Death is not the end—it is the beginning.

For the believer, our true home is with Christ. And for husbands and wives, our marriage is a temporary covenant that refines and prepares us for an eternal reality.

Marriage with Heaven in Mind

Jesus made this bold statement about marriage in eternity: "For in the resurrection they neither marry nor are given in marriage, but are like angels in heaven" (Matthew 22:30 NASB1995).

That means your marriage is temporary. But what you do in your marriage has eternal consequences. Our marriage is not the final destination—it is the training ground for our forever with Christ as "the wife of the Lamb" (Revelation 21:9).

Here's the eternal perspective:

- Marriage as worship: Love and reverence beyond your spouse.
- Holiness before happiness: Seek godliness, then marital joy.
- Eternal legacy: Model Christ for future generations.
- Marriage reflects God: Display His image and Christ and the church.
- Unconditional attitudes: Love and respect show godly obedience apart from a spouse.
- Heavenly rewards: Serve to hear "well done."
- Spirit of forgiveness: Reflect God's mercy in marriage.

Have You Had a Lightbulb Moment Like These Folks?

For some, it came through Scripture. For others, it came through failure and repentance. But for each, it changed not only their marriage but their view of God, eternity, and themselves.

These aren't just marriage tips. They're eternal turning points.

A Husband's Eternal Lightbulb Moment

FROM EARTHLY LEADERSHIP TO SPIRITUAL SHEPHERDING

A man I met with believed that being a good husband was restricted to providing for his family, making wise financial decisions, and ensuring their security.

"I thought leadership was about keeping things in order—working hard, making sure we had a stable home, and being a good father. But then I read Ephesians 5:25: "'Husbands, love your wives, just as Christ loved the church and gave himself up for her.'

"My leadership wasn't about provision alone—it was about laying down my life for my wife, spiritually and emotionally. I needed to imitate Jesus. This was about the vertical, not just the horizontal."

> WHAT YOU DO IN YOUR MARRIAGE HAS ETERNAL CONSEQUENCES.

At first, it was a struggle. Sacrificial love wasn't instinctive, especially when she criticized him, albeit rooted in her care. But when he became more proactive and started praying with his wife, listening instead of fixing, and loving her by responding to the little requests she made, he not only knew he pleased the Lord but he saw his wife begin to honorably respond to him in a way she never had before.

Every husband can have a moment in time when he realizes his leadership isn't just about his family's earthly well-being—it's about him imitating Jesus and living in light of heaven.

PRAYING WITH OUR WIVES

Each of us needs to consider Matthew 18:20: "For where two or three are gathered in my name, there am I among them" (ESV).

It's one thing to pray for your wife. It's another for the two of you to gather in the name of Jesus, coming together to pray in the bedroom, living room, or car. When you pray together, you're not just speaking into the air—you're inviting the risen Christ into your marriage. It's about shifting out of autopilot and making space to be vulnerable together, turning to Him together in prayer.

If you've felt unsure, awkward, or hesitant to pray out loud with your wife, you're not alone. Many men fear they'll stumble over their words or say the "wrong" thing. But here's the reality: God isn't grading your eloquence—He's honoring your willingness.

A simple, sincere invitation, "Can we pray together before bed?" may be the very moment your wife has been waiting for. Most Christian women I know yearn for this, to come under a husband's umbrella of protection in prayer.

You don't have to be a perfect prayer warrior. Just talk to the Lord about the concerns you both have and remember to give thanks for the many blessings.

And when you stand before Christ, what will matter isn't whether you covered everything flawlessly—it's whether you covered your wife in prayer at all.

I have known numerous husbands who've had the aha moment that asking just one question could shift everything: "Can we pray together about this?" They realized that God would be pleased, their wives would be grateful, and they themselves would be stepping into true spiritual leadership as well as vulnerability with their wives simply by initiating prayer. Many wives leap at the opportunity, longing for that sacred moment of shared faith. This, in fact, highlights one of the great gender differences in marriage: When a husband initiates prayer, most wives embrace it with joy, but when a wife makes the same request, it doesn't always cause the same positive response.

RESISTING SECULAR NOISE

A husband shared how worldly distractions—money, career, social media—were pulling him away from his wife and his faith. He justified these things as normal. "Everyone's busy," he said. But deep down, he knew he was slowly drifting from both God and his marriage.

Most believers come to that same quiet realization. And many have read verses like 1 Corinthians 3:13 where Paul said, "Each one's work will become evident . . . and the fire itself will test the quality of each one's work" (NASB).

That kind of verse forces these questions: *What am I building? When I stand before Christ, will I be proud of how I loved my wife and served His purposes? Or will I regret how I wasted my time?*

That realization should change how we spend our lives. Some of us put down our phones, stop scrolling, and start investing in eternity. We begin talking and listening to the Lord more, reading the Bible, giving thanks in trials, joining small groups, fellowshipping with believers, and stepping into ministry.

For others, it's not so easy. It takes more intentionality to stop the behaviors that have become ingrained in us. In these cases, practically speaking, it can help to lean on friends for support in your efforts. Talk to them about your struggles and lay out a plan for how to make new habits and let go of others. Spiritually speaking, beginning the day by asking Jesus to give you the grace to spend your time according to His will can keep you from drifting off the path.

The choices I make today—and really, what in life is truly mundane?—will either be rewarded or regretted in eternity. As one man said to me, "This is no joke."

TEACHING HIS CHILDREN TO LIVE WITH HEAVEN IN MIND

Many husbands embrace the roles of provider and protector but overlook the role of spiritual example. One husband told me how that realization came into focus the night he heard his son repeat something he had said in frustration to his wife. "It stopped me cold," he said. "I realized—my kids are watching. Always."

And that's true for many of us. We forget that our marriage is one of the most powerful sermons our children will ever hear. They are learning—every day—from how we speak, how we serve, and how we love. It's not just about correcting their behavior. It's about modeling Christlike love under pressure.

Ephesians 6:4 calls fathers to raise children "in the discipline and instruction of the Lord" (ESV). That begins not with lectures but with lived-out faith at home.

Interestingly, we often hear a father of his firstborn describe the wake-up call this event produced in his life—in that moment, he realized it was no longer just about him. A sense of weight, purpose, and responsibility settled over him. He was now shaping another life, and the stakes felt eternal.

If we want our sons and daughters to know how to love, respect, and serve their future spouses, it has to start with how we love, respect, and serve ours. Our marriage isn't just affecting our wives—it's shaping our children's eternity.

A Wife's Eternal Lightbulb Moment

Many wives report their newfound biblical perspectives that produced the feeling that they were doing marriage God's way, and this brought them a deep-seated satisfaction.

LETTING GO OF BITTERNESS IN LIGHT OF ETERNITY

Every Christ-follower is familiar with the verse "Forgive as the Lord forgave you" (Colossians 3:13). But for wives, living it out in a marriage full of real, repeated frustrations is something else entirely.

One wife admitted she spent years quietly keeping score—tallying every mistake, thoughtless word, and unmet expectation. She wasn't bitter on the surface, but underneath, the resentment was growing.

Eventually, the truth she had heard for so long caught up with her heart: Would she stand before Christ someday and try to justify why she held on to bitterness? Or would she hear "Well done" for choosing to forgive as Jesus did?

She didn't ignore problems. She still addressed hurts. But now she did it without the poison of resentment—because Christ had already shown her a better way. A way that included regulating her own responses and not allowing her husband's behavior to cause her to move into negative patterns. She could remain in control of how she responded and, using Christ's strength, show compassion and not judgment.

When we forgive freely, we mirror Christ's forgiveness of us.

SHIFTING FROM TEMPORARY ANNOYANCES TO THE UNSEEN KINGDOM

We've all heard it quoted: "Fix [your] eyes not on what is seen, but on what is unseen. . . . What is seen is temporary" (2 Corinthians 4:18). And yet, so often, the temporary and immediate is what consumes us—especially in marriage.

WHEN WE FORGIVE FREELY, WE MIRROR CHRIST'S FORGIVENESS OF US.

One wife confessed she often obsessed over her husband's little flaws. She stewed over dishes left out, plans forgotten, habits that annoyed her. And while the issues were real, they weren't eternal.

But she began to let those Sunday sermons sink in: Was she investing her energy in what would last? Would her reactions hold up before Christ one day?

That shift didn't make the small things disappear, but it put them in their proper place. She found grace growing where irritation once lived. Yes, this was a process. She learned that by beginning her day in prayer, asking Jesus to help her remain in control of her responses, she could overlook her husband's absent-minded actions. She also found a way to communicate to him in gentle ways how his oversights affect her.

When we fix our eyes on the unseen, we stop magnifying what won't matter in eternity, though another's shortcomings may trouble us.

SEEING HER HUSBAND AS AN ETERNAL SOUL IN GOD'S HANDS

One of the most glorious promises in Scripture is "he who began a good work in you will carry it on to completion" (Philippians 1:6). But many wives wrestle with how to apply it to their husbands, especially when spiritual growth in Christ feels slow or absent. This is magnified in parenting. A wife may grow weary of carrying the spiritual load, longing for her husband to step into that role. She feels the urgency, especially while the children are young, knowing these formative years are fleeting.

One wife shared how she had spent years frustrated with her husband's spiritual pace. She compared him to other men and longed for him to lead in ways he didn't naturally step into.

But then came the realization: She was not her husband's Holy Spirit. God was already working—in quieter, slower, yet no less sacred ways.

When she stepped back from pushing and started truly praying, she began noticing things she had missed before. One evening, without her prompting, he gathered the kids and read a short Bible passage before bed. Another week, he initiated a prayer over a family decision. These were small moments, but they were clear signs of God's hand at work. Her posture shifted from critiquing to trusting, and her joy in those moments far outweighed the frustration she once felt.

Some wives readily confess that they fixate on what isn't happening, stop praying, and grow resentful. But praying like this wife—looking expectantly for signs of God responding—enabled her to see her husband's positive steps as part of the journey of God continuing the work He began in him.

When we trust God with our spouse's growth, we stop trying to do what only the Holy Spirit can—and we begin to see and celebrate what He is already doing.

Let me add an important observation. Research consistently shows that many wives struggle with being overly critical or frequently complaining—not always from malice but often from *idealism*. They carry in their hearts a picture of the "perfect" marriage, and when reality falls short, they fixate on the flaws. The tragedy is that this lens can blind them to the good that *is* happening and even breed resentment toward those good moments—because they believe such things should happen all day, every day. This unrelenting standard leaves them chronically disappointed and robs them of joy in the real progress God is making.

MARRIAGE, FAMILY, AND THE BIGGER PICTURE: LIVING WITH ETERNITY IN MIND

Many of us know these verses by heart: "Do not store up for yourselves treasures on earth. . . . But store up for yourselves treasures in heaven" (Matthew 6:19–20). Still, it's easy to chase the appearance of a perfect marriage, family, and life.

One wife admitted she was doing just that—pouring her energy into a beautiful home, ideal routines, admirable kids, and a secure future. But late one night, she wrestled with the truth she'd heard so many times: Was she storing up eternal treasure? Or just creating something to impress others and make her feel good about herself but all of which would eventually fade?

That question changed her prayers and her purpose. She began focusing on the invisible investments—her gentleness, her intercession, her encouragement, her quiet obedience. These, she realized, were the true treasures heaven records. This did not mean she stopped caring about herself or having healthy routines, but she held them loosely, no longer finding her identity or worth in them. Instead, she viewed them as a backdrop for what mattered most—how she loved, served, and honored Christ in the midst of it all.

When we prioritize eternal investments over earthly appearances, we build what heaven never forgets.

Living for Glory, Living to Hear "Well Done!"

Our marriages are not just for this life. Glory is coming. That's not a poetic ending—it's our destiny.

- We will appear with Christ in glory. (Colossians 3:4)
- We will share in His glory. (Romans 8:17–18)
- We will be made like Him. (1 John 3:2)
- Suffering prepares us for glory. (2 Corinthians 4:17–18)
- We will have glorified bodies. (Philippians 3:20–21)
- Jesus wants us to see His glory. (John 17:24)
- God Himself will restore and strengthen us for eternal glory. (1 Peter 5:10)

A grand finale is coming. Each conversation, prayer, sacrifice, and act of love and respect in your marriage is part of that divine staircase. Yes, Scripture motivates us with eternal rewards, but the greatest reward is not a crown—it's the King. We aren't living for eternity merely for what we'll get; we're living for the day when we see Him face-to-face, hear His voice, and join Him in the glory He's prepared for us. Every step of obedience in marriage is really a step toward *Him*. Eternal glory is not just our destination, it's our motivation, because at the top of that staircase—the stairsteps we climb every day, as my mom penned in her poem—is Jesus Himself, the glorified One, whose face shines like the sun in all its brilliance (Revelation 1:16).

THE GREATEST REWARD IS NOT A CROWN—IT'S THE KING.

FOUR

OUR WORLDVIEW: THE HOLY WORD, NOT HOLLYWOOD

Reality reset: Hollywood's reel love feels real because it promises excitement and ease. But only the Holy Word reveals the joy, wisdom, and eternal purpose God designed for marriage.

The Allure of Reel Love

One of our dearest friends shared how she almost lost God's calling in her life. As a single woman ministering faithfully on a college campus with a parachurch organization, she led sixty young women to Christ in just one year. Eventually she became engaged to a wise, godly man. Their calling was clear: They would mentor and equip the next generation of Christian leaders. And they did, eventually mentoring ninety people into full-time ministry.

But one evening, before marriage, after watching *Funny Girl* starring Barbra Streisand, she began doubting her own engagement. Hollywood's romanticized, unrealistic portrayal of love whispered to her heart: *Do I really love him? Shouldn't love feel more dramatic, passionate, overwhelming?*

Maybe he's not really my soulmate.

Seductively, Hollywood's false light started to blind her heart. She actually called off the engagement, nearly forfeiting a lifetime of fruitful ministry and joyful companionship. Thankfully, someone confronted her lovingly and directly: "Are you committed to reel love (R-E-E-L) or real love (R-E-A-L)?"

That simple question broke the spell of deception. She recommitted herself and married her fiancé, and their love-filled and fruitful ministry became a powerful testament to God's faithful design. But the false light allured her to such an extent that she almost swam straight into the jaws of regret.

The Allure of Reel Sex

Many men never imagine they'll face this battle—until one day, they realize they've been quietly drawn in. One man wrote:

> "I never thought I would struggle with this. I was a committed Christian, married to a wonderful woman, and in my mind, I had done everything right. But somewhere along the way, I started believing a lie—a lie sold to me by Hollywood and reinforced by the pornography industry.
>
> I don't remember when it started, but I do remember the growing resentment. At first, it was subtle—just small disappointments. My wife didn't initiate intimacy as often as I thought she should. She wasn't as eager as I imagined a woman should be. I'd watch a TV show where the female lead was passionate, seductive, and uninhibited, and I'd think, *Why isn't my wife like that?*
>
> Then came the justifications. *She's depriving me. I have needs. This isn't adultery—it's just looking.* I started indulging in pornography, convincing myself it was a harmless outlet. But it wasn't harmless. It changed the way I saw my wife.
>
> I judged her. *Why isn't she more like those women? Why does she need emotional connection first? Why doesn't she crave me the way I crave her?*
>
> One night, after another cold interaction between us, I sat alone in my office. I had been on my phone, mindlessly scrolling, when I felt the Holy Spirit convict me so clearly it was almost audible: *You're grieving Me.*
>
> My walk with Christ had been slowly poisoned by my own choices.

Then, another thought hit me like a brick wall: *What if my daughter finds my search history?* My heart stopped. My little girl, the one I had prayed over since birth, the one I wanted to raise to love and honor God—what if she saw what her father had been looking at? What would that do to her? That moment shattered me.

I knew I had to change. I joined a men's accountability group. It was humbling, but it was also freeing. I wasn't alone. And I realized I had been allured by a falsehood."

These aren't just isolated struggles. They grow out of two radically different ways of seeing the world.

Two Worldviews

The Western world is divided by two fundamentally different perspectives on life and truth: One sees humanity guided by the revelation of God (the Judeo-Christian worldview). The other insists that humanity must be governed solely by what can be proven through human reason and scientific observation—placing ultimate authority in personal autonomy and self-defined truth (the secular worldview).

People of faith do not deny established scientific facts, and honest scientists will acknowledge that science cannot answer the deepest questions of why we are here, what our purpose is, and where we are going. The real divide is over which authority is ultimate. These opposing lenses influence how we understand love, respect, marriage, morality, and even the very meaning of life itself.

Consider the famous words of two scientists:

- Blaise Pascal: "There is a God-shaped vacuum in the heart of every man which cannot be filled by any created thing, but only by God, the Creator, made known through Jesus."
- Stephen Hawking: "There is no God. No one created the universe, and no one directs our fate."[1]

Two drastically different perspectives—one embraces divine revelation, the other rejects it entirely. One sees humanity guided by God's revelation about Jesus, the other sees humanity guided merely by human reason. These opposing worldviews do not just influence scientific thought or philosophy; they radically shape how we approach marriage and family.

During my PhD studies in child and family ecology, I encountered the secularist worldview head-on. I remember reading an author's ecological worldview (though I cannot find the exact quote) with the stark declaration: "We reject a revelatory worldview." As a pastor, I recall thinking, *That's a bold claim to put in writing about family ecology—especially to someone like me and many others seeking to serve families through the church.* I knew such authors held to this belief, but this was in your face. To these secular academics, my worldview was nothing more than a subjective preference, while theirs was the supposed enlightened and rational position. To them, I believed in myths. They believed in factual science. Yet all truth is God's truth, whether revealed in Scripture or discovered in creation. The real question is not whether truth exists but whether we will acknowledge its Source.

Usually, the rejection of divine revelation is woven into academic discourse—presumed rather than directly articulated. But here it was, laid out in black and white: "We reject a revelatory worldview." In other words, "We reject Jesus Christ and the Bible." Why state it so bluntly? Why poke people like me in the eye? Perhaps because, deep down, revelation threatens the assumption that human reasoning alone is sufficient. But that same secular mindset creeps into the marriages of some Christians.

Some husbands and wives long for more from their marriage than what God's Word promises this side of Eden. They feel dissatisfied when their relationship doesn't meet the heightened emotional and sexual expectations set by the world. Culture tells them that true love should always feel exhilarating, that passion should never fade, and that their spouse should be their ultimate source of happiness and fulfillment. While emotional connection and sexual intimacy are good and God-designed, the expectation of perpetual romantic euphoria is not biblical—it is a modern myth that sets couples up for disappointment. When reality falls short of these unrealistic ideals, disillusionment sets in, making them vulnerable to resentment or temptation, or even to seeking fulfillment outside of God's design.

Some doubt that God's Word is sufficient for the struggles they do have. "Our problems are too complex for simple prayers and Bible verses. We need counselors trained in modern psychology, personality assessments, and the latest relationship theories. We need practical strategies, not outdated religious ideals." While professional counseling can be helpful, the danger lies in believing that biblical truth is secondary—or even irrelevant—to marriage struggles. "We want therapy, not theology!" When Scripture is treated as optional rather than foundational, couples inadvertently reject the very wisdom that can truly guard and guide their relationship.

Some couples conclude that Scripture pales in comparison to a psychological insight that seems to explain why they are unhappy because of their spouse's shortcomings. They chase after the aha moment that allows them to shift blame and justify their own behavior, conveniently leaving out God's clear instruction to be the person He calls them to be, regardless of their spouse's failures.

For them, obedience to Scripture isn't part of the equation. Focusing on Scripture takes place only when highlighting passages that expose their spouse's wrongdoing. Then, suddenly, they entertain the idea of strategically positioning the holy text on the refrigerator so when their spouse walks by, they will read and repent.

Whether intentional or not, this mindset diminishes the authority of Scripture in their own lives—substituting worldly wisdom for divine truth. In doing so, they demand more than God has promised and reject the very help He has already provided.

Living by Divine Revelation

Jesus declared with authority, "It is written: 'Man shall not live on bread alone, but on every word that proceeds out of the mouth of God'" (Matthew 4:4 NASB1995).

At its core, this statement affirms that life is about far more than mere survival of the fittest. It is about God and His truth. This God is the Father of Jesus Christ. While bread sustains the body, God has spoken, and Jesus calls us to live by what is written (Matthew 4:4, 7, 10). While we must run the race to win, being fit to survive life's trials, we do so based on God's Word and with eternity in mind (1 Corinthians 9:24–27).

This perspective, the Holy Word, should shape every aspect of life, including emotional and sexual intimacy in marriage.

Consider the Implications of This Revelation

ABSOLUTE AUTHORITY

God's Word is our ultimate guide. Scripture is not a collection of human-authored inspirational quotes. It is the infallible Word of God, written by human hands under the inspiration of the Holy Spirit. Peter wrote, "Men moved by the Holy Spirit spoke from God" (2 Peter 1:21 NASB). Scripture teaches us, without error, the truth God intends for us to know and apply. Every major decision in life, especially concerning how we treat our spouse and build our marriage, must be rooted in the unchanging principles and commands of the Bible, not fleeting cultural trends.

THE WORD OF GOD PROVIDES A CLEAR AND UNWAVERING STANDARD FOR WHAT IS RIGHT AND WRONG, LOVING AND RESPECTFUL, FAITHFUL AND COMMITTED.

OBJECTIVE MORALITY

The Word of God provides a clear and unwavering standard for what is right and wrong, loving and respectful, faithful and committed. Paul wrote, "All Scripture is God-breathed [given by divine inspiration] and is profitable for instruction, for conviction [of sin], for correction [of error and restoration to obedience], for training in righteousness [learning to live in conformity to God's will, both publicly and privately—behaving honorably with personal integrity and moral courage]" (2 Timothy 3:16 AMP). Biblical truth does not fluctuate with societal trends or personal emotions. Instead, it anchors us in God's design, protecting us from false expectations about emotional and sexual intimacy that the world often promotes.

ETERNAL PURPOSE

If we trust and obey the words revealed in Scripture, we live with eternal significance: to glorify God with our lives. Marriage is not of human invention, a human contract, or a cultural tradition—it is a sacred covenant designed by God to reflect His image (Genesis 1:27) and the relationship between Christ and the church (Ephesians 5:25–32). Every act of kindness, sacrifice, honor, and forgiveness in marriage carries weight in this life by reflecting the character of God and His relationship with us. What we do in our marriage counts for eternity.

EARTHLY GUIDANCE

A revelatory worldview provides clear guidance when marriages experience tension, disappointment, or unmet expectations (1 Corinthians 7:28). God's wisdom directs us to trust Him, the One who joined us together (Matthew 19:6), knowing He works all things together for good for those who love Him and are called according to His purpose (Romans 8:28). This commitment to His Word empowers couples to weather storms, not viewing trials as mere misfortunes but rather as opportunities to trust and honor Him, even with a spirit of thanksgiving in anticipation of His leading.

Because of this foundation, a wife once declared to me with unwavering confidence, "If Jesus said it, that's good enough for me."

Rejecting Divine Revelation

Yet, in the West, we live in a world where many hold a radically different perspective. They explicitly assert, "We do not live by a revelatory worldview. There is no divine revelation."

This perspective insists that there is no absolute authority, objective morality, eternal purpose, or divine guidance. It directly contradicts Jesus' words, effectively declaring that we live by bread alone (Matthew 4:4). To them, Jesus is wrong—nothing is written, no divine revelation guides us. Humanity is left to fend for itself, a collection of autonomous beings among whom power, not truth, prevails. No God has spoken—only human reasoning and might reigns.

Having said this, some honestly stumble along, groping for truth. At present, they view Jesus as wrong or even imaginary. Since there is no God, there is no divine revelation. From their perspective, no higher power is looking out for us, so we must fend for ourselves. Without the gift of faith, a person doesn't see or hear God, so they look to science as the one thing that is unconditional. This perspective is rampant in the Western world and influences our culture in negative ways. The good news is that the Lord in His love opens their eyes and they come to Him for forgiveness, peace, and purpose.

Consider, though, the implications of this worldly approach to marriage:

- In marriage, there is no external reference point defining love, respect, sacrifice, or commitment. Each spouse determines what seems right or fair, and conflicts often become battles over whose preferences should dominate.
- Marital decisions—whether about finances, fidelity, communication, or parenting—are based not on absolute truth but on personal desires and priorities. This does not mean unbelievers necessarily make worse decisions than believers, as Jesus noted that "the sons of this age are more shrewd in relation to their own kind than the sons of light" (Luke 16:8 NASB). Yet, in their worldview, life is a brief existence between birth and death, managed as best as possible for personal fulfillment, survival, or societal expectations. Many who do not profess faith still pursue what is good, noble, and beautiful—whether serving others, creating art, or working for justice. The difference is not in the capacity for admirable actions but in the foundation and ultimate aim. Why does it ultimately matter? Without an eternal reference point, even the most noble pursuits end in the same place—a life that fades into history. If there is no ultimate meaning, then is there meaning at all?

- Sadly, for too many, the marital relationship lasts only as long as it "works" or "feels right." When emotions wane or challenges arise, divorce or separation often seem like the most practical solutions. Those who remain together may do so for financial, social, or practical reasons, while others, perhaps instinctively, uphold faithfulness without a deeper philosophical foundation for why it is morally right.

The Contrast

This contrast between a revelatory worldview and a purely humanistic one determines how we approach marriage, morality, and meaning itself. Without revelation, marriage becomes a personal arrangement to be evaluated, altered, or abandoned based on personal fulfillment. With revelation, marriage becomes a covenant before God, rooted in divine purpose and upheld by His sustaining help.

The question remains: Which worldview will we live by?

What About You?

Let's assume you fully embrace the Holy Word. You believe in the authority of Scripture as God's divine revelation to humanity. You affirm Jesus' words: "Man shall not live on bread alone, but on every word that proceeds out of the mouth of God" (Matthew 4:4 NASB1995).

You believe this wholeheartedly—at least in principle.

But here's the challenge: Many followers of Christ, who claim in the church that they firmly hold to Scripture's authority, still allow their hearts and minds to be subtly influenced by the anti-revelation worldview. Some, in the face of these voices, become ashamed of Jesus and His words (Mark 8:38).

When applied to marriage, this influence becomes clear in the battle between Hollywood and the Holy Word.

The Subtle Whisper of Hollywood

Hollywood, the voice of the carnal world, seductively whispers:

- "You are missing out on emotional fulfillment—your husband doesn't cherish you as passionately as he should."
- "You are being deprived sexually—your wife should crave intimacy just like the actresses on-screen."
- "Your marriage is mediocre compared to the excitement you see in movies or read in novels."

In other words, Hollywood plants a seed of doubt in your heart: God's Word may be good, but you're missing out on something better.

This is precisely how false light operates. It doesn't appear evil—it appears enticing, appealing, even beautiful. It promises happiness, excitement, and fulfillment. But ultimately, for the follower of Christ, it leads to emptiness, disillusionment, and discrediting. We must not have one foot in the world and one foot in the kingdom, for that leaves us attempting the impossible—to call ourselves followers of Jesus while living in ways that align with antichrist (2 Corinthians 6:14–15; 1 John 1:6). That is not conformity; it is contradiction. That is not devotion; it is distortion.

Scripture explicitly warns us: "Satan himself masquerades as an angel of light" (2 Corinthians 11:14). Satan rarely tempts us with blatant wickedness. Instead, he disguises deception as something desirable, something that seems like it will fulfill us but ultimately pulls us away from God's design.

Aggressive Mimicry: The Trap of False Light

In nature, there is a predatory tactic called aggressive mimicry, when a predator uses deception to attract its prey.

Consider the anglerfish:

- It has a luminous lure on its head that resembles a small glowing organism.
- Unsuspecting prey follows the light, thinking it leads to food.
- Instead, it swims directly into the predator's jaws.

This is exactly how false light works in our lives. The world presents a glowing illusion—an idea of love, honor, intimacy, or personal fulfillment that promises to meet our every desire and need. We chase after it, believing it will satisfy us. But instead of finding joy, we find destruction.

The Choice Before You

Will you follow the false light of Hollywood, or will you stand firmly on the Holy Word?

One leads to frustration and discontent—always believing you're missing out. The other leads to a life that pleases God and, in the end, hearing His words: "Well done, good and faithful servant."

This is not to say that when an atheistic man leaves his wife and four kids for another woman, his life will automatically be filled with misery. No, he may find emotional and sexual satisfaction in his new relationship. If that were not so, people wouldn't have affairs, divorce, and remarry. Temporary pleasure and emotional highs can be found outside of God's design.

Scripture constantly refers to "lovers," which suggests that forbidden relationships can indeed feel passionate and provide a measure of love (Hosea 2:5; Jeremiah 3:1). But the Bible is equally clear that the Christ-follower who pursues such a relationship quenches and grieves the Holy Spirit (Ephesians 4:30; 1 Thessalonians 5:19), erodes a clear conscience, and undermines the fruitfulness God intended for His kingdom purposes. Chemistry cannot excuse covenant-breaking and does not erase the call to holiness, the command to faithfulness, or the consequences of sin. Having a new lover, where one tastes of new love, cannot undo God's design for marriage or shield the believer from the spiritual fallout of disobedience.

Yes, Jesus forgives all who genuinely repent. But forgiveness does not halt the holy, loving discipline of God (Hebrews 12). David was forgiven for his adultery with Bathsheba, yet he and his household still endured devastating fallout for a lifetime (2 Samuel 12). God's forgiveness is complete, but his discipline remains because His purpose is not only to pardon but also to correct choices and reshape the character of those who rebel against Him. We deceive ourselves if we cling to forgiveness while closing our eyes to the reality of God's earthly judgment. Those standing on the front end of such temptation would do well to heed this warning.

I am not arguing that if one loves Jesus, a spouse will automatically fulfill all of one's emotional and physical needs. Scripture acknowledges the reality of unmet desires in marriage. A spouse can deprive us of emotional and sexual intimacy (1 Corinthians 7:5), and some marriages will face separation or abandonment (1 Corinthians 7:10–11).

But the question is not about short-term satisfaction—it's about ultimate fulfillment and obedience to God. The world offers temporary highs, but God offers eternal rewards (2 Corinthians 4:18). True peace comes not from chasing personal fulfillment but from trusting and obeying God's Word, even when it requires sacrifice. That's how I read Jesus and the Scriptures.

Will you chase after fleeting illusions, or will you anchor yourself in the truth of God's Word? The answer to that question will shape not just your marriage but your life, your legacy, and your eternity.

Which voice will you listen to?

The Biblical Truth About Emotional and Sexual Intimacy

God designed marriage to be deeply satisfying yet realistic. A godly marriage is profoundly fulfilling emotionally and sexually, yet it rarely matches Hollywood's exaggerated portrayals.

A wise, loving husband may never write romantic poems, serenade, or execute grand gestures of romance. Yet he faithfully protects, provides, listens patiently, solves problems, sacrifices willingly, and steadily expresses his love through quiet, consistent actions.

A faithful, godly wife may never drool at the thought of sexual intimacy or burn with unending sexual desire. Yet she joyfully engages with her husband, offering her heart and body as an expression of commitment, intimacy, and shared affection. She genuinely enjoys intimacy—not as Hollywood portrays but as God beautifully designed. She finds pleasure in pleasing.

THE WORLD OFFERS TEMPORARY HIGHS, BUT GOD OFFERS ETERNAL REWARDS.

Here is the core question for each of us: Will we choose the genuine, realistic, yet deeply fulfilling marriage offered by Scripture, or will we be seduced by Hollywood's illusion of perfect emotional or sexual fulfillment?

Ask yourself honestly:

- Have I been subtly influenced by Hollywood's portrayals of romantic or sexual intimacy?
- Have I compared my spouse unfavorably to a fictional standard rather than valuing their genuine love and faithfulness?
- Am I unknowingly punishing or accusing my spouse because of unrealistic expectations fostered by Hollywood?

Aha Moments in Marriage

Marriage is full of defining moments: some painful, some redemptive, all transformative. What follows are stories from real husbands and wives who experienced an aha moment—a revelation that changed not only how they saw their spouse but how they walked with God inside their marriage.

Wives: Letting Scripture Redefine Romance

FANTASY IS NOT REALITY

One wife confessed she frequently escaped into romance novels. Her inner world was filled with imagined scenes of perfect connection: a man who always understood her, anticipated her needs, and pursued her with relentless charm. But her husband, though loving and steady, didn't meet those fictional standards.

"I was setting my husband up for failure—no real person could live up to those ideals," she realized.

Her breakthrough came not through confrontation but through reflection. She saw that the man beside her was faithful, hardworking, and deeply committed. As she let go of fantasy, she began to notice what had been there all along: a husband who loved her in quiet, consistent ways. The moment she released her imaginary expectations, their marriage became a place of peace and gratitude, not disappointment.

SCRIPTURE NEVER TALKS ABOUT SOULMATES

Another wife shared how movies had shaped her expectations about marriage. She believed love should be effortless if she married "the right person." So when her relationship hit conflict, she panicked.

"When we started facing challenges, I thought maybe he wasn't my soulmate after all."

But as she sought God's Word and wise counsel, her mindset shifted. She saw that marriage wasn't about discovering a perfect match but becoming the kind of person who could love sacrificially.

"Marriage isn't about finding the perfect person—it's about becoming the right person."

That realization helped her move from fear to faith. Her marriage didn't need to feel cinematic to be holy.

FEELINGS CAN MISLEAD

A third woman shared how her desire for emotional connection took a dangerous turn. She developed an emotional attachment to a man who wasn't her husband—someone who made her feel admired and alive. Meanwhile, her husband was steady but emotionally restrained.

Conviction came unexpectedly as she read Scripture.

"I read in 2 Timothy 3:6–7 about being 'led by various impulses,' and it pierced me. I realized I had been following feelings, not faith."

Then she encountered Ezekiel 6:9: "How I have been hurt by their adulterous hearts which turned away from Me" (NASB). That verse stunned her. Her heart, though unfaithful in silence, had been drifting from both her husband and God.

She confessed everything. Her husband, though hurt, chose forgiveness. In the months that followed, they rebuilt—not on feelings but on faith and mutual grace.

Husbands: Letting Scripture Redefine Leadership

EMOTIONAL CONNECTION FIRST

A husband came to realize he had been pursuing physical intimacy without cultivating emotional closeness. He felt rejected when his wife didn't respond, assuming she lacked desire. But one night, she voiced what she had been feeling for years: "I feel like you only show affection when you want sex."

That line broke through his assumptions. He began to change—listening without an agenda, initiating prayer, giving affection without expectations. Over time, his wife softened.

"She enjoyed our times sexually—she no longer felt used," he reflected.

His transformation didn't begin with better technique; it began with better love—rooted in patience and spiritual leadership.

LOVE ISN'T A TRANSACTION

This husband lived by an unspoken formula: Do nice things, expect intimacy in return. He would plan date nights, help with chores, and silently wait for his reward. But his wife saw through it.

One evening, she confronted him gently but clearly: "I don't want to feel like I owe you something. I want to feel wanted, not obligated."

He was crushed—but grateful. Her words exposed a subtle manipulation he hadn't realized. She proposed a new approach: scheduled conversations and intimacy. At first it felt mechanical, but soon it brought comfort and safety.

"I learned love isn't a trade—it's trust," he said.

And that trust changed everything. He began serving without strings, and she responded with renewed affection.

THE CHOICE TO BE WORTHY OF TRUST

A professional athlete described the slow drift of his heart toward temptation. He never acted on the flirtations he received, but he entertained the attention, believing it was harmless.

One night when he came home, his wife greeted him with joy and full trust. In that moment, he broke inside.

"She trusted me completely. And I hadn't been guarding that trust."

He was convicted by Proverbs 6:27: "Can a man scoop fire into his lap without his clothes being burned?" He knew he had been playing with fire.

"Trust isn't just something you receive," he said. "It's something you choose to be worthy of."

From that moment, he made a vow: to walk in purity, not just for his marriage but for Christ. He shut temptation down before it could take root. The emotional connection with his wife deepened, not because of big changes but because he chose daily integrity.

Why the Holy Word Is the Ultimate Way Forward

Ultimately, Hollywood's version of marriage is a fleeting illusion, while the Holy Word offers a marriage of enduring significance and deep, lasting fulfillment. When we choose to live according to the Holy Word rather than Hollywood's script, we experience

- a marriage grounded in truth, not illusion;
- realistic yet satisfying emotional and sexual intimacy;
- growth in godly character through trials and misunderstandings;
- God's call to fulfill His kingdom purpose as a couple;
- long-term joy and spiritual peace, even amid struggles.

By aligning our marriages with Scripture's principles, we escape the empty deception of false light and discover the profound joy of authentic intimacy. This intimacy may never match Hollywood's script, but it will surpass it, producing a marriage rich with meaning, warmth, respect, and steadfast love.

> Blessed rather are those who hear the word of God and obey it. (Luke 11:28)

This is the secret Hollywood never shares: True fulfillment comes not by chasing elusive fantasies but by embracing God's perfect design for marriage—a marriage built on the enduring, life-giving foundation of His Holy Word.

What Do You Believe About the Scriptures, Really?

Let me invite you to join me in standing on these truths. When I first learned these as a new believer many decades ago, they not only profoundly affected my heart but have served as the foundation of what I believe and what I teach.

- Jesus Himself declared in Matthew 4:4, "Man shall not live on bread alone, but on every word that proceeds out of the mouth of God" (NASB1995). Do you believe that God's Word is essential to your married life?
- The writer of Hebrews affirms that God has spoken—not just in the past but now, through His Son. "God, after He spoke long ago to the fathers in the prophets in many portions and in many ways, in these last days has spoken to us in His Son" (Hebrews 1:1–2 NASB1995). Do you trust that Jesus is the final and fullest revelation of God?
- Peter urged us to remember that the words of Scripture are not merely human opinions but divinely inspired truth. "That you should remember the words spoken beforehand by the holy prophets and the commandment of the Lord and Savior spoken by your apostles" (2 Peter 3:2 NASB1995). Do you believe that the words of the prophets and apostles are still relevant and authoritative today?
- Jesus Himself declared to His disciples, "For all things that I have heard from My Father I have made known to you" (John 15:15 NASB1995). If

Jesus, the very Son of God, made known everything the Father revealed to Him, do you trust that Scripture contains all that we need to know about God's will?

- Peter made a bold statement about the origin of prophecy: "But know this first of all, that no prophecy of Scripture is a matter of one's own interpretation, for no prophecy was ever made by an act of human will, but men moved by the Holy Spirit spoke from God" (2 Peter 1:20–21 NASB1995). Do you believe that the Bible is not just a book written by men but a divine message inspired by the Holy Spirit?

TRUE FULFILLMENT COMES NOT BY CHASING ELUSIVE FANTASIES BUT BY EMBRACING GOD'S PERFECT DESIGN FOR MARRIAGE.

If these verses are true—and I believe they are—then we cannot treat God's Word lightly. We cannot twist it to fit our preferences or ignore the parts that challenge us.

The question is, Will we submit to God's revelation, trusting that He has spoken clearly, or will we choose to live by the wisdom of our culture?

Martin Luther championed *sola Scriptura*, meaning "Scripture alone," as the ultimate authority in matters of faith and practice. He believed that the Bible was the final and sufficient source of truth for the believer.

In today's world, what do you believe—the Holy Word or Hollywood?

PART B

ENHANCING SKILL—OUR EFFECTIVE INTERACTIONS

1. Our Clarity: Understanding Each Other, Not Just Talking
   Translation breakthrough: This couple struggled with miscommunication, even when intentions were good. One of them reflected, "I used to think if I could tell my spouse my feelings, everything would improve. If we could just talk more, we'd get on the same page." But clarity didn't come from more words. Many think communication is the key to marriage, but it is mutual understanding. She speaks pink and he speaks blue, and therefore we need to understand what each means by what they say and do. The turning point came when this couple began asking questions, laying down assumptions, and prioritizing understanding over simply expressing their own thoughts and emotions. As pink began to understand blue, and blue understood pink, real connection emerged. In the end, clarity wasn't found in more talking but in making sure both hearts felt heard and valued. That shift changed everything.
2. Our Harmony: Same Team, Same Goal, Different Plays

Unity insight: Another couple found themselves clashing over how they handled daily life—decision-making, stress, responsibilities. Each believed their own approach was best. "I assumed my way made the most sense," one admitted, "but so did my spouse." The constant tug-of-war created distance, not because they wanted different things but because they were blind to each other's perspective. Then came the breakthrough: They weren't adversaries—they were allies taking different roads to the same destination. When they stopped insisting on their own way and started appreciating each other's strengths, something shifted. Trust replaced control. They no longer competed to be right. Instead, they partnered to move forward—together.

3. Our Acknowledgment: Not Wrong, Just Different Shades of Right

   Mutuality epiphany: Another couple faced daily friction, not over values but over approach. One of them reflected, "For a long time, I saw my way as the right way. The way I handled problems, planned my day, or made decisions just made sense to me." When their spouse did things differently, it felt like resistance. Frustration brewed, fueled by the quiet assumption, *My way is better.* But prayer revealed a deeper issue: pride. "Different wasn't wrong—it was just different," they realized. That insight changed everything. By acknowledging the strengths in their spouse's approach, appreciation replaced irritation. They began to see how their differences weren't barriers, they were balance. What once caused tension became a source of unity.

4. Our Tension: Don't Let the 20 Percent Define the 80 Percent

   Refocus moment: This couple found themselves stuck in cycles of irritation, caught up in the little things that rubbed them the wrong way. "I used to focus too much on the things that annoyed me," one of them admitted. "Small habits, communication quirks, minor disagreements—I let them overshadow the bigger picture of who my spouse really was." Then they heard about the 80:20 ratio: That is, 80 percent of a person is what you love, 20 percent is what you wish you could change. "I realized I was letting the 20 percent take center stage." That insight prompted a shift. They chose to focus on the good—on the 80 percent. As their perspective changed, so did their heart. The 20 percent didn't disappear, but it no longer defined the relationship. Appreciation replaced frustration, and grace took the lead.

FIVE

OUR CLARITY: UNDERSTANDING EACH OTHER, NOT JUST TALKING

Translation breakthrough: Speaking more doesn't fix confusion—true communication means understanding each other's "pink" and "blue" language.

She says, "I have nothing to wear." She means nothing new. He says, "I have nothing to wear." He means nothing clean.

That joke always gets a big laugh—and reveals a deep truth. We can say the same words but mean completely different things.

WE CAN SAY THE SAME WORDS BUT MEAN COMPLETELY DIFFERENT THINGS.

She sees through pink sunglasses, hears with pink hearing aids, and speaks through a pink megaphone. He does the same through blue. This isn't stereotyping, it's recognizing that equal doesn't mean identical.

Many couples assume, "If we're equal, we should automatically understand each other." But equality isn't sameness, and without clarity, communication falls flat.

That's why I often challenge the common phrase "Communication is the key to marriage." Not quite. *Mutual understanding* is the real key. Without it, we just keep talking—and missing each other—using the exact same words.

Let me give you an example.

"You Never Listen to Me"

When a wife says "You never listen to me," she's usually not accusing. She's seeking emotional understanding. What she means is "You're not hearing my heart. I feel unseen, unheard, unconnected, and unloved." Her core pain is feeling ignored, which sounds like "You don't care how I feel. I'm not worth engaging with. I don't matter to you."

She isn't trying to attack. But if her tone becomes sharp or frustrated, it's often a cry underneath: "Will you engage emotionally and show me I matter?"

What he hears, however, is "You're an uncaring human being. You're not good enough as a husband. I don't respect you." So rather than hearing her cry for connection, he feels judged, like he's failed again. Now he pulls away to guard his heart.

When a husband says "You never listen to me," he's not trying to control. He's offering input, protection, or a solution. What he means is "You ignore my advice. You don't trust my judgment. You dismiss my input."

His core pain is feeling disrespected, which sounds like "You value my ideas only when they align with what you already want. You don't think I know what I'm talking about. You don't value my insight or leadership."

What she hears is "You're incapable of following instructions. You're inferior. You're selfish and just do what you want." So instead of hearing his desire to help, she feels demeaned. He's trying to contribute, but she feels talked down to. Both are now hurt.

Here's the honest misunderstanding: Neither spouse is trying to wound the other. Both are speaking from pain. But because they are wired differently, their emotional filters translate the same words into very different meanings.

She thinks, *Why doesn't he care how I feel?*

He thinks, *Why doesn't she trust what I'm saying?*

Ephesians 5:33 is often at play here: The wife feels unloved; the husband feels disrespected. That's why I say talking more isn't the solution.

The Honest Misunderstanding

Often, they're not really disagreeing about the issue—they're missing each other emotionally. What began as a simple topic, like a scheduling conflict or a budget concern, morphs into something deeper: a threat to emotional safety. She's fighting to feel loved. He's fighting to feel respected.

When a wife feels unheard, she often interprets it as unloving. When a husband feels disregarded, he usually experiences it as disrespectful. These perceptions can lead to reactions that escalate tension rather than resolve it.

That's why clear communication is more than just getting your point across. It's recognizing how the other is wired and choosing to speak in a way that honors both love and respect.

Why Conversations Escalate So Quickly

Husbands and wives don't just exchange words. They navigate conversations loaded with history, emotion, and expectation. At first glance, many conversations seem routine: a discussion about finances, parenting, schedules, or weekend plans. But what should be a logical dialogue quickly escalates into frustration, hurt, or even withdrawal.

Why does this happen?

Because marriage conversations aren't just about facts—they're about feelings.

A husband may think he's simply making a point, but his wife feels dismissed. A wife may believe she's sharing a concern, but her husband feels criticized. Both are confused when the other reacts so strongly: *Why are they upset? That's not what I meant at all!*

This is where communication breaks down—not because of intent but because of emotional filters. One feels unappreciated. The other feels misunderstood. What began as a factual discussion now feels personal.

MARRIAGE CONVERSATIONS AREN'T JUST ABOUT FACTS—THEY'RE ABOUT FEELINGS.

This doesn't mean one spouse is overly sensitive or the other is emotionally detached. It means we interpret communication through different emotional needs. Unless couples recognize and honor these differences, even simple conversations can go off track.

That's why clarity matters—not just in what is said but in what is understood. When love and respect are missing, even the right words can feel wrong.

The Emotional Charge Behind Miscommunication

Do you agree, generally speaking, that beneath most marital tension lies an emotional trigger tied to love and respect (Ephesians 5:33)? Do you also agree that when a wife feels unloved and the husband feels disrespected, this sets off the Crazy Cycle: Without love, she reacts without respect, and without respect, he reacts without love? Regardless of the issue at hand, once the Crazy Cycle spins, more words will not move them forward until each acknowledges how the other feels—and does so without a dismissive attitude that says "Quit being so childish."

But when love and respect are emotionally restored—both feeling loved and respected even slightly—the cycle can be broken and a healthy conversation on the issue at hand can take place.

Sometimes, the Crazy Cycle reverses. The wife's deepest need is not just to feel loved but to be honored as an equal (1 Peter 3:7). The husband's deepest need is not just respect but the warmth of love and friendship (Song of Solomon 5:16; Titus 2:4).

Peter commands husbands to "show her honor as a fellow heir of the grace of life" (1 Peter 3:7 NASB1995). The Greek *aponomentes timēn* means to assign value; *sunklēronomos* declares her a coheir—equal in Christ, a full partner in God's grace. Her pain point here is not merely lack of affection but feeling diminished or disregarded.

Titus 2:4 tells wives to love their husbands—*philandros*, from *philos* (friend) and *anēr* (man). This is not only *agapē* love but friendship-love: warmth, enjoyment, companionship. Like the Shulammite's words in Song of Solomon 5:16 (NASB1995), "This is my beloved and this is my friend," a husband longs to feel that his wife likes him, not just loves him by duty.

I can say with certainty that both spouses need love and respect. So, when a husband sounds dismissive or harsh, his wife doesn't just feel disrespected—she feels unloved. And when a wife sounds critical or intense, a husband rarely says, "You're not loving me." Almost never. He says, "Why are you being so disrespectful? Why are you so negative and unfriendly?" That's where he lands.

This emotional filter is where conversations begin to derail.

Couples don't always realize this is happening. What starts as a simple discussion becomes emotionally charged and frustrating. The actual topic—budgeting, parenting, chores—fades. Now they're reacting to how they feel treated.

- A budget discussion becomes a conversation about judgment and rejection.
- A parenting decision becomes a standoff over who's truly valued.
- A practical concern turns into personal hurt.

The issue isn't a lack of communication, it's a lack of emotional clarity. And when one spouse expresses feeling unloved or disrespected, the other may respond with logic: "You shouldn't feel that way." But feelings don't vanish when explained away. They need to be acknowledged.

Here's the good news: This cycle doesn't have to dominate your marriage. Once you recognize why conversations go sideways—and commit to handling them with clarity and grace—you can break the pattern. You can begin working as a team again.

Sarah and I have had our share of "Crazy Cycle" moments. But once we named what was really happening, everything changed. That lightbulb moment prepared us for the next time—and we've needed it.

The Budgeting Conversation

Let's take a common issue, budgeting, and watch how quickly things escalate when emotional needs aren't acknowledged.

Kelly has overspent on gifts this quarter. Scott sits down with her to address the budget.

Numbers should be neutral, but they rarely are. Money often carries emotional weight: It represents values, priorities, and even love and respect.

Scott says, "You overspent again this month on gifts. I thought we agreed not to do that."

Kelly hears criticism without empathy. To her, the gifts were expressions of love. She feels misunderstood.

She responds, "Yes, I gave gifts to people I care about. I wasn't spending on myself. Maybe we need to change the budget and take from your recreation category."

Now Scott feels accused and defensive. She's not owning her mistake. She's just deflecting and blaming him, so he feels.

At this point, the discussion isn't about the numbers—it's about how they feel treated. (This story could just as easily be reversed, with Scott overspending and Kelly confronting the issue; the emotional dynamics, however, are usually the same.)

The Crazy Cycle ignites. She feels unloved and responds with disrespect. He feels disrespected and responds without love. The original issue disappears. Now it's about tone, trust, and whether either one truly feels heard and understood.

They're sidetracked, emotionally distanced, and nothing is resolved.

In many marriages, one person will then try to reconnect. Let's say Kelly circles back, hoping Scott will acknowledge her intentions. But Scott, like many husbands, shuts down. Now they're not just unreconciled financially—they're unreconciled relationally.

To reset the conversation, each spouse must start by asking the right question:

- Scott: "Am I sounding unloving?"
- Kelly: "Am I sounding disrespectful?"

That simple self-check can stop the spiral. Truth is, when this is asked sincerely, few questions possess the power to put a couple back on track more. But if they don't ask, frustration will grow, assumptions will fester, and the issue will go unresolved.

Here's what healing sounds like:

- Scott: "I wasn't trying to be unloving. I'm sorry. Will you forgive me?"
- Kelly: "I wasn't trying to be disrespectful. I'm sorry. Will you forgive me?"

When they own and hone their tone, they reset the dialogue.

Is there power here? Well, what happens to your heart when your spouse genuinely makes this statement and asks for forgiveness of you? What happens when they approach the conversation again but this time with words that sound loving and respectful?

This isn't about being perfect—it's about being aware. The budget isn't the real battleground. It's how they make each other feel in the process of solving problems. The good news? When love and respect are restored, even money conversations can become moments of connection.

Breaking the Cycle: How to Reset the Pattern

If the Crazy Cycle has taken over, the solution isn't more words—it's better words. Talking more won't fix miscommunication, but talking differently will.

That means shifting from reacting to responding. From defending to understanding. From trying to win to seeking connection.

Couples can break the automatic patterns of hurt and begin replacing frustration with clarity. That change begins with humility, awareness, and two key practices.

Two Practical Ways to Break the Cycle

1. Acknowledge Intent Before Jumping to Conclusions

Instead of assuming the worst, start by assuming the best. Acknowledge your spouse's likely intent, then express how it landed on you.

- A wife can say, "I know you're not trying to shut me out, but when you go silent, I feel disconnected."
- A husband can say, "I know you're not trying to criticize me, but when you bring up my mistakes, I feel like I'm never good enough."

Acknowledging goodwill disarms defensiveness. It shifts the conversation from blame to mutual care.

2. Set a Time Limit on Difficult Conversations

Many husbands fear endless conflict.

Many wives fear unresolved silence.

The solution? Create a time boundary.

- A husband can offer fifteen focused minutes daily—engaged, not distracted.
- A wife can agree to stay concise and focused.

Research backs this up: Relationship studies by John Gottman, Howard Markman, and others show that most productive conversations aimed at resolving an issue take about ten to twenty minutes. After that, the likelihood of emotional escalation rises, especially if one or both spouses feel flooded. For many men in particular, a time limit signals safety, keeps the conversation on track, and prevents shutting down.

INSTEAD OF ASSUMING THE WORST, START BY ASSUMING THE BEST.

Are there times when fifteen minutes isn't enough? Absolutely. If an issue needs more, pause the discussion and agree on a specific time—later that evening or the next day—to finish it. The key is that you're choosing to continue, not drifting into an unending, exhausting exchange.

Short, structured conversations protect both spouses from emotional burnout. And more importantly, they create consistent opportunities for clarity, connection, and healing.

The Five-Step Word Picture of How Conversations Get Off Track—and How to Get Them Back on Track

Conversations in marriage are meant to bring clarity, but often they bring conflict. What starts as a simple talk about visiting the in-laws, rearranging work schedules, scheduling when to have friends over, and using mobile phones at the dinner table quickly spirals into frustration and hurt. Why? Because when something is said that sounds unloving and disrespectful, the facts fade and feelings take over.

This five-step framework shows you how to stay on topic, recognize emotional misfires, and stop spiraling before it's too late. Each step gives you a phrase to use—a reset moment. Miss it, and the tension will likely carry you to the next stage. But if you catch it in time, you protect both your clarity and connection.

Step 1: Envision the Whiteboard—Will We Keep the Issue the Issue?

Picture a whiteboard. Both spouses write their perspectives:

- He writes: "We need to follow the budget."
- She writes: "I want more in the gift-giving category."

At this point, the issue is clear and constructive. The whiteboard helps both stay on task.

But here's where it breaks down. He adds, "You're already spending too much on gifts that people don't need." She counters, "You're just stingy." Emotion replaces reason. Now, instead of solving a budgeting question, they're launching personal accusations.

Phrase to use: "Let's keep the issue the issue."

This small redirect protects the conversation. But if no one says it, the next step is inevitable: emotional deflation and reaction.

Step 2: Acknowledge the Air Hoses—Will We Step on Them or Stay Off Them?

Now imagine each spouse connected to an emotional air hose. Her air hose connects to a love tank, his to a respect tank.

- A wife breathes love. Even small critiques can make her feel unseen (unloved).
- A husband breathes respect. A sharp tone can make him feel diminished (disrespected).

Each has a vulnerability where the other does not. What she feels is unloving toward her, he doesn't really see that way. What he feels is disrespectful toward him, she doesn't really see that way.

What often happens: She says, "Why do you care more about numbers than people?" He replies, "You never steward as God intends, which is why we have a budget." They step—or stomp—on each other's air hoses. Both deflate.

Phrase to use: "Are we stepping on each other's air hoses here?"

If you say this, you restore awareness and hopefully can apologize and get back on topic. If you don't? You both feel wounded and your defenses rise. That's when the whiteboard begins to teeter. We are throwing verbal elbows and banging into the whiteboard.

Step 3: The Whiteboard Teeters—Will We Knock It Over or Leave It Standing?

At this stage, it's not about money anymore—it's an emotionally charged room that has squeezed out rationality, understanding, and empathy.

- He feels accused and reacts unlovingly. He'll show her that she can't say such disrespectful things and think he will bow to her.
- She feels dismissed and reacts disrespectfully. She'll show him that she's no doormat, and he's not the boss of her.

What this looks like: He accuses her of being totally irresponsible. She calls him cold and controlling. The whiteboard crashes. No one is solving the issue—they're in attack mode and verbally lunging at each other. Hopefully they come to their senses, go a bit quiet, and say things differently.

Phrase to use: "I think our whiteboard just got knocked over. We need to stop attacking each other and attack the issue. We need to get back on topic."

If this isn't said, you're no longer in a conversation—you're in a clash. And now, you're spinning. You've entered the Crazy Cycle.

Step 4: Spinning on the Crazy Cycle—Will We Call a Time-Out or Not?

Why does the Crazy Cycle cause so much damage?

- She feels unloved and reacts disrespectfully, maybe with contempt.
- He feels disrespected and reacts unlovingly, maybe with hostility.

Contempt and hostility are deadly toxins in marriage. Hostility is like fire, devouring everything in its path. Contempt is like acid, eating away at the very foundations of intimacy. Together, they leave nothing but ashes and ruins where love and respect once lived.

Such reactions trigger emotions so deeply that no healthy conversation will ensue. Our defensive reactions are offensive. Offending another person makes it next to impossible for them to hear the deeper and even noble message we seek to send. We may be right but are wrong at the top of our voice. We need a time-out. Hopefully, one person can gain enough composure to call for a time-out.

Phrase to use: "Let's pause for fifteen. I care more about us than this argument. Let's come back and finish this with calmer hearts."

This is not abandoning the conversation—it's protecting it. But if you don't call time-out, bitterness takes over. Even if the conflict quiets, you're both internally detached. And the whiteboard is lying on the floor.

Step 5: Returning to the Whiteboard—Will We Set It Back Up and Start Again, or Not?

After a pause, you can begin again. Put the whiteboard back up and return to what was written earlier. Then say . . .

- "Here's what I meant. I appreciate your generous heart, but how can we also maintain a budget?"
- "Well, here's what I meant. I need your great capabilities at budgeting, but help me put my generosity leanings somewhere in the budget, if that can work for you."

Now, you're reengaging—not to win but to resolve. Love and respect are restored, and the real issue is back on the board.

Phrase to use: "Let's push reset and take another run at this."

If you skip this? Malice and scorn linger. The issue stays unresolved. But when you push reset, conversations become collaborative, not combative.

How Can We Avoid Repeating This Conflict?

Couples who move through these five steps not only resolve the moment but build a pattern for future peace. Here's what helps them stay out of the Crazy Cycle:

- **They keep the issue the issue,** focusing on the topic at hand instead of drifting into personal criticism.
- **They stay off each other's air hoses,** avoiding emotional deflation and maintaining mutual dignity.
- **They catch the whiteboard before it falls,** recognizing when emotions start taking over and redirecting the conversation.
- **They call time-outs wisely,** interrupting the spiral instead of letting it spin into deeper disconnection.
- **They reset quickly,** not because they ignore hurt but because they've dealt with it lovingly and respectfully and are ready to reengage.

It really comes down to five decisive questions, each one a moment of choice:

- Will we keep the issue the issue—or let it get personal?
- Will we stay off each other's air hoses—or step on them and deflate our spouse?
- Will we catch the whiteboard before it falls—or let our emotions knock it over?
- Will we call a time-out—or let the Crazy Cycle control us?
- Will we push reset—or let frustration and resentment push us apart?

In conclusion, communication isn't just about what's said—or about saying more or saying it louder. It's about what's felt, interpreted, and understood. Behind every word is a heart either reaching out or protecting itself.

When couples recognize that they speak different emotional dialects—often filtered through gender, personality, and past experiences—they can stop reacting and start relating. That's where mutual understanding is born. And mutual understanding is what turns communication from a point of conflict into a path toward connection.

BEHIND EVERY WORD IS A HEART EITHER REACHING OUT OR PROTECTING ITSELF.

When we slow down to listen not just to the words but to the heart behind them, when we apply love and respect even in disagreement, we move from miscommunication to meaningful conversations as friends—good, good friends. That's the real breakthrough.

SIX

OUR HARMONY: SAME TEAM, SAME GOAL, DIFFERENT PLAYS

Unity insight: Your differences allow you to brainstorm and find the best route to the same destination.

Not long ago, Sarah and I were in southern France with our daughter Joy; her husband, Matt; and their three children. They live in Paris, seven hours away by car. After our time together, they returned to Paris. Sarah and I stayed a couple of more weeks in southern France. Then came the question: How should we get to Paris to see them? We had the same goal—reuniting with family. But the route? That was up for discussion. Fly (efficient and quick) or take the train (slower but scenic). Same goal. Two different approaches.

And isn't that often the story in marriage? It's not that we disagree about what we want, it's that we differ on how to pursue it.

We want financial security for the future—but how best do we pursue it? By saving aggressively, cutting back, or working longer hours to generate more income?

We want a satisfying marriage emotionally and sexually—but how best do we cultivate that? By connecting emotionally first to awaken sexual desire or by connecting sexually to draw our hearts closer?

Same desire and destination. But often very different routes.

If most couples thought about it for a moment, they would realize they have a shared vision and common goals on most things. They both want to live with peace in the home, enjoy financial stability, and stay healthy and active into their later years.

I need to make a strong statement: Christ-following husbands and wives have more in common than where they differ.

We Share Twenty-Seven Common Goals

IF MOST COUPLES THOUGHT ABOUT IT FOR A MOMENT, THEY WOULD REALIZE THEY HAVE A SHARED VISION AND COMMON GOALS ON MOST THINGS.

Yes, twenty-seven. That number may sound arbitrary, even a little contrived. But at the deepest level, it isn't arbitrary at all. These goals reflect the absolutes of God's design for marriage—truths that transcend culture, personality, and preference. The point is simple: You and your spouse already want the same things more often than you think. Highlighting them brings into focus the unity God has woven into your relationship from the start.

You want clear, Christ-honoring goals. Shared convictions that reflect the heart of Jesus for your home, your character, and your impact on the world.

These goals fall into three big categories that shape every part of life: faith, formation, and fruitfulness.

Let's walk through them, lightly and quickly, so you get a "feel" for how true these twenty-seven are.

Faith: Our Upward Devotion and Walk with God

1. Trust Jesus together—not just for salvation but in daily stress and decisions.
2. Experience God's power—not rely on our own strength.
3. Learn from Scripture—not be driven by culture or emotion.
4. Worship with gratitude—not grumble or forget His goodness.
5. Value each other's gifts and callings—not compare or compete.
6. See life through a biblical lens—not a self-centered or worldly one.
7. Invite the Holy Spirit to renew us—not force our way.
8. Leave a legacy of faith—not just memories.
9. Live to hear "Well done"—not just live for today.

Formation: Our Inward Character, Home, and Relationships

1. Grow in spiritual and emotional maturity.
2. Build a warm, satisfying friendship—not just share space.
3. Understand each other better—not make assumptions.
4. Resolve conflict instead of avoid or escalate it.
5. Create a peaceful, Christ-centered home.
6. Raise children with wisdom and faith.
7. Steward finances, health, and time well.
8. Enjoy healthy emotional and sexual intimacy.
9. Balance life wisely—not run on fumes.

Fruitfulness: Our Outward Life and Impact on Others

1. Nurture deep, life-giving friendships.
2. Serve others with our time, gifts, and resources.
3. Share the gospel naturally and boldly.
4. Mentor others with purpose and humility.
5. Give generously, not fearfully.
6. Offer hospitality with joy, not obligation.
7. Care for family and friends in need.
8. Embrace later years with meaning—not just comfort.
9. Model a Christ-centered identity—not just a functional life.

So Yes, We Share Twenty-Seven Common Goals

You don't have to memorize the list. These goals are already in you because God put them there (Romans 5:5; Philippians 2:13; Hebrews 10:16). The Holy Spirit Himself is writing God's desires into your heart, shaping your prayers, guiding your choices, and nudging you toward love and respect. This is the promise of the new covenant: God has written His law on our hearts (Jeremiah 31:33; Hebrews 10:16). His truth is already within you far more than you realize (1 John 2:27). Yes, we can resist or suppress these truths, but doing so takes effort, and it leads only to a hardened, calloused heart (Hebrews 3:12–13). But here is the good news: Beneath the resistance, the deeper reality remains. God has already planted His truth within you, waiting to be embraced.

Thus, you're not as far apart as you may think. You're not aimless, you're aiming at the same destination.

Of course, different seasons call for focusing on specific goals while postponing others. That's normal. We cannot—and should not—try to pursue all twenty-seven every single day. That's not the point of the list. The point of the three categories is to give you a clear picture of your shared common ground.

And when you differ on how to reach those goals, you can speak to each other: "Remember! Same Savior. Same team. Same goals."

Different Routes

Tension usually comes not from wanting different destinations but from disagreeing on how to get there—and which goal takes priority in this season.

Often, we're simply studying different routes on the same map. She says, "Let's take the train to Paris." He replies, "Let's fly." Both are aiming at Paris, but now the question arises: Who decides, since a decision must be made?

Let me illustrate.

End-of-Life Care for Grandma

- **Same destination:** We both agree we have a responsibility to care for our dying grandmother with dignity and compassion.
- **Different route:** One believes she would be better cared for in a retirement center with full-time staff and medical oversight. The other feels strongly that keeping her at home with part-time nursing allows her to remain in a familiar, comforting environment.

Church Involvement

- **Same destination:** We both want to serve meaningfully in our local church for the cause of Christ.
- **Different route:** One spouse wants to volunteer for a time-consuming ministry opportunity based on the pastor's appeal. The other values church service but feels the family's current schedule requires a more sustainable level of involvement, enabling a long-term vision of service without exhaustion.

Dealing with Extended Family

- **Same destination:** We both want healthy boundaries and peaceful relationships with extended family as an expression of our love.
- **Different route:** One believes in direct, honest confrontation (speak the truth in love) when something inappropriate happens. The other prefers to stay quiet, extend grace, and avoid stirring up conflict, remembering that love covers a multitude of sins.

Each of these situations reinforces—or should reinforce—that we're not divided because we want different outcomes. We're divided because we see different ways to get there.

That's not a sign of dysfunction; it's an opportunity to sharpen our focus and brainstorm the best path forward. Most of these choices fall into the gray areas of life where Scripture doesn't give a direct command. No verse says, "Thou shall not put grandma in a nursing home."

And even when Scripture calls us to love, for instance, that love can take different forms. Sometimes love means speaking the truth in love (Ephesians 4:15). Other times, love means remembering that love covers a multitude of sins (1 Peter 4:8). Both are biblical. Both aim at the same destination. The difference lies in discerning which route best applies in a given circumstance.

Okay, what do we do?

Begin Here: The Lightbulb Moment

Years ago, Sarah and I had a lightbulb moment: We're on the same team. We both have goodwill. We both want God's will. We want the same outcome—we just disagree on how to get there.

Same team. Same goal. That insight doesn't solve everything, but without it, resolution is nearly impossible. You can't build unity while acting like opponents.

Sadly, many couples never name this truth: Same team. Same goal. They slip into seeing each other as adversaries—not due to opposing goals but to differing routes. Suddenly, a disagreement becomes a battle. And like in combat, "friendly fire" happens—you end up wounding the very person you vowed to love and honor. And repeated friendly fire? It can kill a marriage.

"We Shouldn't Have These Differences!"

Is something wrong if conflict keeps showing up in your marriage?

Yes, if every disagreement turns into yelling, ultimatums, or power plays. That's not a routing problem—it's a rowdy problem. It signals a breakdown in humility, goodwill, and mutual respect.

But no, not if you keep returning to the truth: Same team. Same goal. You want the same outcomes, even if you see different paths. Strategy differences don't break a marriage—self-righteousness, contempt, and coercion do.

Healthy couples still argue. But they don't weaponize their preferences or make their way the moral high ground. Instead, they say, "Let's talk this through. Help me understand your view. Let's blend our ideas."

Conflict isn't the problem. How you walk through it—together—is what makes all the difference. Handled with humility, your differences won't divide you. They'll refine you.

YOU CAN'T BUILD UNITY WHILE ACTING LIKE OPPONENTS.

The Normalcy of Challenges

Challenges in marriage aren't signs of failure or evidence you married the wrong person. They're simply real-life pressures that God uses for your growth.

Paul shared an astonishing truth in 1 Corinthians 7:28 "Those [who marry] will have troubles" (AMP). Not might—will. He's not being cynical; he's simply grounding us in reality. Marriage is beautiful, but it isn't trouble-free. What trouble? Earlier, he conveyed an even more stunning revelation: "The wife does not have authority over her own body, but the husband does; and likewise also the husband does not have authority over his own body, but the wife does" (7:4 NASB1995).

In the bedroom, both husband and wife have an equal authority—an equal voice and equal say—when it comes to sexual and emotional intimacy.

So, who decides? That's where the beauty and challenge of marriage meet. Both long for the same destination—deep physical and heart-to-heart connection—but sometimes they prefer different routes. She may long for emotional intimacy first, which then opens the door to sexual arousal and pleasure. He may desire sexual intimacy first, anticipating that emotional closeness follows in its wake as they lie together and share their hearts.

Neither approach is wrong. The wisdom comes in recognizing the shared goal and learning to honor each other's preferred route when possible. This is how "trouble" and equal "authority" are transformed into teamwork: mutually meeting each other's needs and vulnerabilities (1 Corinthians 7:1–5). She listens and responds to his need for her without dismissing him as selfish. He slows down to hear her words and heart, without minimizing her as overly emotional. In the end, they find themselves holding each other, body and soul. Both feeling loved, respected, and understood.

God calls two flawed but well-intentioned people to step into the realities of marriage, including the honest differences and challenges in the bedroom. But that friction isn't a red flag. As Proverbs 27:17 says, "As iron sharpens iron, so one person sharpens another." Sparks fly, but something meaningful is being forged.

So when challenges arise, and they will, don't interpret them as proof of dysfunction. They are opportunities for growth and mutual satisfaction, protection, and agreement. In the list below, none of us want these difficulties and stressors, but we all encounter some regularly. How do you navigate these?

First Things First: We Are on the Same Team

Will simply saying "Same team. Same goal" solve the issue? Yes and no.

The mindset of being teammates (allies, not adversaries) won't fix everything, but it's the essential beginning. Without it, true resolution rarely takes root.

Saying "Same Team. Same Goal"

Saying "Same team. Same goal" can be a powerful shift in any marital moment of tension. It helps both spouses lower their defenses and truly listen, creating space for honest, gentle collaboration. This mindset reminds each person that the relationship is a partnership, not a battleground. It's not *me versus you* but *us versus the issue*. When this phrase becomes part of the conversation, it builds security, allowing both parties to work through disagreement without fear of attack. It encourages humility: "I don't have all the answers, but I'm with you." It also invites the Holy Spirit to guide both hearts toward unity. Most importantly, it transforms the moment from a personal victory into a shared mission, replacing pride with purpose and division with direction.

Why Does This Work?

When hearts align, minds can collaborate. It's no longer "your problem" or "my problem." It becomes *our* problem. And this isn't just a good relational principle—it's a biblical one. The Lord Himself expects us to embrace this mindset. He made us equal but not identical. Genesis 1:27 says, "Male and female he created them." Equal in worth. Distinct in wiring. So it's no surprise we process, decide, and respond differently.

The trouble begins when "becoming one" gets misinterpreted as "you should agree with me." An honest difference is recast as a personal deficiency, and disagreement quickly slides into disapproval. That shift doesn't just spark conflict; it fuels a reactive cycle of frustration, hurt, and defensiveness.

But God didn't design your spouse to be your clone. As most of us have heard, "If you are the same, one of you is unnecessary." In fact, many of the very differences that now frustrate you are the same ones that first drew you in when you were dating, courting, and choosing to marry. So instead of assigning blame, reach back for that early appreciation.

Most Strategy Tension Falls Into Four God-Woven Categories

These aren't signs of dysfunction. They're part of God's plan to stretch and strengthen your ability to make wise, united decisions—as a team. The truth is, you once valued these differences. Opposites attract . . . then opposites attack. But what if those tensions are invitations to deeper understanding, not threats to unity?

GOD DIDN'T DESIGN YOUR SPOUSE TO BE YOUR CLONE.

Design Differences

God made us unique. Our wiring, instincts, and relational patterns are not mistakes, they're intentional. Gender differences, for example, affect how we process emotion, respond to stress, and relate in conflict. As Genesis 1:27 reminds us, male and female are equal in value yet different by design. Personality differences also play a key role. Some are structured and task-driven, others more flexible and relational. Temperament adds another layer: A naturally upbeat, talkative person may approach life very differently than someone who is introspective and steady. Even our emotional and sexual needs differ, often along lines of gender or personality. These variations can easily be misinterpreted as flaws when, in truth, they're part of how God shaped each of us. Traits aren't defects—they're defaults. When we stop trying to "fix" our spouse's design and start understanding it, empathy begins to grow.

Developmental Differences

While design is about wiring, development is about shaping. Our life experiences—past joys, wounds, family patterns, and spiritual history—form how we engage in the present. One spouse may come from a loud, expressive household, while the other was raised in an environment of quiet restraint. Trauma, loss, or even great success can mold our fears, values, and expectations. Sometimes spiritual maturity is also out of sync: One may feel vibrant and faith-filled, while the other is walking through doubt or exhaustion. And then there's communication style. Some people process out loud, while others reflect internally before speaking. None of these differences are wrong, but they must be respected. Understanding your spouse's background doesn't excuse sin, but it often explains patterns. Compassion deepens when we stop saying, "What's wrong with them?" and start asking, "What shaped them?"

Situational Differences

Some tension isn't about personality or history, it's about the season you're in. Stress, grief, health challenges, or sheer exhaustion can shrink our capacity to love and respect well. When one spouse is maxed out with responsibilities—whether through work, caregiving, or mental load—and the other has more flexibility, it can feel imbalanced and unfair. It's easy to interpret this mismatch as laziness or neglect, when it may just be a matter of differing capacity. Parenting demands, job changes, extended family needs, or even disrupted sleep patterns can all affect how we show up for each other. These situational pressures don't define your relationship, but they unquestionably affect it. And seasons change. What worked before may not work now. Naming the season helps soften the tension and reminds both of you: This is temporary, and we're in it together.

Processing Differences

Even when spouses share the same goal, they often take different paths to get there. One may prefer to leap in faith, while the other wants to pause and pray. One moves fast, the other needs more time. One processes by solving problems, the other by seeking connection. You may both care deeply about grace, truth, or stewardship but rank those values differently when a decision needs to be made. These aren't signs of division. They're evidence of diversity in how God refines unity. You may want the same thing—a peaceful home, a wise decision, a flourishing relationship—but you simply prefer different routes. That's not a threat. It's a call to deeper trust. Learning to understand each other's processing style can turn friction into forward motion—not by demanding agreement at every turn but by honoring the journey together.

Emerson, This Is Too Much!

Now, before you throw up your hands and sigh, "No wonder we can't get on the same page!" pause, take a deep breath, and hear this: This isn't a list of four categories to overwhelm you. It's a lens to help you, like the twenty-seven goals of commonality.

These reasons for differences aren't indictments—they're insights. You and your spouse are not broken just because you approach things differently. Yes, when misunderstood, these differences create tension. But when seen through the right lens, they become God's raw materials to build understanding, empathy, unity, and resolution.

This list isn't meant to discourage you. It's here to normalize what's actually very common and to equip you to handle it with wisdom. These reasons for strategy conflict should relieve the anxiety you feel over having them in the first place.

You are not doomed. You didn't make a mistake in marrying this person. You are just different. And you are going to be okay.

Let's Assume a Stalemate—and Your Way Is Best

Let's say you're stuck. You both care, both have a perspective—but neither is budging. Each feels, "I know what is the greater good, the better way, and the best option. So, we're doing it my way."

Here's the danger: When one spouse declares, "We're doing it my way—take it or leave it," the issue is no longer about strategy. It's now about control. That posture silences dialogue and replaces unity with dominance. The unspoken message becomes "I don't need to seek your alliance—just your compliance."

Even if the plan is wise, a unilateral decision can cause deep damage. Why? Because over time, your spouse begins to wonder, *Do my thoughts even matter?* Eventually, they may stop speaking up—not because they agree but because they've given up. Unilateral decision-making slowly erodes trust, stifles input, and shuts down the kind of brainstorming that creates true partnership. It violates the one-flesh design of marriage.

This is not how God intended marriage to function. Jesus, in John 17, prayed for His followers to be one "just as We are one" (v. 22 NASB1995), reflecting the deep unity of the Trinity. And in Matthew 19:5–6 (NLT), He reaffirmed God's original design for marriage:

> And he said, "'This explains why a man leaves his father and mother and is joined to his wife, and the two are united into one.' Since they are no longer two but one, let no one split apart what God has joined together."

You may be heading toward the right destination, but if you're dragging your spouse behind you—or forging ahead without them—you're violating a sacred process. Marriage isn't just about efficiency. It's about unity. As Amos 3:3 asks, "Do two walk together unless they have agreed to do so?" The answer is no, not when agreement has been replaced with intimidation and domination.

Even if you believe your plan is the right one, the more important question may be, Are you willing to trust God's design by giving your spouse time to process it? Your wisdom carries its own weight. It doesn't require forceful imposition. Sometimes it just needs time to settle into the heart of the one you're called to walk with.

Counsel to the Husband

Husband, maybe you see yourself as a strong leader. But if you consistently move forward without your wife's voice, you may win a few decisions but lose the relational trust that makes leadership meaningful. Jesus prioritized unity. So should you.

Ray Blackwell, once third in command at the California Highway Patrol, modeled this well. At home, he never forced decisions. He patiently gave his wife, Connie, space to think, question, and contribute. His quiet strength left a lasting impression on younger men like Josh, who later reflected, "My wife isn't my employee." That's the truth. Authentic leadership in marriage isn't just about steering the ship—it's about honoring your wife as your equal heir. As Scripture says, "Husbands, love your wives, just as Christ loved the church" (Ephesians 5:25) and "Treat them with respect . . . as heirs with you of the gracious gift of life" (1 Peter 3:7).

Counsel to the Wife

Wife, you may be strong, wise, and highly capable. But if your leadership consistently sidelines your husband, the message he hears—whether you mean it or not—is "I don't need you." That kind of dynamic can stifle his initiative, erode his confidence, or even breed quiet resentment.

Your strength is not a threat to the marriage. It's a gift. But Scripture calls you to express that strength through respect, collaboration, and trust. One Christian CEO once told me, "I will never CEO my husband. That's not leadership—that's pseudo-leadership. I want to honor God's call for my husband to lead, not override it." Her strength wasn't diminished by that statement—it was dignified. She went on to say it made no sense to prove her strength, her independence, or even her spiritual insight at the cost of ignoring the sin of lording it over her husband.

She acknowledged something many wives struggle with: Some women lead both themselves and their husbands, then wonder why he keeps stepping back from being the spiritual leader she longs for. The answer isn't for you to shrink back from your gifting. You may be gifted with leadership and administration (Romans 12:8; 1 Corinthians 12:28). It's to remember the call: Submit to each other out of reverence for Christ (Ephesians 5:21), and trust that God's design gives both husband and wife a voice but also calls the husband to imitate Christ's servant-hearted headship (Ephesians 5:23, 25; Colossians 3:19).

Even the most capable person must sometimes yield for the sake of unity. In marriage, that means not just reaching the goal but arriving together, as one.

Working Through Differences

To agree on the same route (though several could work, and yours may indeed lead to the greater good, better way, or best option in your opinion), this process is about two things more important than your belief that your spouse ought to comply:

1. Honoring the unity God designed for marriage, where decisions are made together, not dictated
2. Creating the space for your spouse to process, contribute, and engage, not just comply with your conclusion

With Sarah, I have to ask myself: *Is the Lord more concerned with the outcome of this decision or with how I make the decision with Sarah?* The answer is clear—until I selfishly really want what I want! Then I rationalize pushing my agenda. In that moment, I'm no longer leading but lording, no longer loving but leveraging.

I recommend this four-step process for honoring both the Lord and your spouse. Trust me, it will save time, prevent headaches, and spare heartache in the long run.

Let me also say this: In most cases, you'll end up following these four steps anyway—but only after yelling, pressuring, or doing whatever it is you do to force compliance. And by then, the cost is greater: bruised trust, wounded hearts, and delayed decision and happiness.

Eventually, when the dust settles, two people return to these steps, unless one has decided "It's my way, because I have control of this decision." And that's not a marriage according to Jesus—that's a clandestine dictatorship. It may look like leadership on the surface, but underneath, it's control without consent.

Unless the house is on fire and death is imminent—when barking "*Flee for your life, this is not up for debate*" is warranted—marriage isn't built on commands; it's built on collaboration.

So why not choose wisdom for 99 percent of the routing problems?

MARRIAGE ISN'T BUILT ON COMMANDS; IT'S BUILT ON COLLABORATION.

The Four STEP Framework

When emotions rise and clarity fades, couples can get stuck—not because they don't care but because they don't have a process. The STEP Framework offers a four-step path to move from disagreement to unity.

S – State the Immediate Issue Clearly

Clarity calms conflict. Start by naming the actual decision in front of you, usually a "this or that" choice. For example: "Are we going to take the new job and move, or stay and say no?" or "Are we going to homeschool, or enroll our children in private school this fall?" When the issue is clear, confusion decreases. You can't move toward unity if you're arguing about five different things and suddenly shouting, "And another thing—it's about your mother!" One decision at a time. One topic at a time. Clarity comes first.

T – Talk Through Your Perspectives

Next, create space to express your personal thoughts, fears, and hopes—without interruption or rebuttal. The goal is not persuasion but understanding. Whether rooted in personality, past experiences, present pressures, or how decisions are processed, all of us will have honest differences of opinion. Neither is wrong, just different. One spouse may say, "I feel energized by this opportunity. It feels like a door we've been waiting to open," while the other may express, "I feel anxious. This would change everything about our rhythm and security." You're not just managing a decision—you're learning how each other thinks, processes, and feels. That mutual understanding lays the groundwork for teamwork.

E – Evaluate Using Shared Vision Statements

Now shift from individual opinions to shared spiritual values. These aren't vague ideals—they're biblical convictions you've named as a couple. Turn to the list of twenty-seven common goals. Ask questions such as "Which of our shared values speaks to this situation?" "How do we stay aligned with what matters most?" and "What does trusting God look like here?" You might affirm, "We both want to walk in God's will. We both want to protect our peace. We both want to provide stability for our children." Let your shared vision—not just your preferences—shape your direction.

Keep this in mind: Though no plan is perfect, and hardships may come, the way you plan can draw you closer as husband and wife. Many couples look back and say, "Even though things didn't work out exactly as expected, the way we approached it brought us together. The struggle didn't pull us apart—it pulled us closer."

P – Plan Forward with the 5 W's and H

Now it's time to cocreate the path forward. This is where brainstorming happens—and it matters. Brainstorming together often triggers creativity, compromise, and unexpected clarity. Things neither spouse had considered alone begin to emerge when curiosity is invited into the room. The 5 *W*'s and *H* provide structure for that shared exploration.

Thesc questions form one of the most time-tested and widely used frameworks for problem-solving, brainstorming, and planning. They're not just academic tools, but many wise and successful leaders, entrepreneurs, journalists, and even investigators use them to structure their thinking. They force you to look at a matter from every angle, leaving fewer blind spots. The questions are basic, but the answers can uncover profound insights. They separate assumptions from facts, feelings from evidence. Many refer to the 5 *W*'s and *H* as "The Checklist."

Start with *Why?* Why are we even considering this? What's the deeper purpose that makes this worth exploring?

Then *What?* What needs to happen? What are the implications—logistical, emotional, relational?

Next, *Who?* Who is best positioned to lead or support this in this season? Who has capacity, gifting, or experience?

Then *When and Where?* When should this happen? Where will this affect our home, marriage, and family rhythms most?

After that, *How?* How will we know whether this is working? How will we check in, adjust, or course correct without blame?

And finally, *What If?* What if this goes sideways? What's our backup plan?

Let's Go Deeper: Applying STEP to the Job Opportunity

A husband receives a job offer out of state—higher pay, meaningful work, and clear advancement. He's thrilled. His wife is hesitant. The move would disrupt their kids' school, distance them from extended family, and strain their relational routines. They use STEP to walk through it—not quickly but prayerfully.

S – State the Immediate Issue

They begin by naming the decision: "Are we going to say yes to the job and relocate—or stay and decline?" This single question provides a clear target and helps prevent getting lost in an emotional maze.

T – Talk Through Your Perspectives

He shares, "This feels like an answer to prayer—provision, purpose, opportunity." She responds, "I feel like this will shift everything. Our kids' routines. Our sense of rootedness. I'm not saying no—I just feel heavy about the cost." They both take time to really listen. They are not enemies. They are teammates facing a crossroads.

E – Evaluate Using Shared Vision

They open their shared vision list and reflect. *We value each other's gifts and callings and will not compare and compete. We desire a peaceful, Christ-centered home. We intend to raise our children with wisdom and faith. We will steward our finances, health, and time well.* From that twenty-seven-point list, they remind themselves of their common ground. They are allies, not enemies. Yes, they that recognize the way to achieve these goals will differ, but acknowledging their commonality comforts them and unites them because of their shared goals.

P – Plan Forward with the 5 W's and H

They move into brainstorming—slowly, honestly, and humbly.

Why: They affirm, "This is a strategic step toward long-term financial stability and calling—but not at the cost of our spiritual or relational peace."

What: They list the changes: commute shifts, school transfers, increased household load, and potential emotional toll on the kids. They also name what must stay intact: date nights, prayer rhythms, and weekend boundaries.

Who: He will negotiate the best family-honoring terms possible. She will assess logistics on the home front and explore community support if they relocate. Together, they'll seek counsel from mentors.

When: They'll give themselves thirty to sixty days to discern. If they proceed, the first ninety days will be a trial period with open communication. They agree not to call it a "forever" decision just yet.

Where: They name what must remain sacred: dinner as a family, no laptops in bed, and protected Sabbath rest. The "where" isn't just about geography; it's about maintaining connection in the places that matter.

How: They commit to biweekly pulse checks—not to assess performance but to ask, "Are we still okay?" "Do we feel aligned?" "Is anything drifting that needs attention?"

Counting the Cost: The Fallback Plan

They know risk is real, so they create a wise plan B. If after a year the job proves unsustainable, they'll explore new roles without panic. He begins quiet networking now—not as an escape but as foresight. They build a flex fund for unexpected shifts. Most importantly, they make a relational commitment: "If this doesn't work, we don't blame—we adjust. Together."

The Real Win

Even if the decision changes, they've already succeeded. Why? Because they moved through it with spiritual clarity, emotional honesty, and relational unity. As Proverbs 16:9 reminds us, "The mind of man plans his way, but the Lord directs his steps" (NASB1995). STEP doesn't guarantee success. But it guarantees connection. You're not just making a plan. You're making sure no one is left behind in the process.

So Why Do Things Still Derail?

Because of unguarded emotions. We lose emotional control. We stop listening and start defending. We move from humility to hostility. And suddenly, it's not about finding a solution—it's about proving a point, protecting turf, or punishing the other. When that happens, even the best frameworks can be abandoned mid-sentence.

But if a couple is willing to pause, breathe, and come back to the table with soft hearts and shared goals, these tools become more than conflict resolution techniques. They become on-ramps to unity, and that's the real goal: not just agreement but deeper unity. But let's remember: God doesn't call us to unity because it's easy. He calls us to it because it's essential. Jesus said, "If a house is divided against itself, that house cannot stand" (Mark 3:25).

This process may feel slow, awkward, or even frustrating at times, but I truly believe that God's wisdom often emerges in the space between two humble, surrendered hearts. When a husband and wife commit to listening, honoring, pausing, and praying together—even if the steps aren't perfect—something sacred begins to take shape. I know He honors the individual who practices these things.

What If We Still Don't Agree?

Sometimes you won't reach consensus right away. That's okay. Start again on the four steps. When agreement stalls, fall back on these truths and say, "We're on the same team. We want the same things. We have goodwill. God is still leading us."

And please—oh please—don't blurt out, "If we really loved each other, we wouldn't have these conflicts." Maybe. However, what that usually means is "If you loved me, you'd see things my way and serve my preference, because I'm the more loving one here." That's not love. That's self-centeredness dressed in virtue to get your way. Conflict isn't the absence of love, it's an opportunity to grow in love, respect, and wisdom.

The Third Party

If you're gridlocked, don't despair. Invite a wise, godly third party. Not to pick sides but to help you both see a bigger picture.

When the decision is weighty and lack of resolution remains, and we must go right or left, turn to a third party for input. The apostle Paul would say to us what he wrote in 1 Corinthians 6:5 (NASB1995): "I say this to your shame.

Is it so, that there is not among you one wise man who will be able to decide between his brethren?"

While Paul is speaking specifically about believers taking one another to court, the heart of the verse applies deeply to marriage and conflict resolution. Actually, in the next chapter Paul addresses marriage, and he no doubt had in mind husbands and wives going to the courts to divorce, and Paul counsels them against that (1 Corinthians 7:10–11).

Paul's challenge is clear: Is there no one wise enough among you to help resolve this in a godly way? The question is rhetorical: There is always such a person. So, let's consider who we can recruit to help us decide since a decision must be made. I predict they will add tremendous insight, and quickly, since we have done our homework on these four steps.

Who should we invite into this? Choose wisely—and humbly.

- Do we both trust them?
- Are they spiritually grounded and relationally wise?
- Can they stay neutral and listen well?
- Will they guide us toward unity, not just a quick fix?
- Are we both open to their counsel—even if it's hard to hear?

Here's what I believe with all my heart: When two people commit to this four-step process—and include a trusted third party when they hit a stalemate—wisdom usually emerges. And more often than not, both parties walk away satisfied with the solution.

It's not that the four steps don't work. It's not that a third party can't offer valuable insight. The issue is usually this: We don't stay with it. We get weary. We get defensive. We reach for control. We revert to old patterns instead of leaning into the slow work of humility, listening, and team play.

But I urge you, don't give up too soon. Every couple needs this reminder: It is always too soon to quit. Don't assume the process has failed just because the path feels messy or progress feels slow. Growth in marriage is rarely linear; it zigs and zags, two steps forward and one step back. Collaboration takes effort. But the fruit from the process is worth it.

When you honor your shared vision, acknowledge your differences with humility, brainstorm, seek win-win not win-lose, and invite godly counsel when needed, you create the kind of atmosphere where God's wisdom comes down from above. The Lord directs your steps (Proverbs 16:9).

So press in. Keep at it. Whether by train or by plane, either route to Paris works, as long as the goal is the same: being together with family.

Emerson must never say to Sarah, "Thus saith the Lord, fly to Paris," when it's Emerson saying, "We must fly because I don't want to take the train since it's too long."

Who does Emerson think he is—God? That's not spiritual leadership; it's personal preference dressed up as divine direction. And Sarah? She'll see right through it—and tell him to hitchhike.

SEVEN

OUR ACKNOWLEDGMENT: NOT WRONG, JUST DIFFERENT SHADES OF RIGHT

Mutuality epiphany: Marriage thrives when differing preferences and perspectives are acknowledged as valid in the gray areas—different shades of right.

At our Love and Respect Conference, I often ask, "If I am right, then my spouse is . . . ?" The crowd responds, "Wrong!" But is my spouse really wrong? Not necessarily—at least not in the countless gray areas of life.

A statement I once heard captures the heart of this principle: "In culinary philosophy, there is no disputing taste." Exactly! Your spouse isn't wrong for preferring only pepper on their eggs, just as you're not solely right for wanting only salt. These are not moral absolutes—they're just different preferences. It does not become the eleventh commandment: Thou shalt never use pepper.

We often say, "Two wrongs don't make a right," and that's true in moral matters. But here's a truth we overlook: In marriage, two people each believing they are right doesn't automatically make one of them wrong. And sometimes the issues aren't even significant. One person once said, "I found marriage to be very educational. I had no idea there was a wrong way to put milk in the fridge."

How many ways can a milk carton be placed? Dozens. Shelf location, direction, proximity to other items, or space-saving priorities. Is there truly a wrong way? Only if it's stored upside down or blocks the door. But emotionally, we assign "rightness" to our habits because they feel familiar, efficient, or respectful. Yet what matters most isn't how the milk is placed but how we respond to the difference.

TWO PEOPLE EACH BELIEVING THEY ARE RIGHT DOESN'T AUTOMATICALLY MAKE ONE OF THEM WRONG.

Small things become symbolic. When you do something your way, not my way, I might interpret it as uncaring or disrespectful. But the real issue isn't the milk. The issue is moralizing and judging.

The goal is not to win arguments over personal preferences but to understand and honor the other's perspective, especially when no biblical or moral absolute is at stake. Most situations have two shades of right.

When "You're Wrong" Ends the Conversation

Sometimes what begins as a simple difference of opinion quickly escalates into moral judgment. We stop seeing our spouse's view as a preference—and start seeing it as a problem. A few common scenarios make this painfully clear.

Take the parenting schedule conflict. He wants to let their teen sleep in on Saturdays; she insists they wake up by 8:30 a.m. to build discipline. Her approach feels purposeful and structured, while his seems enabling and indulgent. Without discussion, her way becomes the "right" way, and the conversation ends before it begins.

Or consider home organization. She's content with a little clutter; he craves clean counters and minimalist order. Rather than viewing this as a matter of comfort or aesthetics, he sees his preference as the morally superior lifestyle. Compromise is off the table—not because it's impossible but because it's already been ruled "wrong."

Then there's conflict timing. During heated moments, he tends to walk away to cool off, while she wants to talk things out immediately. His silence feels like punishment to her, even if he's seeking space to avoid escalating. But instead of exploring why he withdraws, she labels his method as abusive. Her way is "engaged and right." His is "emotionally unavailable and wrong." End of story.

In social dynamics, it happens too. She thrives on hospitality and enjoys inviting people over; he prefers solitude and tight-knit family time. When she suggests hosting a gathering, he shuts it down with finality: "That's not who we are." His value—protecting margin and quiet—becomes the only valid one. Hers is dismissed as exhausting or excessive. The discussion shuts down.

Each of these reflects a nonmoral difference that becomes emotionally charged the moment we treat our preference as a moral absolute. What starts as a differing instinct becomes a battleground for identity and values. And once we feel we've reached the moral high ground, we raise the gavel with phrases like these:

"This isn't up for debate."
"There's nothing more to talk about."
"Case closed."
"That's final."

But the truth is—our spouse isn't always wrong. They may simply be seeing a different shade of right.

An Escalating Power Struggle

Telling your spouse "You're flat-out wrong" immediately puts them on the defensive and escalates the conflict—not because of the actual issue but because

THE TRUTH IS—OUR SPOUSE ISN'T ALWAYS WRONG.

of how it's framed. What began as a difference in preference now feels like a courtroom verdict. The spouse doesn't just feel misunderstood—they feel condemned, unloved, and disrespected.

Welcome to the power struggle. Instead of collaborating, couples compete. They dig in—denouncing the other's view and defending their own at all costs.

Everyday Gray-Zone Differences—Often Resolved Without Conflict

Not every difference escalates into judgment. Many couples navigate preferences with grace. Sometimes, both live out their convictions side by side. Other times, one defers because the matter feels less important or they've come to appreciate the other's view.

Here are common examples where couples resolve differences with flexibility:

- **Dietary choices:** She's vegetarian; he enjoys meat. They prepare both without conflict.
- **Morning vs. evening preferences:** One's a morning person, the other a night owl. They adjust routines with mutual respect.
- **Church service styles:** She attends traditional service; he prefers contemporary. They discuss the message together later.
- **Parenting bedtime rituals:** One values structured prayer time; the other prefers spontaneous conversation. They blend approaches.
- **Vacation planning:** One loves adventure; the other prefers rest. They alternate or mix activities.
- **Home decor tastes:** She likes color; he prefers neutrals. They compromise or assign different spaces.

In chapter 6, we explored how to brainstorm win-win solutions. These examples show that many preferences can coexist, even when firmly held. The danger arises only when we insist our way is the only right way and judge our spouse for differing.

The Gray Zone Is Not Black-and-White

In the gray areas of life—those everyday decisions not explicitly addressed in Scripture—a husband and wife can both be right. Each may sincerely seek what is good, better, or best. Yes, my way may in fact represent the greater good, but that doesn't make my spouse's preference inherently bad and wrong.

I may see the greater good, but that only makes their view the lesser good—not no good. I may promote the better way, but that only makes their way "less better" or less effective, not a bad way. I may prefer what I believe is the best option, but that only makes their opinion the second-best option in this situation.

A friend once said, "I really like the different shades of right. Anything that removes an accusing finger or the impression that something is wrong with my partner due to legitimate differences is life-changing for a relationship." One of the most loving and respectful things I can do is validate my spouse's differing opinion. After all, a point that may be less valid than mine does not make it invalid.

Is There a Biblical Basis for Different Shades of Right?

Years ago, my thinking shifted dramatically when I studied Romans 14. It revealed a stunning truth: I could be wrong—even when I was right.

In the early church, believers clashed over food laws and sacred days. Some Jews refused to eat meat; some Gentiles saw no problem with it. Friday Sabbath versus Sunday worship became another dividing line. But Paul didn't settle the disputes—he addressed the underlying problem: judgment, pride, and contempt.

In this chapter, my goal is not to resolve every disagreement but to echo Paul's plea: "Start here: Stop declaring the other person wrong." You can say, "I believe my way is the greater good, better way, and best option," but don't moralize a preference.

When we elevate our opinions to moral absolutes, we fuel judgment and division. Even if I'm "right" in my conviction, I can be "wrong" in my spirit—becoming proud, dismissive, unloving, and contemptuous. Paul's message is clear: The greater sin may lie in the way we judge others, not in the opinion they hold.

Yes, you may be free to eat meat, but if you do so while despising your spouse's conviction, you've already violated a greater principle—love and respect.

But Isn't There a Right and Wrong Way of Doing Things?

That's the question many couples ask when frustration builds over differences. And the answer?

In the gray area of life, there is no inherently wrong way—just the lesser good, the less better, and the second-best option. We must never make the gray area black-and-white.

Granted, if a husband says, "I think we should let the toddler roam the neighborhood without us," that crosses into what is both illegal and against God's clear command for parental responsibility. That's not a gray area; that's black-and-white, and wrong.

Or, if he says, "We only need to go to the grocery store once a month to save on gas, not four times," he may simply be operating outside his wheelhouse. What he needs is more information about what's required to manage things efficiently, such as how soon milk spoils or the need for bulk storage. And once clarified, the "wrong" way isn't truly bad—it's just incomplete. He needed to shift his attention from saving on gas to stocking groceries. He approached things from a different frame of reference. Though he isn't wrong per se, and his rationale isn't entirely invalid, once he sees the money lost from spoiled food, he'll recognize the wisdom in her reasoning.

In most episodes (unlike the two above), both husband and wife have valid input. In many everyday moments, what we call "wrong" is just different. But when we elevate those differences into verdicts, we don't just disagree—we condemn. What began as an honest difference of opinion devolves into a damning judgment.

IN MANY EVERYDAY MOMENTS, WHAT WE CALL "WRONG" IS JUST DIFFERENT.

Let's explore some examples, some brief snapshots, of how we mistake differences for deficiencies—and wrongly declare the other wrong.

Telling Stories (Wife Condemned)

She's animated and detailed at dinner. He grows restless and says, "Get to the point." She feels dismissed; he wanted efficiency, she wanted connection. Neither was wrong, but he condemned her style as if it was a flaw and she was inherently inferior.

Dishwasher Loading (Wife Condemned)

She loads the dishwasher her way. He snaps, "You're doing it wrong, just like you do so many things." She was trying to serve him and the family with a good heart and goodwill. But he not only turned this into a failing report card in his eyes, he went further and assassinated her character. The issue wasn't her method; it was his damning verdict.

Spending Habits (Husband Condemned)

He buys generic groceries to save money. She criticizes, "You don't care about quality or our health." He was trying to be wise with resources; she was hoping for freshness. Neither was wrong, but she blasted his intent and efforts as foolish and cruel neglect.

Showing Affection (Husband Condemned)

He shows love by folding laundry and checking locks. She says, "You never say anything romantic." He feels unappreciated; she feels unseen. His acts weren't wrong, just different. But instead of recognizing his effort, she wrote him off with a sweeping condemnation. Her unmet expectations blinded her to the love already offered. Love doesn't always speak in words; sometimes it warms coffee or folds towels.

In the Gray Zones

In the gray zones—those matters not right or wrong in Scripture—we must be vigilant not to weaponize our position or bulldoze our preferences. A Gentile in the first century telling a Jew, "Here, eat this ham sandwich and be quiet," doesn't foster peace.

How can you tell whether you've picked up the gavel to judge your spouse as wrong? Chances are, you're doing several things Paul warned the Roman church to stop doing. My meditations on Romans 14 have been some of the most enlightening I've received from Scripture, and I hope they both challenge and encourage you. I want to live by God's revealed truth.

Paul's Wisdom Speaks Directly to Everyday Marital Tension

Disputable matters are inevitable. Different shades of right are standard between two good-willed people. But judgment, contempt, and superiority must never be present.

Instead of defending our position at all costs, we must ask the kinds of questions Paul urged in Romans 14. He used more rhetorical questions in this chapter than in any other part of his letters, for a reason: to provoke humility and heart-checks.

Below are ten questions drawn from Paul's instruction that are designed to help you reflect on recent disagreements where you may have felt "right" but perhaps handled the difference in a way that risked judgment versus promoting love and respect.

Again, the priority for Paul isn't about settling the issue, whatever that issue might be, but first and foremost about examining the spirit we bring to the conflict. Often, God isn't focused on which of you wins the point but on how you both carry yourselves through it.

Ten Questions Every Spouse Must Ask in the Gray Zone of Conflict (at Least Sometimes)

Think of one or two recent disagreements where you felt right. As you reflect, consider whether any of the following questions apply. These may reveal profound insights that can free you to engage honest differences and avoid igniting hostility and contempt—the poisons that prevent marital success and satisfaction far more than the "disputable matters" themselves.

Remember: God is less concerned about which of you *wins* the preference and far more concerned with how you *handle* the disagreement.

1. Quarreling over preferences. Did I take a legitimate difference in a gray area—a disputable matter where Scripture gives no clear moral command—and turn it into a quarrel, making my spouse feel unacceptable or wrong for holding their view?

   "Accept the one whose faith is weak, without quarreling over disputable matters" (Romans 14:1).
2. Despising their view. Did I emotionally despise my spouse for seeing the disputable matter differently than I do—treating them as obviously wrong—when the Lord Himself has welcomed and accepted them and their preference?

   "Let not the one who eats despise the one who abstains . . . for God has welcomed him" (Romans 14:3 ESV).
3. Judging like God. Did I stop to ask, "Who am I to play God by judging

my spouse as wrong, when they, too, are sincerely trying to serve the Lord and His purposes?"

"Who are you to pass judgment on the servant of another?" (Romans 14:4 ESV).

4. Dismissing their reasoning. Did I dismiss my spouse's carefully formed conviction simply because it differed from mine—forgetting that both of us must be fully convinced in our own minds before God, not coerced into agreement with each other?

   "Each one should be fully convinced in his own mind" (Romans 14:5 ESV).

5. Ignoring honorable motives. Did I overlook my spouse's sincere desire to honor the Lord and thank Him for allowing their preference—because I focused more on their disagreement with me than on their heart for Him?

   "The one who abstains, abstains in honor of the Lord and gives thanks to God" (Romans 14:6 ESV).

6. Demanding an account. Did I expect my spouse to give an account to me—as if I were the final authority, needing to approve their choice—instead of recognizing they ultimately answer to God?

   "Each of us will give an account of himself to God" (Romans 14:12 ESV).

7. Tripping them up. Did I put a stumbling block in my spouse's path—not merely by accident but by intentionally trying to prevent them from moving forward in what seemed right to them but was wrong to me?

   "Decide never to put a stumbling block . . . in the way of a brother" (Romans 14:13 ESV).

8. Abandoning peacemaking strategies. Did I stop pursuing peace—anything that fosters harmony, reduces conflict, and promotes understanding—not because peace was impossible but because I wanted control instead of seeking a mutual, equal win-win?

   "So then let us pursue what makes for peace and for mutual upbuilding" (Romans 14:19 ESV).

9. Never keeping quiet. Did I keep pushing on my spouse what my faith told me was right instead of trusting God and allowing us, so to speak,

to sit at the same table, one eating meat and the other abstaining, both quietly honoring the Lord in their own faith, since in some situations we can both act on what is right for us?

> "The faith that you have, keep between yourself and God" (Romans 14:22 ESV).

10. Pressuring against conscience. Did I pressure my spouse to align with my position, even though they moved forward with doubt instead of faith, and in doing so, their sin wasn't their original preference but violating their own conscience?

> "Whoever has doubts is condemned if he eats, because the eating is not from faith. For whatever does not proceed from faith is sin" (Romans 14:23 ESV).

A Word of Caution

If more than half of these questions are answered yes, this is a red light. Slow down. Stop. It is not the time to claim your way is right—or even the greater good, better way, or best option. Your heart is becoming too judgmental, and at this moment, your person, not your position, must be the priority.

This "disputable matter" may expose a deeper issue: a character flaw of self-righteousness, a judgmental spirit, and a desire for control. And perhaps, without even realizing it, you are playing God (or representing Him), presuming not only that you know what is best but that your spouse's view is not just different but beneath God's will.

You may have a strong case for your perspective. You may be operating in good faith. The Roman Jews did. The Roman Gentiles did. But if your approach dishonors your spouse, dismisses their conscience, and disturbs the peace of your home, then you've already lost—even if you "win" the argument.

When we apply Paul's wisdom from Romans 14 to marriage, we see that many of our conflicts are not about right versus wrong but about learning to honor each other's convictions, preferences, and shades of right with humility and grace. That's the marital aha moment that changes everything.

The Marital Aha Moment

Many couples have never had this simple but life-changing insight: Many of the tensions we experience in marriage aren't rooted in sin. They're not violations of biblical commands—they're different shades of right. We forget that two people with goodwill can differ without either one being inherently wrong. Sadly, for some, they have never realized this, with the result that they have fought for decades and are utterly exhausted, living as roommates and tiptoeing around the emotional land mines.

In the heat of disagreement, instead of shouting, "I am right, and you are wrong!" ask, "Is it possible we're both right in different ways?"

Clunky, Uncomfortable Word Choice

Part of the challenge is that we lack a shared language for different shades of right. We don't say things like "I disagree, but I just think your way is . . . less better." That feels clunky, maybe even dismissive.

MANY OF THE TENSIONS WE EXPERIENCE IN MARRIAGE AREN'T ROOTED IN SIN.

In fact, we often struggle to say what we really mean: "I see the rightness in what you're saying; it's just not how I see the full picture," or "That's a solid idea. I'm just having trouble letting go of mine."

So instead, we either stay silent (and simmer) or speak up (and sound superior). Neither builds the bridge we're looking for. Both create emotional distance where there should be safety.

We Fear Making a Concession

Why do we do this? Often it's not disrespect—it's fear. We fear we'll lose ground if we acknowledge our spouse's viewpoint.

"If I say their way is good, mine will be dismissed."

"If I validate their perspective, I must give up mine."

Acknowledging your spouse's point of view isn't the same as agreeing with it. It's about creating a shared language where couples can say, "Neither of us is wrong. We just see different shades of right."

If you don't recognize, accept, and appreciate this, you'll find yourself in repeated arguments—not because the issue is moral but because you've framed it as if it is.

When one spouse says, "You're wrong!" the other instinctively replies, "I'm not wrong! Why are you making me out to be the bad guy?" And just like that, you're no longer discussing the original issue—you're defending yourself against a judgment.

The conflict has escalated not because of a difference in desire but because of how that different opinion was labeled.

Faulty Inner Script

Many spouses operate under a faulty inner script: "If I know I'm right about what needs to be done, and my spouse disagrees, then they must be wrong. We both can't be right." And in that moment, the one who claims to be right assumes the moral high ground. We slam the gavel. We shut down the conversation before it even begins.

We must distinguish between God's moral absolutes (the nonnegotiables) and personal preferences (the negotiables). Yes, a spouse can be morally wrong when they lie, steal, or cheat, and we need to see the sin for what it is: sin.

But what if it isn't sin?

Bias: The Hidden Delusion Behind Certainty

Let me say a word about bias, because it's often the silent culprit behind our strongest certainties. Bias in our own favor is subtle, even invisible to the one who holds it. But it powerfully shapes how we interpret reality—especially in moments of tension. In marriage, unchecked bias doesn't just distort how we see the issue. It distorts how we see each other.

Bias can quietly transform sincere disagreement into a standoff. A conversation becomes a courtroom. A difference in perspective becomes a character flaw. And often we don't even realize it's happening.

Are you aware of how bias may be operating in your heart?

- Confirmation bias causes us to see only what supports our own viewpoint and dismiss what supports our spouse's.
- Assumption bias convinces us we already know their motives—especially the worst ones—without taking time to ask.
- Moral superiority bias subtly tells us that our conviction is not just preferable but righteous. And if our spouse disagrees, they must be spiritually inferior—or even unrighteous.

Bias left unexamined hardens into self-righteousness. And when that happens, every disagreement becomes a battle to win rather than a moment to understand.

Scripture speaks to this reality with refreshing clarity. Proverbs 18:17 reminds us, "The one who states his case first seems right, until the other comes and examines him" (ESV). This doesn't necessarily imply dishonesty. More often, it reveals how narrow our vision can become when we've seen from only one side. When another voice is heard, or when someone probes gently with a question, what once felt obviously right starts to look more complicated.

BIAS LEFT UNEXAMINED HARDENS INTO SELF-RIGHTEOUSNESS.

Similarly, Proverbs 21:2 cautions, "Every way of a man is right in his own eyes, but the LORD weighs the heart" (ESV). We may believe our logic is sound and our motive is pure, but God sees the layers we don't—and the bias we've failed to notice.

You may be operating in sincerity. But you may also be operating with limited sight. That's the heart of Paul's message in Romans 14. He doesn't just ask us to examine our convictions. He asks us to examine how we treat those who hold different ones. In marriage, that begins by admitting, "My perspective may be incomplete, and I need your perspective to see more clearly."

The Vital Distinction

Okay, what's negotiable and what's nonnegotiable?

Every couple must navigate decision-making, but not all decisions are created equal. Some are clearly black-and-white. Others are shades of gray. And some fall into a third category altogether: matters of conscience. Recognizing which is which can help us avoid unnecessary conflict, clarify priorities, and walk in greater unity.

Moral Absolutes Are Black-and-White (Nonnegotiables)

Moral absolutes are the commands of God—especially those clearly revealed in the New Testament—that apply to every Christian couple. These are not negotiable. They don't flex based on feelings, personality, or season of life. The only question is how best to obey them.

We see this in areas like these:

- Trusting and Following Jesus Boldly
  - "Whoever is ashamed of me . . . the Son of Man will be ashamed of them" (Luke 9:26).
  - "If anyone wishes to come after Me, he must deny himself" (Matthew 16:24 NASB1995).
    - There's no place for denying Christ or fearing man more than God.
- Faithfulness and Sexual Purity in Marriage
  - "The marriage bed is to be undefiled" (Hebrews 13:4 NASB1995).
    - No room for adultery, pornography, or betrayal.

- Honesty and Integrity
  - "Speak truth" (Ephesians 4:25 NASB1995).
  - "Let your 'Yes' be 'Yes'" (Matthew 5:37 NKJV).
    - Deception and manipulation are never justified.
- A Forgiving Spirit
  - "[Forgive] each other, just as in Christ God forgave you" (Ephesians 4:32).
    - We can't harbor bitterness or weaponize silence—even when reconciliation takes time.
- Love and Respect Within Marriage
  - "Each one of you also must love his wife as he loves himself, and the wife must respect her husband" (Ephesians 5:33).
    - Contempt, hostility, and neglect have no place in Christian marriage.
- Gratitude in All Circumstances
  - "In everything give thanks" (1 Thessalonians 5:18 NASB1995).
    - Chronic grumbling and entitlement reveal a heart out of alignment with God.
- Submitting to What's Right—Even When You Could Get Away With Wrong
  - "Submit yourselves for the Lord's sake" (1 Peter 2:13 NASB1995).
    - Integrity means obeying even when shortcuts are available.

These truths are not optional. None of us live them perfectly, but when we fall short, we don't redefine the standard. We return to it. That return begins with confession, repentance, and a renewed commitment to God's Word.

Personal Preferences Are Gray-Area Issues (Negotiables)

Once we've identified the nonnegotiables, we realize something freeing: Most of what couples argue about isn't sin—it's preference. These issues are shaped by personality, background, and season of life. Scripture offers freedom and flexibility here, not rigid rules.

Unfortunately, this is where many couples get stuck—treating a personal preference like a divine mandate. We adopt a "Thus saith the Lord" tone about things God hasn't clearly spoken on.

Here are six areas where couples might differ, not because one is wrong but because both see different shades of right:

- Letting a child go to a sleepover: She trusts the host family and says yes. He feels hesitant and wants to say no. Both want to protect their child but differ in discernment.
- Social media boundaries: She enjoys sharing their life online to encourage others. He prefers privacy. Both value integrity but differ in visibility.
- Technology use for kids: She's okay with supervised screen time. He prefers outdoor play. Both want healthy development but express it differently.
- Holiday travel vs. staying home: He loves visiting extended family. She finds deep rest in quiet holidays at home. Both value family, just not the same expression of it.
- Health and fitness styles: She thrives on structure and progress tracking. He prefers casual activity. Both prioritize wellness but have different rhythms.
- Cash gifts to adult children: She wants to give generously to their adult children with families, especially when urgent needs arise. He voices concern that while her generosity is admirable, human nature being what it is, the kids may quietly compare amounts or question fairness. Both care deeply about family but differ in how they weigh immediate need versus long-term equity.

These are not issues of right or wrong. They're opportunities to practice humility, flexibility, and empathy. The deeper goal isn't getting your way—it's preserving unity while making space for difference.

Honoring Each Other's Conscience

Not every issue fits neatly into the "command or preference" framework. Some matters stir up strong internal convictions in one spouse—often rooted in past experiences, upbringing, or deeply personal values. These are areas where one feels free and the other feels bound. In Romans 14, Paul calls us to handle these differences with tenderness, not force. He doesn't say to pick a side; he says to honor both.

Consider these real-life examples:

- **Wine Drinking:** Josh enjoys wine in moderation. Rebekah, scarred by her father's alcoholism, feels anxious even seeing it, and she fears what could happen if Josh overindulges or sets the wrong example for their kids. Josh doesn't dismiss her fears. Instead, he assures her of his boundaries, chooses to limit his drinking to specific settings, and remains accountable. Rebekah, in turn, resists shaming him and respects his freedom. Mutual care—and mutual reassurance—win.
- **Grace at the Beach:** Ethan is honest about his struggle with temptation surrounded by half-naked women at crowded beaches. For him, it isn't just discomfort—it's spiritual vulnerability. Emily loves being near water and initially feels frustrated, worried that he's limiting her joy. And further, if he loves her, why look at other women? But she realizes men are visually oriented and knows Ethan loves the Lord and wants to walk in purity. Instead of dismissing each other, they find creative solutions: quiet lakefront spots, less crowded beaches, or weekend trips to rivers and pools. He protects his purity; she still enjoys the refreshment of water. No control, just compassion and compromise.
- **Birth Control Choices:** Elena feels convinced against hormonal birth control. Marcus doesn't share that conviction but honors her conscience. They agree on a natural method, not because they fully agree but because they're fully committed. They use the calendar method to track the cycle days to estimate fertile and infertile windows. They also chart her waking temperature daily to pinpoint ovulation. It took work,

but it also created a new sense of partnership and actually enhanced their sexual life.

- **Educational Philosophy:** Jason leans toward traditional schooling, convinced it provides structure and stability. Emily is deeply passionate about Montessori, shaped by her own experience, and feels strongly that this is the best fit for their children. At first, tension rises: Jason worries Montessori will be too unstructured; Emily feels dismissed and unheard. After honest conversations, Jason recognizes that her conviction runs stronger, especially since she will carry the daily load of teaching. He sees her passion and commitment and chooses to honor it. At the same time, she commits to involving him in shaping the details so their children benefit from both structure and creativity.

In each of these examples, love and respect limit liberty but never erase freedom. The issue isn't who wins. Romans 14 shows us that unity doesn't require uniformity. It requires humility, deference, and trust in the Spirit's work in each other.

Yes, deference. Harmony often calls for the simple principle I used to repeat in my church board meetings among the elders when decisions had to be made after sufficient debate: "Can I defer to what the others prefer?" That posture doesn't diminish me; it dignifies the relationship and strengthens unity with us so we can move forward. We had to decide. And if, down the road, it turned out the decision wasn't the greater good, the better way, or best option, I relinquish the right to say "I told you so." After all, the lesser good wasn't evil. One way might have been better, but what we chose was still good. And though we didn't land on the very best option, it was never a bad option.

Based on Acts 15:28, we did what "seemed good to the Holy Spirit and to us" at the time. And in parenting, according to Hebrews 12:10 (NASB), parents act based on what "seemed best to them" at the time. Thus, we move forward without regret, trusting God's Spirit to redeem even our lesser goods and to bring His greater purposes out of our imperfect choices.

Bottom line: Know what's black-and-white. Discern what's gray. And when it comes to conscience, be tender. Because marriage isn't about always agreeing—it's about walking together in a way that honors Christ and each other.

The Teeter-Totter

Most successful and satisfied couples don't keep score. Instead, they develop a sense of what is fair and maintain what I call a healthy teeter-tottering—a balance that shifts gracefully as each spouse honors the other's conscience and conviction.

In marriage, not every issue is about logic, leadership, or compromise. Sometimes it's about bearing with each other in love and respect. Sometimes it's about deferring not because you're convinced but because you care.

Many spouses confuse deferring with losing. But in matters of conscience, deference is often the highest form of love and respect. Nobody is coerced. Nobody is condemned. Liberty and conscience remain intact, while the relationship stays strong.

This doesn't mean there's always a clear formula. Even Romans 14 doesn't give us steps to solve every tension. That's why discernment matters.

Below are five prayerful, thoughtful criteria—not formulas but discernment tools—for weighing who may lovingly and respectfully yield in a specific moment.

1. Greater Vulnerability: Who Feels the Greater Risk—Physically, Emotionally, or Spiritually?

A Corinthian husband, recently converted from idol worship, felt spiritually unsettled at community feasts where meat had been offered to idols. His wife, unaffected by the associations, had no issue attending. But when she saw the toll it took on him, she declined the invitations. She didn't mock or dismiss him—she honored his journey by adjusting her freedom for his sake.

This reflects 1 Corinthians 8:9: "Be careful . . . that the exercise of your rights does not become a stumbling block to the weak." Strength isn't insisting on your freedom; it's knowing when to yield it for the one you love and respect.

2. Greater Concern or Disapproval: Who Is More Unsettled, Grieved, or Conscience-Bound?

Romans 14 calls us to defer in love and respect when something troubles our spouse's conscience, even if it seems minor to us. Imitating Christ means lifting their burden, not proving a point.

A wife told me, "I demanded we buy a vacation condo, even though my husband didn't support it. Later, I realized I'd disrespected his conviction to live within our means. When I told him I supported his decision not to buy, it restored peace. I wasn't stripped of dignity—I was stripped of my contentiousness."

Another husband said, "I wanted to buy a vacation home, but my wife had serious financial concerns, shaped by her childhood experiences with debt and instability. Though I disagreed logically, I deferred. We didn't move forward until we had enough saved—and I had no problem with that in the end. She wasn't wrong."

3. Greater Responsibility or Consequence: Who Will Carry More of the Weight Based on the Outcome?

When one spouse will bear more of the emotional, logistical, or spiritual weight, that burden should be considered.

One couple said, "We decide based on whose lane it is." In other words, they defer to the one most directly responsible.

Now, how does this fit with biblical headship? Especially when mutual submission leads to an impasse?

If that impasse begins to erode unity—or consistently places final authority in the wife's hands—then yes, headship matters. In those rare but real moments, Scripture calls the wife to trust God by deferring to her husband—not because she agrees but because she honors his spiritual responsibility and because God will judge him, not her, for issues of headship.

One husband sensed a calling to leave his corporate job to plant a church. His wife was concerned—college tuition loomed, and one child needed extra support. They prayed, fasted, and sought counsel. In the end, though still unsure, she chose to support him. "If this calling is from God," she said, "He'll sustain us. If not, you'll bear the responsibility—and grow through it."

She honored his headship and sense of calling and duty. This was not blind obedience but rather trust in God, the One who "causes all things to work together for good to those who love God, to those who are called according to His purpose" (Romans 8:28 NASB).

Here's another example. A wife felt strongly called to homeschool. Her husband initially preferred a Christian school. But after prayer and dialogue, he said, "You'll carry the daily burden. I'll support your conviction."

This wasn't abdication; it was servant leadership. Later, when she felt overwhelmed, he didn't say, "Told you so." He stepped in and helped. That's what headship looks like—authority expressed through empathy and shared responsibility.

4. Greater Hardship: Who Will Face More Difficulty If the Decision Goes Against Them?

When one choice creates greater emotional, relational, or spiritual hardship, deference may be the wiser path.

One husband confessed, "I used to ignore my wife's wishes unless she could argue her point successfully. Over time, I realized that pattern shut her down emotionally. I've since changed my approach. Now I listen for her pain and consider the cost of my decisions on her heart."

The hardship wasn't from one decision but from a pattern. And when he changed, the wall between them began to fall.

Another wife shared, "We disagreed about moving for a job. I wanted to stay near family. But I realized that staying meant my husband would face long commutes, less security, and the emotional weight of missed opportunity. I chose to defer. God gave me the strength to adjust—and it honored my husband's burden."

5. Greater Insecurity or Unresolved Fear: Is One Spouse Reacting from Past Trauma or Deep Fear?

Sometimes what seems like an overreaction is really rooted in old wounds. If the fear is sincere—not manipulative—this may be a moment to defer, protect, respect, and love.

Every husband must understand that many wives interpret silence or withdrawal as rejection. To her, it feels like "I don't love you enough to stay engaged." Her fear is "I'm three conversations away from hearing, 'I'm done with you.'"

One husband said, "I finally realized my silence felt like abandonment to her. Now I choose to reassure her—even when I feel overwhelmed. I still carry the burden of needing space, but I carry it with her, not away from her."

That's wisdom. He didn't just avoid conflict—he chose connection over comfort. He didn't default to "If I want to drop it, we will drop it. If I don't want to talk, I won't talk." Instead, he honored both her fear and his own burden by finding a way to stay present without being swallowed by the moment.

Another wife had her own revelation. Her husband witnessed a purse snatching but stayed with their kids instead of running to help. He was distraught—not because he didn't act but because he felt torn between protector and parent.

Before understanding this, she might've told him, "You had no choice—get over it." Instead, she said, "You were being pulled in both directions. God made you a protector, and you chose the right thing." His spirit lifted.

She didn't dismiss him; she affirmed him. That's the power of deferring to fear when it's rooted in identity and integrity.

Deference is not weakness. It is love and respect in action. It is strength under control. In the eyes of the Lord, might this be the greater good, better way, and best option? Indeed.

The Wrongness of Being Right

The danger isn't the disagreement itself—it's moralizing the difference. When one spouse claims the high ground and casts the other in a lower light, the pursuit of wisdom becomes a battle for superiority.

Being correct doesn't give you the right to be relationally destructive. That's when "being right" goes wrong.

You may believe your path is the greater good, better way, or best option. But if your tone is condemning, your posture is coercive, and your spirit is contemptuous, you are no longer being Christlike. You are being self-righteous—and relationally damaging.

The Practical and Compassionate Way Forward

So what does handling gray-zone conflict look like in real life? Here are ten ways to move forward—not with judgment or fear but with humility and grace—when you and your spouse differ. Pick just one this week and live it out.

1. Validate Your Spouse's Conscience—Even When You Disagree

Your spouse may feel strongly about a decision you wouldn't make. Validation doesn't mean surrendering your view—it means recognizing their intent. It means honoring the sincerity behind their conviction. Instead of dismissing them with "That's ridiculous," say, "I can see you're trying to do what's right before God. Can I share what I see too?" You're building trust, not tearing it down.

2. Drop the Gavel

You're not the judge in your marriage. And when you say "You're wrong," you've already stepped out of partnership and into authority. Instead, put down the gavel. Appeal with your convictions but stay humble. Don't rule with finality—invite conversation.

3. Name the Fear

Behind many intense arguments is unspoken fear: fear of being ignored, getting it wrong, or repeating the past. Instead of accusing—"You're reckless" or "You're rigid"—try to name what's underneath: "I'm afraid we'll regret this" or "I'm scared we're not on the same page." Naming the fear builds bridges, not walls.

4. Pass the Mic

Let your spouse speak—fully—without interruption, rebuttal, or rush. Say, "Tell me more. Help me understand." We often don't do this because we assume we already know, or we're too busy mentally loading our next argument. Stop. Pass the mic. Real listening invites real connection.

5. *Validate the Instinct*

After you listen, affirm what you heard—not the exact conclusion but the motive behind it. Say, "I see the care behind your caution" or "You're really trying to do what's right—I respect that." Validation is not weakness. It's relational maturity. It's saying, "Even if we land differently, I still value your heart."

6. *Never Weaponize Righteousness or Use Spiritual Guilt*

"If you loved me, you'd agree with me."

"God told me what to do."

"If you disagree, you're disobeying God."

These are spiritual power plays, not spiritual leadership. Jesus never used righteousness to crush people. Don't turn truth into a weapon to win arguments. Use it to invite, not impose.

7. *Don't Threaten Under the Illusion of Choice*

Saying things like "It's your call . . . but I'll remember" or "You decide . . . but don't expect me to be okay" isn't offering freedom—it's cloaked control. True partnership requires space to disagree without punishment. Remove the threat if you want real trust.

8. *Don't Mistake Urgency for Moral Rightness*

Sometimes "We must act now! This is the deal of a lifetime!" is more about control than conviction. Urgency doesn't make your position more righteous. When urgency silences your spouse's voice, it's not discernment—it's domination. Love and respect never rush wisdom.

9. *Prepare a "Next Time" Plan*

After the dust settles, ask, "How can we do better next time?" Try "How can we handle this kind of tension with both of our convictions honored?" or "What's one way we can protect our unity when this issue arises again?" Proactive planning builds peace before the next storm.

10. Repair the Damage

Even if you were technically right, your delivery might have caused harm. Say, "I was wrong to declare you wrong. I let fear turn into judgment. Will you forgive me?" The goal is never just to be right. It's to be loving and respectful—even when you disagree.

When we choose to act this way, we reflect a greater wisdom: that love limits liberty, and respect restrains reproach. In many conflicts, the greater good isn't about who "wins" but about how you walk through it together. Especially in matters of personal preference, it's worth remembering: Neither of us is wrong—we just see different shades of right.

EIGHT

OUR TENSION: DON'T LET THE 20 PERCENT DEFINE THE 80 PERCENT

Refocus moment: Frustrations and shortcomings are real, but goodwill and front-side strengths often offset backside weaknesses.

Over the years, I've shared the 80:20 concept with countless couples because it brings clarity to relational tension. The idea is simple: About 80 percent of the time, your spouse acts out of goodwill. They want to love, respect, and serve you, even if they fumble the execution (1 Corinthians 7:33–34).

But 20 percent of the time, things break down. That portion includes:

- Non-sinful deficiencies: quirks, emotional gaps, immaturities
- Sinful distortions: selfishness, deceit, or harmful patterns

Here's the danger: When that 20 percent goes unaddressed or unprocessed, it feels like 100 percent. The mind begins filtering every interaction through disappointment. The emotional courtroom opens. Grievances get rehearsed. Goodwill gets buried.

That's why this chapter matters. I want to help you

- recognize the 20 percent without exaggerating it;
- discern between weakness and sin; and
- respond in a way that protects the 80 percent.

Your marriage doesn't have to be perfect to be good. If you can navigate the 80:20 ratio wisely, your relationship can thrive with empathy, clarity, and resilience.

On the one hand, Scripture reveals that we will have trouble in marriage. First Corinthians 7:28 says, "Those [who marry] will have troubles" (AMP). May I suggest this is the 20 percent? The part that tests us, stretches us, sometimes even wounds us. On the other hand, Scripture reveals we are deeply concerned to please the other. In 1 Corinthians 7:33–34, Paul wrote that a husband is "concerned about . . . how he may please his wife," and a wife is "concerned about . . . how she may please her husband" (NASB1995). Might this be the 80 percent? And might this 80 percent get drowned out when we fixate on the negative marital challenges?

YOUR MARRIAGE DOESN'T HAVE TO BE PERFECT TO BE GOOD.

Her Story: When the 20 Percent Feels Like 100 Percent

At first, she believed she had married well. Her husband was faithful, funny, and steady. He didn't flirt with other women, didn't mock her in public, and didn't abandon his spiritual role. She felt grateful—and confident—that she had made a wise and godly choice.

But as months turned into years, something shifted. He didn't initiate like she had hoped. He rarely picked up on emotional cues. When hard topics came up, his responses defaulted to humor, distraction, or silence. His socks landed near the basket—never in. He forgot important dates. Their conversations hovered on the surface. She didn't want to nag, but she also didn't want to carry everything alone.

At first, she laughed it off. She told herself, *This is marriage. No one gets everything they want.* But quietly, disappointment began to stack up. His quirks turned into irritants. His emotional absence started to feel like rejection. She felt unseen, unheard, unpursued.

So she began collecting mental evidence. He forgot her birthday dinner. He brushed off her concerns about their daughter. He avoided spiritual conversations—again. She wasn't trying to build a case. She wasn't cruel. But emotionally, she began to live like a prosecutor—rehearsing his shortcomings and silently preparing to justify her resentment. She stopped seeing the 80 percent—the man who faithfully provided, protected, showed up, and stayed. She could only see what he wasn't doing.

And, in time, she could predict exactly how he'd respond in the moments that mattered most—dismissive here, defensive there, distracted again—and the more her predictions proved true, the more she was sure she was right . . . even a kind of prophetess.

In my work with couples, I've seen this same shift happen in wives and husbands alike. The 20 percent becomes so loud that it drowns out the 80 percent. The heart stops seeing with grace and starts scanning for fault.

But here's the hopeful turn. One afternoon, while journaling, something clicked. She realized, "I'm not responding to his sin—I'm reacting to his humanity." That moment didn't solve everything, but it softened something in her. She began to notice the good again. She still had needs. But now she also saw a faithful man. Committed. Hardworking. Protective. Competent. Gentle. Sincere. Good-willed.

The Trap of Fixating on the 20 Percent

Why does the 20 percent feel so much bigger than it is?

Because of negative filtering—a subtle shift in focus that changes everything. When someone we love lets us down repeatedly, our mind begins scanning for more disappointment. It becomes a form of self-protection: *If I expect less, I won't get hurt again.*

But in marriage, this habit is deadly.

We stop watching the whole "movie" of our spouse's life—seeing their goodwill, their efforts, their intentions—and instead take mental "snapshots" of the worst moments. Those images become our dominant narrative. A bad day becomes their identity. One failure becomes the defining trait.

This leads to a dangerous thought pattern:

- I withdraw because they always disappoint me.
- I lash out because they never listen.
- I've stopped trying because they don't care.

And this, in turn, fuels the Crazy Cycle: Her lack of respect triggers his lack of love. His lack of love triggers her lack of respect. And around they go, each believing their reaction is justified by the other's failure.

But here's the truth: Your spouse may not have changed, but your focus has.

Fixating on the 20 percent blinds us not only to our spouse's goodwill but to our own responsibility before God. We become so focused on what they lack that we stop asking, *How am I responding? Am I still being the person God calls me to be, regardless of who they are being today?*

The danger isn't only in their weakness. It's in how we interpret and react to it.

His Story: The Burden of Constant Critique

From his perspective, it felt like he couldn't get anything right. What began as small observations from his wife—"Hey, don't forget the meeting" or "I wish you'd ask me more questions"—slowly morphed into what felt like constant corrections. The timing only made it harder: right before bed, just after walking in from work, or in the middle of family gatherings. No matter how hard he tried, his efforts seemed invisible or inadequate. Even when he did make improvements, conversations often circled back to what he hadn't done yet.

He wasn't angry—just tired. He started to retreat. Not because he didn't care but because engagement started to feel like failure on repeat. Eventually, silence felt safer than stepping into another conversation he couldn't win.

But then something shifted. He heard a pastor say, "Offense doesn't always mean someone is being offensive." That line stopped him. Was his wife truly attacking him or was she simply exhausted? Was her tone cruel or was it a cry for closeness she didn't know how to express?

He began asking different questions: "Is she reacting to my failures or is she reaching for connection?" "Am I pulling away from sin or just from her sadness?" "Have I missed her goodwill while focusing only on her frustration?" With that perspective shift, he made a conscious choice: to stay steady. To keep showing love even when her tone sounded sharp. To remember the 80 percent—her loyalty, her heart for the kids, her desire for closeness. He didn't deny the tension, but he stopped letting it define their whole story.

And over time, something shifted in her too. When he didn't withdraw, she didn't escalate. When he stayed present, she began to soften. The change didn't happen overnight, but it happened. And it began not with her behavior changing but with him choosing to see her differently—not as a critic but as a woman who still cared deeply. A woman whose frustration masked her longing for connection. A woman who was passionate and, beneath the moments of negativity, reaching for him—wanting and needing him.

Turning Point: A Universal Awakening

At some point in every marriage, both husband and wife face a sobering realization: *The person I married is not perfect. And neither am I.*

Early admiration gives way to daily life. Quirks that once seemed endearing begin to irritate. Personality differences that once sparked fascination now cause frustration. Emotional gaps—whether in communication, intimacy, parenting, or decision-making—start to feel like chasms.

This is the moment every spouse must ask:

- Is this sin or simply a difference?
- Is this weakness actually the backside of a strength?

Consider this list of frontside abilities but backside deficiencies:

Personality and Decision-Making

- Thoughtful, deep thinker → Overanalyzes, slow to decide
- Carefree, spontaneous → Disorganized, forgetful
- Disciplined, structured → Inflexible, resistant to change
- Visionary, big-picture thinker → Overlooks details, distracted

Communication Styles

- Honest, direct → Blunt, unintentionally harsh
- Good listener, empathetic → Avoids conflict, bottles up frustration
- Expressive, articulate → Talks too much, dominates conversations

Emotional Sensitivity and Relational Energy

- Sensitive, compassionate → Easily hurt, takes things personally
- Logical, steady under pressure → Emotionally distant or detached
- Passionate, emotionally expressive → Overreacts, mood swings

Habits, Preferences, and Stress Responses

- Hardworking, driven → Workaholic, neglects rest and relationships
- Laid-back, easygoing → Procrastinates, messy or unmotivated
- Adaptable, stress-tolerant → Avoids difficult conversations
- Problem-solver, logical thinker → Emotionally disconnected in conflict

Have you found yourself fixating on these backside deficiencies? Have you stopped appreciating the strength and begun resenting the weakness? Do these patterns frustrate you so deeply that you now define your spouse by them?

This is a human marriage, not a perfect one. But it's also not the whole story.

The Backside of Depravity: When 20 Percent Is More Than Weakness

There's something beyond personality limitations—something weightier. There is sin. There is the backside of depravity, the willful distortion of God's design.

This is when a spouse doesn't just forget, fumble, or fall short but rather chooses deceit, betrayal, addiction, rage, control, or cruelty.

If non-sinful actions can cause pain, sinful behaviors can devastate a marriage. These are not flaws. They are violations—of love, of trust, and of God's heart.

Consider the backside of depravity, the sinful distortion of strengths:

Personality and Decision-Making

- Thoughtful, deep thinker → Becomes judgmental and arrogant; exalts self above others; uses intellect to shame or control
- Carefree, spontaneous → Lives recklessly; breaks promises and obligations with no remorse; acts irresponsibly and refuses accountability
- Disciplined, structured → Demands control; enforces rules with harshness; shames others who fail to meet rigid standards
- Visionary, big-picture thinker → Neglects people and commitments; manipulates others to serve personal ambition; tramples others for "the goal"

Communication Styles

- Honest, direct → Speaks cruelly or condescendingly; wounds others with words under the guise of honesty; uses truth as a weapon
- Good listener, empathetic → Deceives by feigning compassion; withholds truth for self-preservation; enables sin through silence
- Expressive, articulate → Lies, flatters, or dominates conversations; talks to impress or control rather than build up others

Emotional Sensitivity and Relational Energy

- Sensitive, compassionate → Manipulates others through emotional outbursts; weaponizes vulnerability; plays the victim to avoid responsibility

- Logical, steady under pressure → Withdraws love and connection; uses silence as punishment; coldly withholds emotional care
- Passionate, emotionally expressive → Rages in anger; emotionally intimidates or controls others; demands others comply emotionally

Habits, Preferences, and Stress Responses

- Hardworking, driven → Neglects spouse and children for personal success; idolizes performance; refuses relational engagement
- Laid-back, easygoing → Lazily avoids responsibility; refuses to contribute; blames others when confronted
- Adaptable, stress-tolerant → Enables sin through cowardice; refuses to confront evil; prioritizes personal comfort over righteousness
- Problem-solver, logical thinker → Mocks emotions; uses intellect to control; shows contempt for emotional or spiritual needs

These are not quirks. In most instances, they are sinful distortions of God-given design—evidence of depravity, not deficiency. They break trust. They violate love and respect. And they grieve the heart of God.

The Theology Behind the 80:20 Ratio

Why does this pattern of tension, goodwill, and brokenness show up in nearly every marriage? Because it reflects a deeper spiritual truth.

Every husband will at times feel his wife is way too negative, critical, contemptuous, and unfriendly. He'll want to exclaim, "Can't we just have one day when everything is okay? All you do is complain." Likewise, every wife will at some point feel her husband is falling short—too passive, too distant, too unimpressive. "He never surprises me, romances me, or makes me laugh. Why can't he make me feel special, like a princess, every day?" These thoughts aren't signs that something is broken in your marriage—not necessarily. They are signs that something is universally broken in all of us. We are no longer in the garden of Eden.

Every person is made in the *imago Dei*, the image of God (Genesis 1:26–27). That means your spouse possesses inherent dignity, a moral conscience, emotional depth, and a God-given capacity for goodwill. Most husbands and wives genuinely want to love, respect, serve, and please each other. As I quoted earlier, Paul wrote in 1 Corinthians 7:33–34 that both the husband and wife are naturally concerned with how to please their spouse. That's the 80 percent. Even when imperfect, most spouses operate from sincere concern and basic goodwill.

But Scripture is also clear: Every part of us is touched by sin. Romans 3:23 reminds us, "All have sinned and fall short of the glory of God." And James 2:10 intensifies the reality: "Whoever keeps the whole law and yet stumbles at just one point is guilty of breaking all of it." This is the doctrine of total depravity—not that we are as bad as we could be but that every part of our nature is affected by sin. Our thinking, our desires, our communication, and our relationships all bear its mark. That's the 20 percent, so to speak.

Even if your spouse is 80 percent consistent in kindness, loyalty, and care, that doesn't erase the 20 percent of brokenness, selfishness, or failure. And even if your marriage is 95 percent good, you still need grace for the other 5 percent. Why? Because one sin is enough to fall short of God's standard of glory (and our marital standard) and render us guilty. That's why goodwill alone can't save a marriage. And it's why no spouse—not even a "mostly good" one—can stand righteous on their own. We all need more than better communication or a new strategy. We need a Savior.

So what do we do with this tension—the reality of the 80 percent that reflects goodwill and the 20 percent that reveals weakness and sin that results in trouble in marriage (1 Corinthians 7:28)? First, we stop being surprised by it. And then we begin to learn how to respond to it.

When couples fail to grasp this, they often interpret flaws as fatal red flags. Thoughts like *If they loved me, they wouldn't do that* or *If this relationship was meant to be, it wouldn't be this hard* start to creep in. But that's not biblical—that's naive. Marriage isn't the absence of sin. It's the presence of commitment in the face of sin.

If you understand the doctrine of sin, you're not shocked by your spouse's imperfections. You're prepared to respond with discernment: *Is this a personality difference or a moral issue?* With grace: *Can I make room for their weakness without minimizing the pain it causes?* With courage: *Do I lovingly confront when sin surfaces?* And with endurance: *Can I stay faithful even when things aren't easy?*

MARRIAGE ISN'T THE ABSENCE OF SIN. IT'S THE PRESENCE OF COMMITMENT IN THE FACE OF SIN.

Hear me. Christlike couples don't deny the presence of sin, but neither do they turn it into ammunition. They don't pretend everything's fine, and they don't use each other's failures as leverage. Instead, they face sin honestly, confronting it with both truth and tenderness. They understand that marriage isn't a courtroom where one wins and the other loses, nor is it a closet where conflict gets shoved out of sight. It's a sacred covenant, a place of grace and growth, where two imperfect people can look each other in the eye and humbly say, "I need Jesus in this and so do you."

We All Need the Savior—Even at 80 Percent Goodwill

Let's be clear: Goodwill is a gift—but it's not enough. Even if your spouse is loving 80 percent of the time . . . even if your own intentions are mostly sincere . . . even if your marriage looks strong from the outside . . . you still fall short. And so do they.

Again, hear me: Your 80 percent kindness doesn't cancel out the 20 percent where harshness and cruelty enter. Their 80 percent good faith effort doesn't erase the 20 percent where selfishness and deception take over. A mostly faithful relationship still needs grace. Why? Because goodwill isn't salvation. And effort doesn't redeem. Only Jesus can deal with the sin in your marriage—both the 20 percent that's obvious and the 80 percent that still falls short of God's perfect holiness.

We don't come to Christ because our bad outweighs our good. We come because even our best isn't enough. That's not a rebuke or condemnation. It's a relief. You cannot be perfect. Your spouse cannot be flawless. You both need a Savior. And in Jesus, you have one.

My Story and the Crossroads of Grace

I came to Christ at age sixteen while attending military school. I watched a Billy Graham film. That night, four truths pierced through the fog of adolescence.

First, I realized that God loved me. Despite my failures and shame, I heard clearly: "God so loved the world that he gave his one and only Son" (John 3:16).

Second, I saw that my sin separated me from Him. No matter how much good I could muster, "all have sinned" (Romans 3:23). That included not just my obvious 20 percent but also my best 80 percent, which still wasn't perfect.

Third, I came to understand that Christ died in my place. His cross wasn't just historic—it was personal. "While we were still sinners, Christ died for us" (Romans 5:8).

Fourth, I knew I needed to respond. That night, I prayed, confessed my sin, and trusted Jesus for salvation. "If you declare with your mouth, 'Jesus is Lord,' and believe in your heart . . . you will be saved" (Romans 10:9).

That decision changed everything. It not only secured my eternity; it shaped my perspective on marriage. The forgiveness I received from Christ now fuels my grace toward Sarah—even when her 20 percent looms large. And when she sees my 20 percent show up, she responds not with shock but from a deep well of mercy. Because we both know the truth: We need the gospel every day—not just for salvation but for sanctification.

So, let's be honest. Your marriage has a broken 20 percent. But that doesn't mean your relationship is broken beyond repair. It means it's normal. Biblical. And redeemable.

When you include sin in your worldview, you won't be blindsided by it. When you remember James 2:10, you'll stop pretending that mostly good is good enough. And when you anchor your hope in Christ, you'll stop placing God-sized expectations on your spouse and begin extending the grace you yourself so desperately need.

Yes, there is tension. On the one hand, you acknowledge and accept the reality of sin. On the other hand, you confront sin as unacceptable and reject the notion of endorsing and enabling sin.

Discernment: Non-Sinful Deficiencies vs. Sinful Distortions

One of the most important skills in marriage is discernment, the ability to know the difference between a non-sinful deficiency and a sinful distortion.

Many conflicts escalate not because of what happened but because one spouse mislabels the issue. If you call a weakness a sin, you'll become harsh and critical, demanding what your spouse cannot (or may not) change. If you call sin a weakness, you'll tolerate what God commands you to confront—and enable behavior that destroys trust.

So what's the difference?

- A *non-sinful deficiency* is a limitation, a gap in personality, maturity, or emotional wiring. It's the backside of a strength.
- A *sinful distortion* is a moral failing, a willful violation of love, honor, truth, or covenant.

Discernment keeps you from overreacting to human frailty or underreacting to genuine rebellion. It gives grace where it's needed and courage where it's called for.

That's why this distinction matters so much in marriage:

- If you mislabel a deficiency as sin, you'll poison goodwill and drive wedges where there should be patience.
- If you excuse sin as a quirk, you'll invite more harm and erode the foundation of safety and respect.

Grace does not mean overlooking sin. And love does not mean avoiding truth. Discernment allows you to be both compassionate and courageous—a spouse who reflects the character of Christ in tone, timing, and truth.

Five Things to See Before You React

When your spouse's 20 percent shows up, whether as a weakness or a sin, you face a choice: Will you react emotionally or respond spiritually?

Here are five things to see before you speak, accuse, withdraw, or retaliate.

See the Real Enemy—So You Fight the Right Battle

If you don't, you'll treat your spouse like the enemy—when the real battle is spiritual.

Scripture says, "Our struggle is not against flesh and blood, but against . . . the spiritual forces of evil" (Ephesians 6:12).

One wife told me, "My husband committed adultery and took 100 percent responsibility. But in time, I realized I wasn't guiltless either. I had withheld intimacy (1 Corinthians 7:5), which left him vulnerable. Satan saw that opening and tempted him. His sin was his own. But he wasn't the enemy—he was a victim of the Enemy's scheme."

Recognizing the Enemy doesn't excuse sin. But it helps you fight wisely—with spiritual weapons, not personal attacks.

See What Jesus Sees—The Human Spirit Behind the Failure

Jesus said, "The spirit is willing, but the flesh is weak" (Matthew 26:41). He sees your spouse's intention, even when their execution falls short.

A husband once shared that after his wife confessed to an emotional affair, he initially saw only betrayal. But later, through prayer, he saw her deeper story—exhaustion, emotional isolation, and unmet longing. Her choice was wrong, but it wasn't fueled by hatred of him or lust toward another. It came from her vulnerability, the misleading of another, and his own neglect. That insight helped him respond with both truth and mercy, especially when he heard her express, "That was never what I wanted. I wanted you. His attention misled me."

Ask, Is this rebellion, or is it weariness, fear, longing, or confusion?

See Your Own Sin—So You Stay Humble

Romans 3:23 says, "All have sinned and fall short of the glory of God." Not just your spouse. You too.

One wife realized that while her husband's pornography use was clearly sinful, her response—coldness, sarcasm, and control—had become a sinful pattern of its own. She recalled Jesus' words: "Let him who is without sin among you be the first to throw a stone" (John 8:7 ESV). Her breakthrough came not by excusing his sin but by owning her own.

Pride points fingers. Humility opens hands. Repentance softens the soil for healing. Because we all need the Savior, we need to realize the only real difference is that we just sin in different areas. Yes, lust toward female images repulses every wife, and rightly so. She cannot imagine coming near such filth. Yet what she often cannot see is that her own self-righteous, angry judgmentalism can be just as deadly—the pharisaical sin Jesus could not break through because it was blinded by self-deception.

See Your Overreaction—So You Don't Become the Bigger Offender

Without self-awareness, we justify destructive reactions that often cause more damage than the original offense.

Romans 12:17 warns, "Do not repay anyone evil for evil."

One husband told me that his wife's withdrawal during a stressful season hurt deeply. But instead of responding with patience, he lashed out with sarcasm, belittling comments, and cold silence. He admitted, "Her weakness became my excuse. But my cutting words, my shaming tone, and my cold shoulder ended up wounding her far worse than her withdrawal ever wounded me." His punishment exceeded her crime. Yes, her flaw revealed her weakness, but his reaction bordered on wickedness. Her silence stung, but his scorn scarred. We must not become inhumane just because another is human.

See Their Deeper Need—So You Respond with Compassion

Behind most destructive behavior lies an unmet need: a longing, a fear, a wound.

One wife learned her husband had lied about finances. She was devastated. But through counseling, she discovered the deeper root: fear of failure, shame, and a desperate desire to prove himself. His actions were wrong. But understanding his fear gave her compassion. She confronted the behavior—but without condemnation.

One husband grew weary of his wife's constant withdrawal in their marriage. It felt like rejection, like she didn't want him. But through counseling, he discovered the deeper route: When she was a girl, her father had yelled, screamed, and called her names whenever she tried to express herself. Over time, she learned that speaking up only invited more pain. So, in marriage, her silence wasn't disrespect—it was fear, a habit of self-protection. Once he understood that wound, his perspective shifted. He still asked her to engage, but he did so with patience instead of pressure, compassion instead of criticism.

Behind every sin is a story. Compassion doesn't excuse sin, but it helps you address the root instead of just punishing the rotten fruit.

Biblical Self-Reflection and Prayer

Before confronting your spouse's 20 percent, take time to examine your own heart. The following questions and prayers are designed to help you engage with humility, discernment, and grace, rooted not in pride but in Christlike love.

Am I Proactively Assuming Goodwill?

"A married man is concerned about . . . how he can please his wife. . . . A married woman is concerned about . . . how she can please her husband" (1 Corinthians 7:33–34). This passage bears repeating as a foundational reminder that, more often than not, both spouses are trying—even when they fall short. So ask yourself: Do I truly believe that my spouse wants to do right by me? Or have I started interpreting everything through suspicion and past pain? Am I giving the benefit of the doubt I would want if the roles were reversed?

> *Prayer: Lord, remind me that both of us are called to care for and please each other. Help me assume goodwill, not ill will. Teach me to see the intention behind the imperfection and to respond with grace rather than suspicion.*

Am I Patiently Bearing Non-Sinful Weaknesses?

"Bear with each other" (Colossians 3:13). Some frustrations stem not from sin but from personality, wiring, or limitations. One translation says, "Make allowance for each other's faults" (NLT). The Greek word *anecho* includes the idea "to tolerate" and "to put up with."

Am I expecting perfection where God is asking for patience? Do I offer grace for my spouse's humanity or only irritation? Have I mislabeled quirks as moral failures?

Prayer: Father, help me bear with my spouse as You bear with me. Teach me to see their limitations as opportunities for compassion, not criticism.

Am I Encouraging—Not Enforcing—Spiritual Growth?

"Restore [them] gently" (Galatians 6:1). The spiritually mature cannot force spiritual maturity on another. That's a contradiction. Growth must be invited, not imposed. Ask yourself: Do I gently invite reflection, or do I push for change? Are my words inspiring growth or shutting my spouse down via shame? Have I approached them in humility as one beggar telling another beggar where the bread is, or have I just tried to control the outcome?

Prayer: Holy Spirit, guide my words. Help me encourage growth without forcing it. Remind me that You are the One who transforms hearts—not me.

Am I Guarding My Own Heart from Superiority?

Jesus warned against self-righteousness through the parable of the Pharisee and the tax collector (Luke 18:9–14). The Pharisee thanked God that he wasn't like "other people." Have I ever thought, *I would never struggle the way they do*? Do I feel morally superior when my spouse sins? Do I see their weakness as proof of my strength? Am I quick to confess my own sin—or quicker to point out theirs?

Prayer: Jesus, protect me from self-righteousness. Help me remember that we both need grace and that pride has no place in love.

Am I Consciously Refocusing on the 80 Percent?

"Love covers over a multitude of sins" (1 Peter 4:8). Peter isn't saying love denies sin but rather that love refuses to keep sin at the center. To cover means to absorb, to overlook, to refuse to make the 20 percent the headline. That's why choosing to focus on your spouse's 80 percent isn't naive; it's obedience. When you celebrate their goodwill, loyalty, and daily faithfulness, you are living out love that covers.

Ask: Have I thanked them lately for what they do well? Am I seeing our marriage as a whole or just reacting to one painful snapshot?

> *Prayer: God, retrain my perspective. Help me see the goodness You've placed in my spouse. Teach me to focus on what's honorable, not just what's hurtful.*

"But Emerson, What About Sin as Part of the 20 Percent?"

While many marital struggles come from personality gaps or occasional failures, sometimes the 20 percent reflects ongoing, serious, or unrepentant sin. In these cases, wisdom and courage are required because the issue is no longer weakness but possible violations of the marriage covenant—and of God's commands. Let me be theologically clear.

Biblical Grounds for Boundaries, Physical Separation, or Divorce

Scripture provides clear, though sobering, grounds for physical separation or divorce. These are never light decisions, but they are sometimes necessary, and they are never outside the scope of God's compassion and wisdom.

Adultery is one such ground. Jesus permits divorce in cases of sexual immorality (Matthew 19:9). While forgiveness and reconciliation are always encouraged when possible, the innocent spouse is not biblically obligated to remain in the marriage. One husband I met with admitted, "My wife gave 110 percent. I'm the problem. I travel, and I have sex with other women. I'm not changing." This wife did everything she could to keep the marriage, but this man, as honest as he was with me, bailed. Years later, she divorced and remarried. Based on my understanding of Scripture, she had biblical grounds for doing so.

Abandonment by an unbelieving spouse is another. Paul wrote in 1 Corinthians 7:15, "If the unbeliever leaves, let it be so. The brother or the sister is not bound in such circumstances." This abandonment can take the form of physical departure or of willful neglect and refusal to engage in the marriage covenant. In such cases, the believing spouse is released. This verse does not apply to two believers since Paul distinguishes that situation from what he writes in 1 Corinthians 7:10–11: "But to the married I give instructions, not I, but the Lord, that the wife should not leave her husband (but if she does leave, she must remain unmarried, or else be reconciled to her husband), and that the husband should not divorce his wife" (NASB1995).

Separation for protection—not divorce—is also affirmed in Scripture. In situations of abuse or persistent, dangerous behavior, 1 Corinthians 7:10–11 allows for physical separation without divorce. As Paul wrote, "Remain unmarried, or else be reconciled." My own mother left my father for five years due to his rage. She didn't yet know Christ, but in that decision, she lived out biblical wisdom. She remained married while protecting herself—and us. That physical separation preserved both safety and dignity. No one is to remain in harm's way physically.

Physical Separation Is Not Rebellion

Choosing to separate is not a lack of faith or an act of vengeance. In some cases, it is an act of stewardship—to protect your life, your children, and the sacredness of what marriage is meant to reflect. If your spouse repents, reconciliation may be possible. But even then, Paul is clear: You are not required to reconcile. Forgiveness is a command. Reconciliation is a process. And safety is a boundary that God honors.

Always Prioritize Safety and Accountability

If you or your children are in danger, get out immediately. God never calls anyone to endure unrepentant, destructive evil in the name of covenant. In these situations:

- Involve civil authorities when abuse or criminal behavior is present.
- Seek godly counsel from trusted pastors, counselors, and legal advisers.

- Surround yourself with truth-tellers—not those who spiritualize suffering or excuse sin.

God is not honored by hiding sin. He is honored when truth comes to light and the vulnerable are protected.

Can There Be Divorce Apart from Adultery?

When asked whether there were any valid reasons for divorce besides adultery, Jesus addressed the question head-on—and He did not broaden the grounds. He didn't soften His stance. Marriage, He taught, is a covenant that can be broken only by death. Moses permitted divorce because of the people's hard hearts, but Jesus reaffirmed God's original design, overturning that concession and allowing only one exception—sexual immorality (*porneia*), meaning adultery.

If someone is abused, the only biblical response is to separate, not divorce and not remarry. As empathetic as we are with the victim—and all of us are—Jesus strictly prohibits remarriage if both spouses are alive and deems it committing adultery (Matthew 19:9; Romans 7:3).

This is why the apostles respond to Jesus' statement in Matthew 19:6 with such astonishment, essentially saying it would be better, in their view, for some to remain celibate than to marry and be bound for life without the option of divorce. To them, Jesus' view felt too strict, too unbending, as is the case with too many today. But their reaction was based on subjective opinion, not the objective truth of the Word of God standing in front of them.

The hope is that through counseling, prayer, and support, the situation will improve. Sometimes it does, other times it doesn't. Jesus knew it would be this way. In those cases, physical separation is the only other biblical response. It is a very hard teaching.

It bears repetition that Paul affirmed the same truth in 1 Corinthians 7:10–11 "To the married I give this charge (not I, but the Lord): the wife should not separate from her husband (but if she does, she should remain unmarried or else be reconciled to her husband), and the husband should not divorce his wife" (ESV).

A Word of Caution

Let me be clear: Genuine abuse is evil, must never be hidden, and must be confronted with both truth and protection. I lived that in my home, witnessing my dad attempt to strangle my mother.

At the same time, the word *abuse* must not be used vaguely as a catch-all justification for divorce. Jesus and Paul restricted the grounds for divorce; they did not broaden them to include vague claims of unhappiness or conflict. Sadly, some stretch the term beyond its biblical or moral meaning. For example, normal marital conflict, a single harsh word, or simple disappointment can be exaggerated into "abuse." Others invoke the word when what they really mean is "I feel unhappy, neglected, or misunderstood." Still others use it as a weapon to gain sympathy, silence their spouse, or rally support on social media—without evidence, context, or accountability. Such misuse not only dishonors Scripture but also cheapens the pain of those who have truly suffered—like my mom—and distorts the gravity of covenant-breaking.

Furthermore, such wrongdoing should be confirmed by "two or three witnesses" (Deuteronomy 19:15; Matthew 18:16; 2 Corinthians 13:1), not from one person on social media making such a claim. That violates Proverbs 18:17 "The first to plead his case seems right, until another comes and examines him" (NASB). Both sides must be heard, not just one. And when there are serious concerns, godly and wise people (or civil authorities) must be sought to weigh the facts and confront the abuse. In every case—whether separation, confrontation, or reconciliation—our hope is not in ourselves but in the God who redeems broken people and broken marriages.

When You Must Confront Sin

Even when your spouse's actions clearly cross the line from weakness into sin, how you respond matters deeply. Scripture never calls you to ignore sin, but it does command you to confront it with truth, love, respect, and spiritual maturity. As Galatians 6:1 reminds us, "If someone is caught in a sin, you who live by the Spirit should restore that person gently."

To approach this in a Christlike way, begin with the first principle: Speak lovingly, respectfully, and truthfully, without character assassination. Ephesians 4:15 calls us to "[speak] the truth in love." That means you name the sin clearly and describe how it is damaging the relationship, but without using contempt, sarcasm, or shame. For example, don't say, "You're a liar, just like your father." Instead, say, "When you hid this from me, it broke trust. That secrecy hurt—and it has to change." The goal is not to attack identity but to confront behavior in a way that keeps the door open to repentance and healing.

Next, invite your spouse to discern what God is saying. Rather than issuing ultimatums or demands, you create space for spiritual reflection. Ask sincere questions, like "What do you hear God saying to you about this?" or "What would a change of course look like—not just to me but to Him?" This removes the temptation to control and allows the Holy Spirit room to convict. Even if your spouse resists initially, these questions can plant seeds that God uses in His time (John 16:8).

Finally, recommend trusted guidance. Some sins—such as infidelity, addiction, financial deceit, or patterns of emotional abuse—require outside help. Don't try to manage it alone. Proverbs 11:14 says, "In an abundance of counselors there is safety" (ESV). This doesn't mean you make the issue public, but it does mean ongoing sin must not remain hidden indefinitely. Bring in a Christian counselor, pastor, or accountability partner as early as possible. The sooner you involve godly help, the greater the chance for restoration.

At the same time, beware of turning to voices who will simply "tickle your ears" (2 Timothy 4:3). In a moment of hurt, it's tempting to seek advice from friends or online communities who affirm your feelings but don't call you to biblical truth. True love doesn't tell us only what we want to hear—it points us toward Christ and His way, even when it's hard.

Confronting sin is never about control—it's about resolution and reconciliation. It's about saying, "This cannot continue. But I still believe that restoration is possible when we both listen to God."

Responding Like Jesus When Confronting Sin

When your spouse sins—whether in a moment or over a season—your response becomes part of the story. The way you handle their failure can either open a path toward healing or deepen the damage. Scripture doesn't just tell us what to confront—it shows us how to do it through the life and example of Jesus. Jesus confronted sin with clarity, naming it without flinching. He maintained the dignity of the sinner, never destroying their worth. He offered hope, inviting restoration instead of despair. And He set boundaries, choosing not to entrust Himself to the unrepentant (John 2:24–25). Having said this, people still walked away from Jesus, like the rich young ruler (Mark 10:17–22). To imitate Jesus does not mean others will respond positively.

Even so, we choose to follow the way of Christ regardless of another's response.

Truth Must Be Spoken Clearly

Sin is not minimized or excused. When a wife discovers her husband has been secretly viewing pornography, she is crushed. The temptation is to scream, shame, or shut down. But a Christlike response might sound like "This betrayal has deeply hurt me. Pornography violates our trust and God's design for intimacy. I love you and believe in your deepest heart you are an honorable man—but this can't be ignored. I want to believe we can heal, but I need to know you're willing to turn from this." Jesus modeled this kind of response in John 8. He didn't ignore the woman's adultery; He addressed it with the words "Go and sin no more" (v. 11 NLT). Yet He also shielded her from public stoning and offered her a new path forward.

Dignity Must Be Preserved

The spouse is not defined by their failure. Suppose a husband discovers his wife has formed an emotional bond with a coworker. He feels betrayed and angry—but he also remembers the woman he married. He might say, "This crossed a line. I won't pretend it didn't happen—but I also won't define you by it. If you're willing to be honest and restore trust, I'm willing to walk toward healing. I am willing to understand your heart better and your needs moving forward." That tone reflects the heart of Christ: grace without compromise. It's a love that speaks hard truth without using sin as a label.

Hope for Restoration Must Remain

If there is repentance and change, healing can follow. When a wife admits to secret spending and debt, the husband is stunned—but she confesses fully and without excuse. Instead of reacting with rejection, he says, "You've damaged trust. But I believe with honesty, support, and accountability, this can be rebuilt. I want to walk through this with you, not against you." Jesus did the same with Peter after his denial. He didn't discard him—He restored him, with both tenderness and truth (John 21).

Let's not kid ourselves. These approaches are tough. But what's the alternative? To respond in an un-Christlike way?

Boundaries Are Necessary

Boundaries can be upheld without bitterness or retaliation. A husband who endures years of verbal disrespect may feel his soul shrinking under constant criticism. He doesn't retaliate—but he also doesn't stay silent. He says, "Your words are wounding me. I love you, but I will no longer remain in conversations where I'm consistently dishonored. I want to get counseling. I believe in our marriage—but I need to protect both of us from deeper damage." Jesus modeled this as well. He didn't entrust Himself to everyone (John 2:24). He withdrew from hostility. He never enabled ongoing harm.

Confrontation, when done Jesus' way, is neither passive nor punishing. It is honest, holy, and hopeful. You can say "This hurt me," without saying "You're worthless." You can set a boundary without setting fire to the relationship. You can confront sin and still leave the door open for redemption.

CONFRONTATION, WHEN DONE JESUS' WAY, IS NEITHER PASSIVE NOR PUNISHING. IT IS HONEST, HOLY, AND HOPEFUL.

Unless there is clear, ongoing harm or

unrepentant sin, begin by assuming your spouse has goodwill. Most spouses don't wake up each day looking for ways to wound. They're trying, just imperfectly.

Final Refocus: Don't Let the 20 Percent Become the Whole Story

The truth is, no marriage is built on perfection—it's built on perspective. And the perspective we choose shapes the reality we experience.

Yes, your spouse will fail. So will you. Some of those failures are just the backside of a strength—a human limitation that can be softened with grace. Others are sins that must be confronted with truth and love. But either way, the question is not only "What did they do?" It's "How will I respond?"

When you respond to weakness with compassion and to sin with courage and clarity, you protect what matters most. You protect the 80 percent—the goodwill, the effort, the daily faithfulness that reflects God's design for marriage.

That's the invitation of this chapter. Not to ignore pain. Not to excuse what's wrong. But to choose what's right: to see the whole story, to respond like Christ, and to walk by faith, not by frustration.

You are not the judge of your spouse's soul. But you are the steward of your own response.

So, ask yourself:

- Will I magnify the 20 percent until it eclipses all that's good?
- Or will I refocus and let grace speak louder than grievance?

Don't let the 20 percent define the story God is still writing. Pray, *Lord, help me see the whole story. Help me magnify what's good, not what's missing. Help me give the grace I need myself.*

PART C

CULTIVATING WISDOM—OUR INNER COMPETENCIES

1. Our Self-Awareness: When I Get Defensive, Do I Get Offensive Too?
   Behavior jolt: I've heard from many spouses who, when finally honest with themselves, recognized a painful pattern: They were doing damage in the name of self-protection. One husband admitted that whenever he felt criticized, he'd snap back—not because he wanted to hurt but because he felt cornered. Another described how he'd talk over his wife, not to dominate but to keep from feeling exposed. And one wife shared how her tendency to withdraw wasn't about giving the silent treatment—it was about shutting down before she said something she'd regret. As one person put it, "I thought I was shielding myself, but I was actually swinging." That realization—seeing how defensiveness often becomes offensiveness—was the jolt that led them toward change.
2. Our Authenticity: Motivation Without Manipulation
   Influence pivot: Over the years, I've had spouses reflect on how their attempts to influence often slid into subtle control. One wife

admitted, "I thought my pouting and whining when disappointed would inspire him to try harder." A husband said, "I'd withhold affection to get her to reconcile and apologize." Neither saw it as manipulation at the time—it just felt like self-protection or strategic motivation. But that's how it landed: pressured, conditional, and performance-based. What changed everything was when they began offering love and respect not as a tactic but as a reflection of Christ. "When I stopped using power tactics—which I didn't even recognize at first—and started responding to my spouse's needs," one wife told me, "he responded so much more positively."

3. Our Forgiveness: Not Offending—Just Misunderstood
   Compassion spark: I've spoken with so many couples who discovered that what wounded them wasn't always rooted in willful offense—it was often a misunderstood intention. One husband shared how his wife's strong tone wasn't contempt; it was a desperate effort to reconnect. A wife described how her husband's retreat wasn't rejection; it was an attempt to avoid saying something hurtful. Once they started asking, "What if this wasn't meant to wound?" something shifted. Compassion replaced assumption. Forgiveness felt reachable. And when real sin did need to be addressed, they could do so without hostility—because wisdom had already entered the room.
4. Our Empowerment: Free and Strong When I Live Out "My Response Is My Responsibility"
   Liberating realization: Again and again, I've seen freedom come through this one truth: My response is my responsibility. A husband told me, "I used to think I couldn't help how I reacted—it was just who I was." A wife said, "I kept waiting for him to change before I changed how I responded." But when they both stopped blaming their reactions on their spouse's actions, everything shifted. They discovered they weren't powerless—they had options. That's when real freedom began. They didn't need perfect circumstances to respond with peace. They just needed the Holy Spirit—and the willingness to take ownership of their response.

NINE

OUR SELF-AWARENESS: WHEN I GET DEFENSIVE, DO I GET OFFENSIVE TOO?

Behavior jolt: We often hurt others most when we're protecting ourselves—our shield becomes a club.

Perhaps the greatest illumination I've ever received came through what we now call the Crazy Cycle. This aha moment, drawn from Ephesians 5:33, revolutionized my understanding of marriage: Without love, she reacts without respect; without respect, he reacts without love.

Decades later, this insight continues to help countless marriages. It has given couples language to describe their experience, built awareness of what's really happening beneath the surface, and offered a clear off-ramp from escalating conflict. It helps spouses pause and choose wiser responses, fostering empathy and mutual understanding.

But what I didn't realize after first discovering the Crazy Cycle was that a second eureka moment waited just down the road—one that would pierce even deeper with a simple vocabulary: When I defend, I can offend. When I am defensive, I can be offensive.

WHEN I AM DEFENSIVE, I CAN BE OFFENSIVE.

When her love tank runs low, she feels unloved. Out of that emptiness, she becomes defensive and reacts negatively, which comes across as disrespectful, and that offends him. When his respect tank runs low, he feels disrespected. Out of that emptiness, he becomes defensive and reacts negatively, which comes across as unloving, and that offends her.

Both feel defeated and deflated, gasping for air.

In trying to defend themselves, each unintentionally pushes the other off their "air hose," and before long, they're not just cutting off the supply, they're stomping on it. These defensive reactions keep the cycle spinning, where both keep feeling offended—but neither sees their own part in it. They see it only in the other.

That realization blew my socks off into the next county.

Here are two episodes on how this plays itself out.

The Dinner Table Disruption

Linda prepares a special dinner, complete with her husband's favorite dessert. Right before she serves the meal, Mark takes a phone call from his boss, keeps talking as he sits there, and absentmindedly begins eating without even looking up.

Linda feels ignored. Hours of planning and effort have been met with silence. Why can't he be more aware and appreciative? Why can't he make her the priority and call the boss back later? Even if she primarily feels disrespected, over time, many wives interpret repeated disregard as unloving. In that moment, the feeling of disrespect toward her husband surfaces. She blurts, "You care more about others than you do about me! You're pathetic!"

Underneath her words is a plea: "Notice me. Appreciate me. Value my effort." She intends to defend her effort and draw out empathy and an apology, but the accusation offends him.

Mark now feels unappreciated for his hard day and judged for taking a quick call from the person with the authority to promote him and increase his salary. He fires back: "I work and make these sacrifices so we can have this home and meals like this, and if I don't always jump through your hoops, you call me pathetic? You're the pathetic one."

Underneath his words is a plea: "Recognize my sacrifices. Respect the way I provide for us."

Both are defending—and both are offending. Each reaction confirms the other's worst fear. Typically, she goes off to another room, heartbroken and feeling unloved, and he sits at the table feeling disrespected and defeated. Neither is trying to be cruel; they're trying to be understood. These aren't power plays—not really. They're defensive reactions that end up stomping on each other's air hose.

Parenting Disagreement

During a family gathering, Mike tells his son sternly to behave. Jackie interrupts, "Honey, don't be so harsh. He's just excited."

Jackie feels that Mike is being unloving toward their son. She defensively corrects him in front of others, which offends Mike.

Mike feels disrespected in front of the group. Defensively, he responds, "Why don't you let me parent without reprimanding me? I am not the child here."

Mike defends his authority as a parent but offends Jackie by accusing her of disrespect and disregarding her concern for their child.

Jackie feels dismissed and retorts, "Maybe I wouldn't have to if you were the adult!"

She defends her position but offends Mike with criticism and sarcasm.

Both are defending, but both are offending. The Crazy Cycle spins.

Couples Get Stuck on the Crazy Cycle

These two stories explain why couples so often stay stuck on the Crazy Cycle. We don't see ourselves as offensive—we see ourselves as defending. A wife sees her husband as unloving but doesn't realize her defensive response feels disrespectful. And if he does feel that way, she thinks he deserves it—or should at least know she doesn't really mean it as her primary aim. A husband sees his wife as disrespectful but doesn't recognize how unloving he becomes in reaction. And if he does, he assumes his response will teach her to show him more respect, since he doesn't deserve this.

WE DON'T SEE OURSELVES AS OFFENSIVE—WE SEE OURSELVES AS DEFENDING.

Sarah and I try to keep two questions in front of us, which I recommend to each couple: Do I realize that my misrepresentation of myself leads to misinterpretation by my spouse? Do I expect my spouse to decode that I'm not being offensive when I'm reacting negatively?

The Reality of Defensiveness: Common to All of Us

Defensiveness takes many forms and often arises from deep, understandable fears and emotions. Below are some of the most common reasons both husbands and wives react defensively—even when their true desire is to protect the relationship.

Fear of Being Wrong or Criticized

A husband feels his wife's feedback about his parenting style as an attack on his competence. His instinct is to explain himself quickly—not to be combative but because the thought of being "a bad dad" is too disheartening to consider.

Feeling Falsely Accused

When his wife was mentally preoccupied and unintentionally less attentive, her husband says, "You never listen to me." She instantly reacts by defending all the times she did listen. She feels the accusation is unfair and wants to correct the record.

Fear of Rejection or Abandonment

During an argument, a husband becomes defensive when his wife expresses dissatisfaction with their emotional connection. His quick denials come from a deep fear: If I admit I've failed her, will she stop respecting me and be so unhappy with me that she wishes she had married her high school boyfriend?

Previous Emotional Wounds / Unresolved Past Hurts

A wife was frequently blamed unfairly as a child. Now, when her husband raises a concern about household spending, it triggers that old fear. She becomes defensive—not only against him but against the echoes of past blame.

Shame or Guilt

A husband forgot their anniversary. When his wife brings it up, he feels a rush of shame. Rather than admitting fault, he defensively minimizes it with an excuse about extra demands at work that distracted him, trying to escape the crushing belief that he's failed again.

Perceived Loss of Power or Control

A wife feels her husband is micromanaging a family decision. Rather than calmly sharing her viewpoint, she jumps in hard—cutting him off mid-sentence, dismissing his reasoning, or pushing through her preference without real discussion. It's not that being strong or voicing her convictions is wrong (strength is a gift in marriage), but fear distorts it. Past experiences or cultural voices have convinced her that if she yields on a decision, she's being controlled or diminished. In that defensive posture, her "strength" becomes a shield that shuts him out and subtly communicates "I don't trust your leadership." Of course, that isn't the message she intends to send.

Fear of Conflict Escalating

A husband, sensing an argument brewing, cuts off his wife's concerns with curt answers. His defensiveness isn't about disagreement; it's a desperate attempt to prevent another exhausting fight.

And Let Me Share My Own Defensiveness

As a husband, I feel a deep responsibility to be the servant-leader in our family. It's something I take seriously. But that sense of calling also comes with a hidden vulnerability: I can get sensitive—sometimes overly so—when Sarah tells me what needs to be done. While she sees it as a mutual, eye-to-eye effort to solve a matter—a simple, matter-of-fact issue—I can sometimes hear it as a directive. It feels less like partnership and more like I'm being managed. I've even said before, "I already have a mother—I don't need another." That wasn't fair. That was my issue. I misread her tone, her intent, and her heart.

Now, to be clear, many times I don't read into her comments or requests. I reply, "Sure, hons! Anything for you!" I receive them for what they are: sincere, collaborative, and helpful. But there are clearly moments when I do read something into them. Something gets triggered in me. I know better, but I still react. And the strange thing is, I know Sarah. I know she isn't trying to control me. I know she's not trying to disrespect me. But even then, I can default into defensiveness.

As I've often said at our conferences, it's not a turn-on to a woman to boss her husband around. That's not what she wants to do. Instead, most women—Sarah included—see themselves as a "helper suitable" to their husband (Genesis 2:18). Not over him, but beside him. Not in competition, but in partnership.

Over the years, Sarah became aware of how some of these moments affected me. At first, it baffled her—she didn't see what the problem was. But she paid attention. She adjusted. She came to see that I had vulnerabilities where she had strengths, just as she had vulnerabilities where I had strengths. And instead of dismissing that difference, she honored it. She began to approach me with more intentional respect—appealing to the strength in me, not the insecurity.

In return, I've had to learn—and continue learning—how to love her through tone, touch, and timing. To speak with care. To avoid sounding harsh or indifferent. And even after all this time, I'm still amazed at how easily I can get defensive—how I can forget her goodwill and read into her remarks something she never meant.

But that's where grace comes in. Grace doesn't pretend the weakness isn't there—it invites us to meet each other with compassion in the middle of it. And when I choose to trust her goodwill more than my wounded instinct, we move forward—together.

As we become aware of the many ways defensiveness can take hold—even in ourselves—we can begin the work of responding with humility rather than reacting in ways that offend and wound.

Defensiveness That Becomes Offensive: Escalation and Hurt

Feeling Devalued or Unheard

A wife feels her suggestions about parenting are dismissed. She defensively snaps, "Fine—do whatever you want. Clearly, my opinion doesn't matter!" Her sarcasm not only silences him but also communicates contempt, deepening emotional distance.

Stressed and Overwhelmed

A husband, feeling overwhelmed by pressures at work, reacts sharply when his wife mentions that several things around the house need attention—the toilet is running, the refrigerator door isn't closing properly, and a bedroom windowpane is cracked. Though she is simply informing him of household issues, he feels accused of being irresponsible. He turns it on her, harshly accusing her of always complaining and never being satisfied.

Miscommunication or Misinterpretation

A wife misunderstands her husband's comment about the budget as a criticism of her spending habits. She fires back with a sarcastic remark about his poor financial choices and the fact that he doesn't make enough money.

Fear of Vulnerability

A wife, hiding emotional hurt and hating vulnerability, becomes defensive when her husband notices her distance and asks whether something is wrong.

She snaps, "Why do you always assume something's wrong? I'm fine. Stop making a big deal out of nothing. Quit psychoanalyzing me like you're some shrink."

What Does Scripture Say About Defensiveness Turning Offensive?

Defensiveness is a universal human reaction. We feel attacked, so we protect. We feel misunderstood, so we push back. But Scripture, with piercing wisdom, shows us how defensiveness, when left unchecked, can quickly shift into offensiveness. And in doing so, it sabotages the very connection we long to preserve.

Let's walk through what God's Word says—not in bullet points but as a conversation between the text and our everyday moments.

Take Proverbs 15:1: "A gentle answer turns away wrath, but a harsh word stirs up anger." It's stunning how quickly things can escalate. One moment, there's tension—something small. But then we answer sharply, and suddenly the whole room changes. A gentle word could have defused it. But defensiveness often doesn't give us that luxury. We fire back. Why? Because we're trying to protect ourselves. But Scripture reminds us: This isn't about what's fair—it's about what's effective. Gentleness can be the very strength that stops a conflict in its tracks.

Proverbs 15:18 echoes this: "A hot-tempered person stirs up conflict, but the one who is patient calms a quarrel." Your spouse may have said something unfair, even unkind. But if your response is hot and reactive, the fire only grows. Defensiveness feels justified in the moment. But patience—real, Spirit-led patience—does what defensiveness never can: It calms. It steadies the ship when everything feels off-kilter.

Then Ecclesiastes 7:9 confronts us bluntly: "Do not be quickly provoked in your spirit, for anger resides in the lap of fools." Many of us don't like hearing that word—*fool.* But there it is. When we're defensive, we often carry unresolved frustration under the surface. Then, when someone touches that tender spot, we explode. But the provocation was already seated in us. Scripture doesn't excuse the other person's comment—but it asks us to take ownership of our internal climate. Am I quick to be provoked? If so, what anger am I still holding in my lap?

James 1:19–20 gives us the sobering why behind this: "Everyone should be quick to listen, slow to speak and slow to become angry, because human anger does not produce the righteousness that God desires." We think our anger is righteous. But often, it's self-righteous. When I'm defensive, I want to be right more than I want to be righteous. And in that moment, I'm no longer led by the Spirit. I'm led by my ego. But God's righteousness is cultivated in listening, not lashing out.

Proverbs 19:11 invites us to rise higher: "A person's wisdom yields patience; it is to one's glory to overlook an offense." There is something deeply spiritual in restraint. Not everything needs a rebuttal. Not every offense needs a courtroom. Sometimes the most glorious thing you can do is quietly let it go. That's not weakness—it's wisdom.

But defensiveness rarely feels like that in the moment. That's why Proverbs 29:11 warns us: "Fools give full vent to their rage, but the wise bring calm in the end." When I vent everything I'm feeling to my spouse, it may feel honest—but it's often destructive. The wise learn to hold space for their emotion without unloading it on someone else. They pursue calm—not catharsis. If you need to vent, talk to Jesus. He's ready and waiting to spend time with you about this.

In Proverbs 14:29, we're reminded again: "Whoever is patient has great understanding, but one who is quick-tempered displays folly." It's not just about keeping your cool. It's about realizing that reacting quickly often means reacting poorly. When I respond with patience, I'm showing that I understand more than just what was said—I understand the person, the history, the moment. That kind of understanding builds trust.

But Proverbs 12:16 pulls no punches: "Fools show their annoyance at once, but the prudent overlook an insult." How many arguments could be avoided if we simply delayed our annoyance? If we paused before reacting? Defensiveness shows up in our sighs, our tone, our muttering under our breath. But the prudent learn to step back—not to suppress but to assess.

That's why Proverbs 17:14 adds urgency: "Starting a quarrel is like breaching a dam; so drop the matter before a dispute breaks out." One defensive comment is all it takes to open the floodgates. What started as a misunderstanding becomes a meltdown. The wise person learns to "drop the matter"—not because it doesn't matter but because the cost of escalating isn't worth it.

And in Proverbs 18:13 we hear a painful truth: "To answer before listening—that is folly and shame." Defensiveness cuts off curiosity. It assumes, reacts, and fires back—before the other has even finished speaking. But when I truly listen, something in me softens. I move from self-protection to self-control. That's when peace can enter the room again.

THE PRUDENT LEARN TO STEP BACK—NOT TO SUPPRESS BUT TO ASSESS.

And finally, 1 Peter 4:8 gives us the anchor: "Above all, love each other deeply, because love covers over a multitude of sins." At the end of the day, love is the antidote to defensiveness. Love doesn't pretend the other person is always right. It simply refuses to let every wrong become the reason the relationship falls apart. Love chooses, at times, to release certain offenses, knowing not every misstep requires confrontation. If the person is already aware and working on it—or if it's something best left for God to address—we can drop it, extend grace, and move forward.

These scriptures don't shame us for being defensive. They illuminate what's possible when we surrender our knee-jerk reactions to the Spirit of God. And as we grow in self-awareness and grace, we find that what once triggered us now teaches us.

You can walk in truth without weaponizing it. You can protect your heart without closing it off. You can be honest without becoming harsh.

Scripture does not condemn the instinct to protect oneself (defense). But it repeatedly warns that defensive reactions, when ruled by pride or fear, can escalate into sinful offensiveness that damages relationships. The wise cultivate patience, restraint, and a heart ready to listen—not merely react.

Even Rachel and Jacob illustrated this dynamic of defensiveness turning into offensiveness (Genesis 30:1–2). Rachel reacts without respect. She becomes defensive, feeling inadequate as a barren woman, perhaps isolated in her burden and even questioning Jacob's and God's love. Out of this deep pain, she appears offensive. Emotionally, unreasonably, and demandingly, she says, "Give me children, or else I die." (Genesis 30:1 NASB1995).

Jacob reacts without love. He is defensive, feeling inadequate and disrespected, but appears offensive when he becomes angry and replies, "Am I in the place of God, who has withheld from you the fruit of the womb?" (Genesis 30:2 NASB1995).

Defensiveness often looks like offense—even when the deeper emotion is frustration, fear, and inadequacy. This has been true since ancient times and remains true today.

But My Spouse Caused My Reaction

When defensive, do we cast blame and excuse ourselves, not realizing how our own responses contribute to the very problem we despise?

This is where maturity steps in. A mature person admits, "Yes, my spouse may be unloving or disrespectful—but that doesn't justify my unloving or disrespectful response." Even more, they recognize, "Just as I feel offended, I am also offending. I'm pouring gasoline on the fire while blaming my spouse for lighting the match."

And that, my friend, is where wisdom—and healing—begins.

But not everyone embraces that wisdom.

A story is told of a police officer who jumped into his squad car and radioed the station: "I've got an interesting case here," he reported. "A woman shot her husband for stepping on the floor she just mopped."

"Have you arrested her?" the sergeant asked.

"No, not yet. The floor's still wet."[1]

We laugh at the absurdity, but beneath the humor of a real situation lies a sobering truth. No doubt the wife felt both disrespected and unloved. She had worked hard to clean, only to feel that her efforts were ignored—or outright dismissed. In her frustration and defensiveness, she overreacted and ended up literally wounding her husband.

Most couples will never take things to such an extreme, but the pattern is familiar. When unchecked, defensive reactions often escalate into offensive actions. What begins as simple self-protection quickly becomes wounding. We leave our spouse leaning against an emotional wall, bleeding, but we don't see it, because we're bleeding, too, from their earlier words or actions that felt unloving or disrespectful to us. Both are hurting, but neither can fully see the other's pain through their own.

As extreme as the wet-floor story sounds, the heart of that situation was something we all experience: defensiveness. It's a natural, self-protective reflex—often a way to shield ourselves from feeling overlooked, underappreciated, hurt, blamed, or misunderstood. We are in disbelief that our spouse walked across our clean floor. However, some of us cross a line. We move beyond simple self-protection and lash out at the one we vowed to love and honor.

What Do I Say to the Person Who Wants to Be Offensive?

What do I say to the person who says they've had enough? They're tired of being the one who tries. Maybe they've felt unheard, unloved, disrespected, so they decide, "Fine. I'm done. I'll hit back."

To that person, I would say this: I understand the temptation. When you've been hurt repeatedly, offense can feel like power. You may feel like this is your way to regain control, to assert yourself, to stop the bleeding. But let me be clear: Choosing to be offensive is not strength. It's a surrender—to bitterness, to resentment, to self-justification.

Yes, you've been affected. But the question is, Are you going to let that pain define your character?

Because when someone wants to be offensive, what they're really saying is, "I'm giving myself permission to violate who God calls me to be to punish who they are." But James 1:20 tells us, "The anger of man does not produce the righteousness of God" (ESV).

You are not powerless, but offense is a counterfeit form of power. It looks strong. It feels strong. But it produces nothing life-giving. Offense tears down what little remains of connection, trust, and goodwill. Offense does not heal. It only hardens.

If you are in Christ, then you are called to something higher. The commands to love and respect are not conditional. They are not contingent on how your spouse behaves. They are expressions of who you are in your obedience to God.

> CHOOSING TO BE OFFENSIVE IS NOT STRENGTH. IT'S A SURRENDER—TO BITTERNESS, TO RESENTMENT, TO SELF-JUSTIFICATION.

Are you becoming the very thing you despise? Are you now justifying your own sin because of someone else's sin?

If so, I invite you to stop. Not because they deserve better but because God does, from you. God has called you to walk in love and respect—not because your spouse earns it but because you reflect Christ.

Choosing offense may feel good in the moment. But it always leads to regret. Choosing obedience to Christ often feels hard in the moment. But it always leads to peace.

So I urge you—don't step into offense. Step into maturity. You don't have to keep going down this road. You can stop. You can turn. And when you do, you'll rediscover the dignity and strength that offense only pretends to offer.

A Gentle Heart Check

Don't be afraid of self-awareness. Those with emotional intelligence aren't those who never fail—they're the ones who can name their reactions without shame, own them without fear, and grow through them with humility. That's a strength. That's maturity. That's the Spirit at work.

With that in mind, which one of these statements best explains why you get defensive?

I fear being blamed unfairly or punished unjustly.

I've developed defensive patterns—often shaped by childhood or past relationships.

I carry unhealed wounds or unresolved emotional trauma.

I fear rejection or abandonment if I admit fault.

I worry that admitting weakness will cost me influence, respect, or control.

I feel shame or fear of being exposed in my areas of struggle.

I rely on pride—the need to always appear right.

I often feel misjudged or unfairly accused, and I react from that place.

I fear losing the argument and looking weak or foolish.

I want to win—or at least control—the tone or direction of the conversation.

I confuse loving correction with personal rejection.

I struggle to regulate my emotions under pressure.

I feel convicted—but I'm not ready to repent, so I deflect or defend.

Which one of these best reflects what you say or do when you're defensive?

I justify myself instead of humbly listening.

"It wasn't my fault." / "You're misunderstanding me."

I blame my spouse to avoid taking responsibility.

"You're the one who started this."

I use sarcasm or mocking to shut them down.

"Wow, I guess I can't do anything right."

I dismiss or minimize their hurt.

"You're blowing this way out of proportion."

I react with a sharp, irritated, or contemptuous tone.

Eye rolls, sighs, harsh tone.

I bring up their past faults to change the subject.

"Well, remember when you . . ."

I withdraw or give the silent treatment.

"I'm done talking about this."

I focus more on defending myself than understanding their pain.

"You're always making me the bad guy."

I flip the conversation to their flaws.

"You have your own issues, too, you know."

I use humor or change the subject to escape accountability.

"Let's not be so serious. Wanna go out instead?"

Every spouse, at times, reacts poorly. The very fact that you're reflecting on your own defensiveness means you're already taking a step toward maturity and healing. You are not your worst moment—and neither is your spouse.

The Lord doesn't withhold grace for things like tone, defensiveness, or impatience. He sees it all—and still extends forgiveness and power to change.

YOU ARE NOT YOUR WORST MOMENT—AND NEITHER IS YOUR SPOUSE.

You can rebound. You can grow. And by God's grace, your humility and self-awareness can begin to break old patterns and build new rhythms of peace.

Not because God expects us to be flawless. Not because our spouse needs us to be perfect. But because growth in marriage starts with growth in me.

What If My Spouse . . .

What if my spouse *never* owns their offensive reactions?

While we each must own our reactions, this does not mean tolerating ongoing disrespect, hostility, or abuse. Self-awareness and humility are not invitations to become a perpetual emotional punching bag. If your spouse repeatedly refuses to own their behavior and escalates into patterns of harm, it is wise and biblical to seek counsel and set healthy boundaries.

What if my spouse misreads me even when I'm *not* defensive?

At times, despite our best efforts to respond lovingly and respectfully, our spouse may still misread us. Their past experiences, fears, or hurts may cause them to see offense where none was intended. In those moments, our role is to patiently clarify—not defensively insist—and gently affirm our goodwill.

What about when my spouse's correction isn't wise or valid?

There will be moments when the correction or feedback we receive is itself defensive, unfair, or inaccurate. Even then, the call is to listen with humility, weigh the truth (if any), and respond calmly. Not every criticism must be accepted, but every criticism can be heard with grace.

Moving Toward Wisdom and Emotional Intelligence with God's Help

Many couples feel discouraged when they begin to recognize the patterns of defensiveness and offense in their relationship. But awareness is not condemnation; it's the first step toward change. One couple, Matt and Jenna, discovered just how transformative self-awareness, humility, and God's grace could be.

Whenever Jenna questioned Matt's spending or his parenting choices, he felt cornered, like a teenager being scolded again. These moments triggered an old wound: the voice of his father accusing him of being irresponsible. Over time, Matt began to realize this fear wasn't just about his wife—it was about his past. That recognition was a breakthrough.

Jenna, too, had her own realization. Her sharp tone wasn't just rooted in anger—it stemmed from years of feeling dismissed as a child. Her voice had often been ignored or minimized, and now, even in marriage, she feared being unheard again. When she finally expressed this vulnerability to Matt, something shifted. He didn't hear her as just critical—he began hearing her as longing to be reassured. And she, in turn, began to understand that Matt's defensiveness wasn't rejection—it was fear.

Together, they began to shift their communication. Instead of sarcasm or shutdown, they started saying things like "I need to bring something up, but I want us to stay connected while we talk." He said, "I don't want to come across as unloving, so help me here." She said the same but used the word *respect*. That small reframe helped lower the heat in their conversations. They practiced pausing before reacting, sometimes even praying silently before answering. It wasn't perfect, but it slowed the spiral.

They also learned to name what was really happening. "I feel defensive," Matt would say, "but I don't want to get on the Crazy Cycle." Just saying it aloud helped disarm what used to feel inevitable. Jenna responded in kind: "That tone wasn't respectful—I'm sorry. Can we start over?"

And when they failed—and they did—they learned to rebound quickly. No drawn-out sulking. No days of silence. Just a simple, sincere apology: "That sounded unloving. Will you forgive me?" "I reacted disrespectfully. I want to do better."

What they discovered was that success in marriage isn't about never failing. It's about failing forward and rebounding with humility. It's about understanding where your reactions come from, owning your part, and choosing to grow.

You don't have to do this perfectly. You simply have to be willing. With God's help, you can respond a little less defensively, a little more wisely, and a lot more lovingly—one conversation at a time.

YOU DON'T HAVE TO DO THIS PERFECTLY. YOU SIMPLY HAVE TO BE WILLING.

Conclusion: Breaking the Cycle with Christlike Humility

At the end of the day, defensiveness is part of being human. We feel attacked, so we raise our shields. But in marriage, those shields often turn into clubs—we hurt the very person we're trying to protect ourselves from. That's why Scripture calls us to a better way.

> When they hurled their insults at him, he did not retaliate; when he suffered, he made no threats. Instead, he entrusted himself to him who judges justly. (1 Peter 2:23)

Jesus shows us what it looks like to absorb offense without becoming offensive. He entrusted Himself to the Father—and so can we.

So what does this mean when the Crazy Cycle starts spinning? It means we can choose an off-ramp. Here are a few:

- Name it: Say out loud, "I feel defensive right now."
- Pause before reacting: Take a breath. Pray silently. Don't fire back.
- Ask, don't assume: "Can you help me understand what you meant?"
- Step away briefly if needed: "This isn't to punish but to regain composure."

These small choices create space for connection instead of escalation.

But none of this works without a foundation of goodwill. If you assume your spouse is malicious, you'll misread everything. But if you assume they mean well—even when their words are clumsy—you'll see a person trying, not an enemy attacking. That shift alone can break the cycle.

Here's the hope: You don't have to do this perfectly. You simply have to be willing. God's grace is not withheld when your tone falters or your patience slips. He sees it all—and He offers power to change.

Maturity in marriage isn't about never failing—it's about rebounding faster, with humility and grace. And when you do, you'll discover what the Crazy Cycle can never deliver: peace, connection, and the presence of Christ right in the middle of your marriage.

TEN

OUR AUTHENTICITY: MOTIVATION WITHOUT MANIPULATION

Influence pivot: Long-lasting influence happens where love and respect are present. The key to motivation is meeting another's deepest need.

In our marriage, Sarah and I have come to believe that when we meet each other's needs, it motivates, not manipulates. That's the distinction we've had to learn (sometimes the hard way). The goal isn't to use or pressure the other; after all, why would I try to control the very woman with whom I am to be one? That's not love or respect.

We've learned—often through trial and error—that this kind of pressure never works long-term. Even from a human standpoint, it just makes more sense to meet the other's need while honestly and gently expressing our own. Sarah and I operate best when we're aligned, when we can look each other in the eye and say, "I need you, you need me. I've got your back, and you've got mine."

But sometimes we can get derailed. This is where it gets dangerous—especially when we're hurt or misunderstood. That's when the temptation slithers in and says, "Just say it. Let it out. Be brutally honest . . ." which ends up just being *brutal*. We've both been there—feeling righteous, justified, even empowered to unload our frustration. And in that moment, it *feels* like authenticity. Like truth. But it's not.

What actually comes out is blame: "You make me so angry. You don't love me. You don't respect me." And with those words, we cross a line. I've done it. Sarah's done it. We call it honesty, but really, it's pain speaking. Or pride. Or fear. And instead of building connection, we tear it down—coming off as unloving, disrespectful, and blind to the damage we're doing . . . all while thinking we're just being "real."

But those kinds of reactions don't reach the other's heart. They provoke instead of motivate.

When I've come at Sarah harshly, assuming it will ignite repentance, regret, and reform, I've only managed to create distance. And when she's confronted me out of her pain without first considering tone or timing, I've shut down. The truth is, we often think our intensity will wake the other up, but it usually pushes them away.

And then we're stuck cleaning up more than just the original issue. We're mending the emotional rift our reaction caused. What began as a conversation about a real need now requires apologies, reassurances, and time to restore that sense of friendly teamwork before we can even get back to the original concern.

That's the high cost of using unhealthy means (unloving or disrespectful reactions) to achieve a worthy end (getting our need for love or respect met). Unless we learn to call it what it is, we'll end up mistaking emotional dumping for honesty—and expecting it to produce empathy and change.

Sometimes in those moments, our words become laced with ultimatums or sweeping accusations that don't persuade—they provoke. The other feels attacked, labeled, boxed in. In that defensive state, ears close. Bodies stiffen. Our words sound like rebuke, not an appeal for connection.

This is the danger of counterfeit authenticity.

Actually, this isn't *real* emotion—it's *raw* emotion. And there's a difference. *Real* emotion, when humbly expressed, is honest, vulnerable, and ultimately helpful. It seeks connection. It builds trust. *Raw* emotion may be honest, yes—but is it humble? Is it helpful? That's the dividing line. Raw emotion often bypasses wisdom. It surges out unfiltered, unrestrained—and in doing so, it wounds. It doesn't heal.

It feels authentic to vent. But when that venting becomes a verbal weapon—driven more by self-justification than by love or respect—it stops being real and starts to offend and wound.

> *REAL* EMOTION, WHEN HUMBLY EXPRESSED, IS HONEST, VULNERABLE, AND ULTIMATELY HELPFUL.

We've learned—slowly and imperfectly—that true authenticity isn't just saying what you feel. It's showing your heart without attacking theirs. It's being honest without being harsh.

Authenticity, in a Christ-centered marriage, is truth expressed with humility and care.

What actually motivates? Meeting each other's needs—freely, sincerely, consistently. Offering love and respect not as leverage but as a gift.

When both husband and wife act in good faith, there's no game playing—just a cycle of mutual motivation.

What About You?

How would you assess yourself?

Let's begin with a brief self-check. It may be one of the most meaningful moments of reflection—an opportunity to consider how you're seeking to influence your spouse and whether your impact is shaped by the love and respect set forth in Ephesians 5:33 or drifting toward pressure and control.

Self-Check: Do I Authentically Motivate or Self-Protectively Manipulate?

Read each pair slowly. Circle, underline, highlight, or pray through the one that most often reflects your behavior in marriage.

1. When I feel hurt, disappointed, or disconnected . . .
   - Motivate: I open up about what's going on inside me without putting them down, and I ask where they're coming from too.
   - Manipulate: I shut down, go cold, or withhold affection—expecting them to feel my disappointment and move toward me.
2. When I want something to change . . .
   - Motivate: I bring it up in a way that says, "Let's figure this out together."
   - Manipulate: I keep repeating my frustration until they give in and do what I want.
3. When I want their help . . .
   - Motivate: I ask clearly and appreciate whatever they can give, even if it's not perfect.
   - Manipulate: I guilt-trip them or drop hints to make them feel bad and step up.
4. When I disagree with them (or they disagree with me) . . .
   - Motivate: I slow down, share my take, ask questions, and look for a win-win.
   - Manipulate: I pressure, exaggerate, or act like my way is the only way.
5. When I feel insecure . . .
   - Motivate: I say, "You have a strength I really need right now."
   - Manipulate: I point out what they're not doing—because it's their job to make me feel better.
6. When I want more intimacy—emotional or physical . . .
   - Motivate: I let them know I need them—not out of desperation but with humility.
   - Manipulate: I turn to anger, criticism, or withdrawal to get my needs met.
7. When things don't go my way or we're making decisions . . .
   - Motivate: I look for a solution we can both feel good about, believing there's a creative third option.
   - Manipulate: I subtly steer things to prioritize what I want—or bypass them and do it anyway.

8. When we handle finances . . .
   - Motivate: I seek open, honest conversations where both of us feel heard, aiming for peace and good stewardship.
   - Manipulate: I steer spending or saving toward my preferences—while calling it "joint decision-making."
9. When we share responsibilities—parenting, chores, or other roles . . .
   - Motivate: I collaborate for the good of our home and family, honoring their input and capacity.
   - Manipulate: I demand agreement with my way or insist on strict equality without flexibility.
10. When I feel unheard or emotions run high . . .
    - Motivate: I pause, ask for a better time to talk, and show I want to understand their feelings.
    - Manipulate: I snap, bring up old stuff, or say things like "You never get it—so why do I even try?"
11. When I'm trying to help them grow . . .
    - Motivate: I encourage their development for their benefit.
    - Manipulate: I push them to change because I'm irritated with who they are right now.

Count how many times you chose a "Motivate" response: ___________

Count how many times you chose a "Manipulate" response: _________

Don't let your numbers define you—they're just a snapshot, a starting point.

- If you mostly chose Motivate: You're learning how to energize, motivate, and influence in a godly, wise manner. Stay encouraged—keep walking in this direction.
- If your answers were a mix: You're in process (as we all are). Identify one or two patterns to shift, and invite God into those moments.
- If you mostly chose Manipulate: You're not alone. Many of us have picked up survival-based habits. But with self-awareness and the Holy Spirit's help, there's a better way forward.

You may be asking, "What's the point?"

May I invite you to pray based on Psalm 139:23–24? Here is my paraphrase of verses many of us know . . .

Lord, search my heart and examine my thoughts. Reveal any fear, pride, or pain that's causing me to react in unloving or disrespectful ways to get what I want. If there's anything in me that's offensive to You or harmful and coercive to my spouse, bring it into the light. And lead me in Your everlasting way—the way of Christlike love and respect.

This isn't about shame. It's about freedom and receiving God's help. We need Him.

Confessions from Spouses

Even with good intentions, you can harm rather than heal. You can try hard and still miss each other. Not because you're ill-willed. Not because you don't care. But because the ways in which you try to connect are sometimes interpreted as too pushy.

Many spouses are doing what they think will work. They're trying to love and even respect. Trying to be strong. Trying to stay steady. But they're unknowingly creating more distance, not less.

Below are the types of confessions I have heard from husbands and wives—brief but powerful reflections from people who, like many of us, had to learn the hard way that intentions alone aren't enough.

From Wives

"I used tears to control him—not connect with him."

"I thought withholding sexual intimacy would motivate him . . . but it only punished him."

"I thought I was being helpful in giving directions—but he felt I was his mother, not his lover."

"I thought I was guiding him with my critiques, but I was actually crushing his spirit."

"I assumed being direct meant being strong . . . but I was just being disrespectful."

"I let myself have meltdowns and vented, so he'd understand my feelings . . . but it only flooded him with anxiety."

Each of these women wanted a connection and to help. But their efforts—though honest—began to feel like criticism, control, or rejection to their husbands.

Here's the critical insight: Even noble aims lose their power when our methods control rather than invite.

From Husbands

"I withheld affection to wake her up—it only pushed her away."

"I thought pulling back would get her attention, but it just made her feel abandoned."

"I kept pressing my logic and solution, but it only resulted in her saying, 'You never hear my heart and why I share these things.'"

"I thought challenging her perspective would make her stronger—but it only made her feel small and dismissed."

"I corrected her when she performed poorly . . . but she eventually just shut down on me."

"I called it leadership . . . but it was really control."

These men weren't trying to hurt their wives. Many thought they were being strong or principled. But their wives didn't feel loved—they felt alone.

These Tactics Don't Work—Not Long-Term

When we feel ignored, unloved, or disrespected, it's tempting to reach for whatever gets a reaction—sarcasm, silence, guilt, or control. These approaches feel powerful because they often provoke a response. But they don't build trust. They don't deepen intimacy. At best, they create compliance. At worst, resentment. Over time, they erode the emotional safety required for meaningful connection and friendship.

Many spouses have confessed to using tactics like these, thinking they'd help, only to find they hurt. Here are a few of the most common:

- Guilt may spark short-term action, but it hardens the heart. "After all I've done for you . . ." only drives your spouse further away.
- The silent treatment often communicates rejection. One spouse may need space, but the other hears, "You're not worth my words."
- Withholding affection or respect makes love feel conditional: "You must earn my heart" instead of "I choose to give it."
- Control—micromanaging, pushing outcomes—may get results, but it costs unity and breeds resentment.
- Comparison deflates. "Why can't you be more like . . ." discourages and wounds.
- Flattery used as a tool for manipulation feels disingenuous. When discovered, it breaks trust.
- Criticism without love wears down the soul. The other feels judged, not helped.
- Emotional outbursts might release frustration, but they often bury the real issue and overwhelm the other.
- Withholding sex or conversation as leverage strikes at the heart of intimacy: "Until you change, I'll keep myself from you."
- Ultimatums don't inspire best-of-friends status. They threaten and create panic and distance.

In all these cases, the method may feel powerful—but over time, it drains emotional energy and leads to discouragement and defeat.

More on Authenticity

Authenticity isn't just about being open; it's about being accountable. The more "real" we claim to be, the more we must consider the impact of our words.

True authenticity requires self-awareness. It doesn't stop at "Am I being honest?" It presses further: "Does Christ shape my honesty?"

And here's the subtle danger: Sincerity can still be self-centered. We can be completely genuine and still be driven by pride, fear, or the need to control.

TRUE AUTHENTICITY REQUIRES SELF-AWARENESS.

Authenticity shaped by Christ doesn't give emotions the final word—it brings them under His authority. It's not about reacting on impulse but responding with spiritual maturity. Truth, spoken in love and with respect, builds trust, fosters connection, and reflects the heart of Christ—even in hard conversations.

The Crazy Cycle vs. the Energizing Cycle

Throughout this book, I've highlighted how we all wrestle with our negative reactions in marriage and how, at times, we feel justified in those reactions because we're trying to get our spouse to stop their mistreatment and respond in a more civil and dignified way. So, crossing a line on Ephesians 5:33, a husband may react in ways that feel unloving to his wife in hopes that she'll stop showing disrespect. Or a wife may react in ways that feel disrespectful to her husband, hoping he'll finally become more loving.

This puts them on the Crazy Cycle, where they trigger each other and spin in reaction. The way forward is choosing the Energizing Cycle—the path to motivating a spouse as God designed. Based on Ephesians 5:33, a husband's love most effectively motivates a wife's respect, and a wife's respect most effectively motivates a husband's love. That kind of sincere purpose and practice replaces manipulation.

Unfortunately, we can keep on negatively reacting to motivate our spouse to be positive. At conferences, I jokingly act out a scenario: After years of marital frustration, a spouse suddenly exclaims, "I get it! I had an epiphany! After thirty years of marriage, I finally realized you were being negative to motivate me to be positive. How did I miss it? What a strategy—you're brilliant!"

The crowd always laughs, because we all relate. Deep down, many of us think our sarcasm, criticism, or silence will influence our spouse to be positive, appreciative, and tender. But they won't. They are defensive reactions that prove offensive. There never is such an epiphany.

I CANNOT BE UNLOVING AND DISRESPECTFUL TO MOTIVATE MY SPOUSE TO BE LOVING AND RESPECTFUL.

The essence of this chapter comes down to this: I cannot be unloving and disrespectful to motivate my spouse to be loving and respectful. That's comparable to shouting, "I will deprive you of your deepest need to coerce you into meeting my deepest need!"

Can I Have Good Motives?

Yes, you absolutely can have good motives. Most husbands and wives don't set out to punish or manipulate. They're not trying to be disrespectful or unloving per se. Their motives are often sincere: to feel heard, stay connected, or fix what's broken. But sincerity doesn't always translate into success. Even good intentions can cause harm when the method contradicts the message.

You may be saying "I need you," but your tone might sound like "You're failing me." You may be asking for closeness, but if it comes across as control or criticism, your spouse may shut down—regardless of your heart's intent.

One wife shared this very struggle. Her motive was love, but her method landed like contempt. She wanted connection but pushed him emotionally when he shut down. She craved reassurance but withheld warmth, hoping to provoke a reaction. She offered criticism when she truly longed for partnership.

"I wasn't trying to hurt him," she said, "but I chipped away at his confidence and didn't create safety." Later, she admitted, "Not everything that hurt me was a sin against me—some of it was my own sensitivity." That insight helped her change. She began voicing needs with vulnerability instead of blame. Slowly, things began to shift.

A husband shared a similar realization. During conflict, he often stayed silent, believing he was being calm. But his wife interpreted his silence as indifference or rejection.

"I wasn't punishing her," he said. "I just didn't know how to handle her intensity without shutting down." Over time, through prayer and intentional effort, he began reengaging—asking better questions and making it clear that his pauses weren't rejection but self-regulation. He didn't become perfect, but he became present.

AUTHENTICITY REQUIRES US TO MATCH WHAT WE INTEND WITH HOW WE BEHAVE.

That's authenticity in action. Authenticity requires us to match what we intend with how we behave. When method and motive misalign, the message gets lost. That's why self-awareness matters. When we consciously and willfully align what we mean with how we express it, our influence increases.

Worthy Desires, Unworthy Tactics

Your need for love and respect is real—and God-given. But how we pursue those needs matters deeply. It's possible to have right needs but use wrong methods. Even when the desire is healthy, the delivery can be harmful. We must remember that pure desires can still use coercive tactics. God-given desires must be guarded in how they're expressed, because a holy need doesn't justify unholy means.

In my book *Love & Respect*, which is rooted in Ephesians 5:33, I explain how God has woven deep desires into the fabric of each spouse. The wife longs for love, captured in the acronym COUPLE, and the husband longs for respect, reflected in CHAIRS. While both men and women need love and respect equally, most husbands don't doubt their wives love them. What many fear, however, is this message: "You're inadequate as a man—and I will never truly respect you." For wives, the deeper vulnerability often sounds like this: "I've never really loved you—and I plan to leave."

These foundational longings are not selfish—they are sacred. They are God-given, as Scripture asserts or implies. I include this section to help you better understand what God's Word reveals about your good desires as a married person—and your spouse's.

But just as important as the desires themselves is the way we respond to them. There are appropriate, Spirit-led ways to motivate your spouse to respond with love or respect—and there are harmful, fear-driven methods that cross the line into manipulation. The former builds trust and connection. The latter undermines both.

COUPLE: A Wife's God-Given Desire for Love

Each of these desires reflects something healthy and holy in a wife's heart. These are not selfish demands—they are deep needs God wove into her being. But a wife must never use disrespect to manipulate her husband into loving her more.

C – Closeness

"A man shall leave his father and his mother, and be joined to his wife; and they shall become one flesh" (Genesis 2:24 NASB1995).

This speaks to your longing for emotional, spiritual, and physical closeness and connection. You were made for intimacy—not just sexually but relationally. You want to feel "one." That's good. But closeness cannot be forced through criticism or control. So, how will you approach your husband?

- **Motivate:** "I miss being close to you—not just physically but emotionally too. Can we spend a little time together tonight?"
- **Manipulate:** "You never want to be around me anymore. What's even the point of this marriage?"

O – Openness

"Husbands, love your wives and do not be embittered against them" (Colossians 3:19 NASB1995).

This speaks to your desire for openness, not coldness. You don't want a husband who shuts down, withholds words, or simmers in quiet anger. You long to feel trusted and emotionally safe. That desire is good. But your response must not be disrespect when he closes off—it must be rooted in gracious strength and trust.

- **Motivate:** "I feel closest to you when you, a man seeking to be honorable, let me in—even just a little. Hearing your thoughts not only helps me feel important to you but also enables me to pray that the Lord would honor you in your endeavors related to your thoughts."
- **Manipulate:** "Of course you're shutting down again. Why do I even try?"

U – Understanding

"You husbands in the same way, live with your wives in an understanding way" (1 Peter 3:7 NASB1995).

You want him to listen, not fix. To care, not correct. That's good. You long to feel heard and known. But this cannot be achieved by condemning his attempts or disrespecting his heart.

- **Motivate:** "Thank you for wanting to solve this burden I feel. But when you simply sit with me and listen—even without solving anything—it eases more of my weight than you realize."
- **Manipulate:** "You just don't get me. You never have."

P – Peacemaking

"The two shall become one flesh. . . . What therefore God has joined together, let no man separate" (Matthew 19:5–6 NASB1995).

This speaks to your yearning for harmony. You feel safe when there's peace. God made you to value relational unity. That's beautiful. But peace cannot be forged by blaming or shaming—it starts with a soft answer and a soft heart.

- **Motivate:** "I want us to be at peace—not just to avoid conflict but so we can feel like we're a team again. What happened felt unloving . . . but did I trigger this with my disrespect?"
- **Manipulate:** "You always make everything worse. Why do I even bother?"

L – Loyalty

"The LORD has been a witness between you and the wife of your youth . . . she is your companion and your wife by covenant" (Malachi 2:14 NASB1995).

You need assurance of his commitment—body, soul, and spirit. That desire is right and good. But you cannot test loyalty through threats or suspicion. Loyalty is fed through respect and trust, not fear.

- **Motivate:** "It means a lot when you let me know we're in this together—no matter what."
- **Manipulate:** "Maybe I should just stop trusting you at all."

E – Esteem

"Show her honor as a fellow heir of the grace of life" (1 Peter 3:7 NASB1995).

You long to feel treasured and valued—not as a burden but as a blessing. You want to know you matter to him. This desire is not selfish; it's sacred. But honor must be drawn out by dignity and mutual respect, not demanded through contempt.

- **Motivate:** "It means a lot when you value my thoughts and strengths. It helps me feel secure. I feel honored by a man seeking to be honorable."
- **Manipulate:** "No wonder I never feel good enough around you. You can't even spell the word r-e-s-p-e-c-t."

CHAIRS: A Husband's God-Given Desire for Respect

These are not signs of ego but rather evidences of how God designed a man's heart to be affirmed. But a husband must not withhold love to punish his wife for a lack of respect. That's not leadership—it's manipulation.

C – Conquest

"Then the LORD God took the man and put him into the garden of Eden to cultivate it and keep it" (Genesis 2:15 NASB1995).

You want to be acknowledged for your desire to work, achieve, and provide. That is healthy. But don't use love as a tool to leverage appreciation. Give love unconditionally—even when you feel unrecognized.

- **Motivate:** "I work hard because I want to provide for you and our family. It means the world when you believe in what I'm building."
- **Manipulate:** "After everything I do around here, the least you could do is show a little appreciation. But I won't hold my breath."

H – Hierarchy

"The husband is the head of the wife, as Christ also is the head of the church" (Ephesians 5:23 NASB1995).

"Wives, be subject to your own husbands, as to the Lord" (Ephesians 5:22 NASB1995).

You want to lead with responsibility and be trusted in your role. That is good. But your authority must mirror Christ's love, not demand submission to earn your affection.

- **Motivate:** "I care about leading us well, and I want your voice in the process. I want to grow in this together. We are one."
- **Manipulate:** "It's your job to follow me. That's what the Bible says, so don't question it. Just submit, woman."

A – Authority

"I do not allow a woman to teach or exercise authority over a man" (1 Timothy 2:12 NASB1995).

"He must manage his own household well" (1 Timothy 3:4 ESV).

You desire to be trusted when offering input or taking initiative. That longing is valid. But love should never be withheld when your leadership feels resisted. True authority is humble and servant-hearted.

- **Motivate:** "I feel responsible before the Lord to make this decision, but I want to be sure I've heard your heart first. God speaks through you to me first and foremost."
- **Manipulate:** "You just need to go along with this. I don't have to explain myself."

I – Insight

"The woman being deceived, fell into transgression" (1 Timothy 2:14 NASB1995).

You want to be respected for your discernment and perspective, serving your wife when her feelings could be misled. That's good and biblical. But your insight must serve, not intimidate, dominate, or incriminate. Lead with humility, not superiority.

- **Motivate:** "Can I share a concern? I think there may be something we're not seeing clearly—and I'd like us to think through it together."
- **Manipulate:** "You're too emotional to see things logically. Just do as I say—I know better."

R – Relationship

"Encourage the young women to love [*phileo*] their husbands" (Titus 2:4 NASB1995).

"Enjoy life with the woman whom you love" (Ecclesiastes 9:9 NASB1995).

You long for companionship—shared activity, shoulder-to-shoulder time, friendship. That's healthy. But relational closeness must include emotional connection too. Don't settle for activity without affection.

- **Motivate:** "I miss just spending time with you. I love shoulder-to-shoulder time. Let's do something together this weekend—just the two of us."
- **Manipulate:** "You're always too busy for me. Maybe I'll just go do my own thing while you make everyone and everything more important."

S – Sexuality

"Let her breasts satisfy you at all times; be exhilarated always with her love" (Proverbs 5:19 NASB1995).

You feel bonded through physical intimacy. That is holy and right. But you cannot demand sex as a reward for good behavior. Sexuality in marriage must always remain sacred and self-giving.

- **Motivate:** "I am grateful the Lord designed me to need you. I feel most connected to you when we share physical intimacy and can talk heart to heart afterward. Thank you for your understanding and for seeing that this isn't just about the physical—it's about feeling known, understood, and appreciated."
- **Manipulate:** "If you really cared about me, you wouldn't say no all the time. You are so frigid. There's something wrong with you."

All of these desires—rooted in love and respect—aren't weaknesses. They are God-given reflections of how He uniquely wired men and women. But when we use them to control rather than energize, motivate, and influence as the Lord intended, they lose their benevolent power.

The Energizing Cycle: Why God's Design Works

When we align with God's design in Ephesians 5, something powerful unfolds. Scripture reveals a pattern that strengthens marriage: His love energizes her respect, and her respect energizes his love.

When a husband loves—even when he feels disrespected—his love often draws out respect. When a wife respects—even when she feels unloved—her respect softens his heart and stirs his love.

This message isn't just rooted in Scripture—it's confirmed by data. In a study I conducted with Dr. Ken Canfield of our Love & Respect attendees, which averaged for over ten years 1,800 people per two-day conference (we did around ten conferences a year), we found that 80 percent of men said they feel disrespected during conflict, while 78 percent of women said they feel unloved. When asked what they most preferred to receive from their spouse—love or respect—74 percent of men chose respect, and 71 percent of women chose love.

After attending the Love & Respect Conference, the clarity only increased. Ninety percent of men said they felt disrespected during conflict, while only 10 percent said unloved. Eighty-three percent of women said they felt unloved, and only 17 percent said disrespected. Most telling, 96 percent of men said, "Love best motivates my wife," and 94 percent of women said, "Respect best motivates my husband."

These consistent results confirm the biblical insight that men and women are wired differently—and thrive when treated accordingly. Love and respect are not just ideals; they are relational oxygen and gender-specific.

When couples align with God's design—where love motivates respect and respect motivates love—they don't just avoid the Crazy Cycle, they enter the Energizing Cycle. And as the research shows, this isn't just biblical; it's observable. Men and women thrive when their deepest God-given needs are acknowledged and met. This message of love and respect rings true for couples.

Biblical Models of Motivation vs. Manipulation

Scripture doesn't just give us commands—it gives us stories. Real people in real relationships, making real choices. Through these accounts, we see a powerful contrast: Godly motivation opens hearts, while manipulation breeds distrust. These stories aren't just ancient—they're mirrors and models for how we influence today.

Consider Hosea and Gomer. In Hosea 3:1, God told Hosea, "Go again, love a woman who is loved by her husband, yet is committing adultery, as the LORD loves the sons of Israel, though they turn to other gods and love raisin cakes" (NASB). Hosea was the husband, and his love wasn't a ploy—it was a holy, faithful pursuit reflecting God's unrelenting and unconditional love. He didn't chase Gomer to control her but to restore her. But imagine Hosea's pain. To Gomer,

Hosea was not enough. Other men were more to her. Yet Hosea heard and obeyed God's truth: "Go . . . love a woman . . . committing adultery."

GODLY MOTIVATION OPENS HEARTS, WHILE MANIPULATION BREEDS DISTRUST.

While the text doesn't tell us whether Gomer ever returned to Hosea with all her heart, there's an underlying assumption: Hosea's love was the God-ordained means to influence, motivate, and invite her back—not through control but through compassion and covenant faithfulness. But he did create boundaries. Hosea didn't excuse her behavior or allow ongoing betrayal. He said, "You shall live with me for many days. You shall not play the prostitute, nor shall you have another man; so I will also be toward you" (Hosea 3:3 NASB). His love was tender, but it was also clear, structured, and rooted in commitment. This love—with boundaries—is the path forward that God intended. This is how He influenced Israel and how He motivates us: not with fear or force but with steadfast love.

Likewise, the wife in 1 Peter 3:1–2 is encouraged to influence her "disobedient" husband—not with persuasive words but with the silent strength of "respectful and pure conduct" (ESV). Her power wasn't in arguments or demands but in the dignity of her demeanor and the consistency of her character. She didn't nag, shame, or preach—she lived the truth. And through that quiet authenticity, Peter said she could win her husband. That's influence rooted in respectful conduct.

Esther is another powerful example. Though she had access to the king, she didn't rush in with demands. Instead, she prepared herself with prayer and fasting (Esther 4:16), approached with respect, and spoke with wisdom and humility. Her dignity, timing, and restraint ultimately influenced the king to reverse a death sentence over her people.

By contrast, Michal, the daughter of Saul and wife of David, showed contempt rather than respect. In 2 Samuel 6:16–23, when David danced before the Lord with all his might and holiness, clothed only in a linen ephod, Michal "despised him in her heart." Later, she confronted him with sarcasm and scorn, essentially mocking his heart and humility before God.

Rather than drawing David closer by honoring his sincere desire to worship God, her contempt drove a wedge between them. The result? Scripture says she was barren the rest of her life—a sobering symbol of what happens when respect is replaced with ridicule, condescension, and self-righteous judgment, fueled by her carnal pride and desire for human applause.

Manipulation is control that breaks trust. Rebekah, in Genesis 27:8, believed she was protecting God's promise by instructing Jacob, her son, to deceive Isaac, her husband. Her motive may have seemed spiritual, but her method was manipulation. The result? A fractured family. Jacob fled. Esau the twin brother raged. Rebekah lost the very relationship she tried to preserve. What began as conviction turned into control. Her faith in God's promise was eclipsed by fear, and fear rarely leads to authentic action.

Delilah didn't appeal to Samson's heart—she manipulated it. In Judges 16:15 (NASB1995), she said, "How can you say, 'I love you,' when your heart is not with me?"—a classic emotional guilt trip meant to question the sincerity of his love and pressure him into compliance. She amplified her offense: "You have deceived me these three times," using accusation and exaggeration to create shame and erode his resistance. Yet the real deceiver in this story was Delilah. Then, in Judges 16:16 (NASB1995), we read, "It came about when she pressed him daily with her words and urged him, that his soul was annoyed to death." Day after day, she wore him down—not through love or humility but through relentless pressure and coercive tactics. She didn't build trust; she weaponized emotion. And Samson didn't just lose his secret—he surrendered his calling. That's the high cost of manipulation: It doesn't just extract compliance; it can derail destiny.

The contrast is clear. Motivation builds. Manipulation breaks.

Before You Accuse Your Spouse of Manipulation . . .

How easy it is to read this information and turn it against one's spouse: "This is you! You manipulate me!" Ironically, that very outburst becomes a form of manipulation itself—doing in that moment the very thing it accuses. It shifts the spotlight, seizes control, and demands change by shaming, not by inspiring. Many have shared with me over the years that they read my content to point a finger at their spouse, and in doing so they violate the very truth they claim their spouse violates.

But beyond your personal hypocrisy, sometimes your spouse isn't manipulating you, contrary to your claims. Not every flawed method in your spouse is rooted in control—sometimes it's fear, pain, or immaturity. Look deeper before you label.

Is your spouse truly trying to control you—or are they expressing a need the only way they know how at this stage of their maturity?

We all have moments when we communicate poorly—clumsily, emotionally, even unfairly. That doesn't automatically mean we're being manipulative. Sometimes it just means we're hurting.

Take the wife who vents but really wants connection. She raises her voice. She gets emotional. She repeats herself. Her husband feels overwhelmed and thinks, *She's trying to control me with her emotions.* But is she? Beneath the intensity may be a deeper plea: "Will you hear me? Will you stay close when I'm scared?" Her method may need work, but her motive isn't control—it's connection. She's not trying to overpower; she's trying to be seen.

Now consider the husband who withdraws but longs for peace. He goes quiet when conflict escalates. His wife feels shut out and thinks, *You're using silence to punish me. You are abusive!* But what if he's not rejecting her? What if he's trying to stay calm to avoid saying something he'll regret? His method may feel cold, but his motive may be peace, not power.

Yes, delivery matters. But don't confuse a flawed method with a manipulative heart.

Assume goodwill unless there's physical harm. In toxic or abusive situations, seek professional help. But in most marriages, what feels like manipulation is often reactions rooted in a lack of knowing how to handle the tension. This is the call of Christlike authenticity: to see past the offense and seek the heart—not to excuse dysfunction but to engage their goodwill and longings.

Before labeling your spouse, ask yourself:

- Are they trying to control me or trying to protect themselves?
- Are they shutting me out or trying not to escalate?
- Are they being demanding or do they just not know how to ask gently?

You Can Influence Your Spouse

Scripture says, "Let us consider how to stimulate one another to love and good deeds" (Hebrews 10:24 NASB1995).

DELIVERY MATTERS. BUT DON'T CONFUSE A FLAWED METHOD WITH A MANIPULATIVE HEART.

We can stimulate a spouse but must "consider how." You can influence—without control—by reflecting Christ through authentic love and respect. There is never a guarantee, but anyone placing a bet would readily wager that a loving husband and respectful wife will stimulate the same in their spouse.

Granted, you can't force your spouse to change. But that doesn't mean you're powerless. You aren't voiceless or irrelevant. You can influence them as you choose to be loving and respectful as a person, regardless of your spouse's choices. Usually, that softens the spirit of a spouse. Why wouldn't it? We are meeting their core need. As I humorously say, "If they don't positively respond, you are married to one bad dude or dude-ess."

You are not responsible for how your spouse receives your love or respect, but you are responsible for whether you offer it as unto the Lord. Saying "I will love because I'm loving—not because they've earned it" or "I will respect because I'm respectful—not because they deserve it" is not weakness. It's maturity.

You can stir your spouse—if there's any goodwill in them—not by demanding they change but by becoming someone who reflects Christ so consistently, so humbly, and so graciously that change becomes hard to resist.

I cannot control the outcomes in Sarah. I cannot force her to change, heal, soften, or see what I see. But I can control my actions and reactions toward

Sarah. And that begins by becoming the real deal—the adult in the room, the authentic person God is calling me to be.

Let these Scriptures guide you:

"Do nothing out of selfish ambition or vain conceit. Rather, in humility value others above yourselves" (Philippians 2:3).

"A person may think their own ways are right, but the LORD weighs the heart" (Proverbs 21:2).

"We are not trying to please people but God, who tests our hearts" (1 Thessalonians 2:4).

Your calling is simple, though not always easy:

I will offer love and respect as a gift, not a strategy.
I will trust God with the outcome, even if I don't see instant results.
I will not mask control as concern.
I will be the peace-bringer, not the chaos-reactor.
I will let the Holy Spirit do His job—and stay faithful in mine.

This is not about being flawless. It's about being faithful.

With God's help—I will be the real deal.

THIS IS NOT ABOUT BEING FLAWLESS. IT'S ABOUT BEING FAITHFUL.

That's how marriages begin to change—not through pressure but through one faithful spouse choosing Christlikeness over control. And when that happens, no matter what your spouse does or doesn't do, you are free.

And oh, when I fail, I will get back up. "For though the righteous fall seven times, they rise again" (Proverbs 24:16).

ELEVEN

OUR FORGIVENESS: NOT OFFENDING—JUST MISUNDERSTOOD

Compassion spark: Often what hurts us may not have been meant to harm us. We can first look past the offense, to their pain, then gently address true sin.

I once heard someone say, "Only marriage can turn a missing spatula into an act of war."

In moments of tension, when a spouse speaks sharply or withdraws emotionally, it's easy to assume, *They meant to hurt me.* And when these moments pile up, hurt hardens into resentment—even bitterness.

But after decades of ministry—and thousands of conversations with couples—I've found most husbands and wives have basic goodwill. As Paul said in 1 Corinthians 7:33–34, he does not intend to displease her, and she does not intend to displease him. In most marriages, intentional harm is the exception, not the rule.

More often, the pain we feel comes from

- misunderstanding—words or actions landing differently than intended;
- miscommunication—withholding or avoiding hard conversations;
- emotional defensiveness—protecting, not attacking;
- fear or fatigue—reactions born from being overwhelmed;
- stress—external pressures that shorten patience;
- unmet expectations—disappointments never expressed;
- personality differences—friction, not sin.

Most marital pain comes from two people of goodwill trying—but sometimes failing—to connect and be understood. And when that's the case, forgiveness becomes not only possible but natural.

Recognizing that most hurt is unintentional softens our hearts. It replaces accusation with empathy and turns marriage into something far more friendly, gracious, and joyful.

Understanding Each Other's Defensiveness

After five decades of marriage, Sarah and I still have to guard against wrong assumptions in moments of tension. When one of us reacts sharply or withdraws, it's easy to assume the worst: *She's choosing to disrespect me. He's choosing not to love me.* But in reality, those reactions are rarely rooted in conscious decisions to wound. Paul reminds us in Ephesians 5:33 that a husband is called to love his wife and a wife to respect her husband—yet in the heat of conflict, we often misread our spouse's heart and assume the opposite.

Many wives, for example, have shared that they used to believe their husband's silence meant he didn't care. Now, they see something deeper: He was trying to calm himself so he wouldn't say something damaging. That shift in understanding made forgiveness easier—because what felt unloving was actually a sign of emotional restraint. In fact, many men go quiet out of a desire to do the respectful thing—holding back words that might wound instead of blurting them out in anger.

Likewise, many husbands once assumed their wife's criticism was an attack. But when they began to decode what she was really saying, they saw something different: She wasn't attacking—she was hurting, reaching out, seeking love and reassurance. What felt disrespectful was, in truth, a plea for connection. In fact, in her world, pressing in strongly toward her husband was not contempt but love—a desperate way of saying, "Don't pull away; I need you."

Sarah and I have lived this too. When she feels unloved, misunderstood, or dishonored—just as 1 Peter 3:7 warns husbands not to let happen—her reactions can feel "unfriendly" to me (Greek, *phílandros*, meaning a lack of warm affection or friendship; see Titus 2:4). When I, in turn, feel a loss of lover-friendship and affection, I can come across as unempathetic and dishonoring to her.

If left unchecked, we soon find ourselves spinning on the Crazy Cycle. Typically, it looks like this: Without love, she reacts without respect; without respect, he reacts without love. But sometimes a reverse-felt-need cycle takes over. Without her warm affection and friendship (*phílandros*, Titus 2:4), he withdraws understanding (*sýnesis*) and honor (*timḗ*, 1 Peter 3:7). Without his understanding and honor, she withholds warm affection and friendship. Round and round it goes.

Now imagine if either of us believed those reactions were intentional. What if Sarah assumed I deliberately wasn't motivated to love, understand, and honor her—despite having written a book on the subject? That would feel like betrayal. Or if I assumed Sarah chose to withhold warm affection and friendliness, showing disdain and knowing how deeply it wounds me, it would be equally hard to forgive. But those assumptions would be false.

This is why love and respect aren't marginal ideas—they're foundational. Ephesians 5:33 isn't just a good suggestion; it's God's design for marriage. And whether a couple is navigating a devastating crisis like adultery or simply dealing with "the little foxes that ruin the vineyard" (Song of Solomon 2:15), this principle holds true: When we forget love and respect—or loving friendship and honorable understanding—even minor moments can destroy connection.

That's how small misunderstandings become major offenses.

- We feel hurt.
- We assume bad intent.
- We stop clarifying.
- Resentment builds.
- Bitterness hardens the heart.
- Forgiveness fades—and walls rise.

But when we step back and remember that most of these moments are not acts of malice, we break the cycle. And in that light, forgiveness becomes possible again.

Understanding the "Why" Behind the Behavior

Understanding what's behind your spouse's behavior is often the turning point in a strained marriage.

The Crazy Cycle thrives on misunderstanding: Unmet needs for love and respect—or friendly, warm affection and understanding and honor—trigger defensive reactions, which feel unloving, disrespectful, cold, and unfriendly. Over time, both spouses begin to believe the worst: *They're doing this on purpose.* Resentment takes root, and an unforgiving spirit isn't far behind.

UNDERSTANDING WHAT'S BEHIND YOUR SPOUSE'S BEHAVIOR IS OFTEN THE TURNING POINT IN A STRAINED MARRIAGE.

But here's what many couples have discovered: The other person wasn't trying to be offensive—they were insecure, overwhelmed, or hurting. And once the "why" becomes clear, the offense often shrinks, empathy grows, and forgiveness feels possible.

One couple clashed almost every weekend in the early months of their marriage. Each time they misread the other's intentions, a little more hurt settled in, and the seeds of resentment began to grow. She often filled Saturdays with errands, projects, or social commitments, assuming he would appreciate a productive day. He, however, saw it as her avoiding time together. Before long, both began to feel frustrated with each other—liking each other less with every misunderstanding.

When they finally talked, she explained that in her family, weekends were for "getting everything done" before Monday. To her, that rhythm was a way of showing care and responsibility, not rejection. What he interpreted as avoidance was actually her attempt at love. And what she assumed was helpful responsibility felt to him like neglect. Misinterpretations like these don't just spark arguments—they quietly plant roots of resentment that only forgiveness can uproot.

Another couple fought over parenting. He often stepped in mid-discipline to handle things "his way," and she felt undermined in front of the kids. But when they finally talked, he admitted that as a child, he had been harshly punished for "getting it wrong." His interruptions weren't about control—they were about fear, a desperate attempt to protect his children from the pain he once knew.

A third couple constantly butted heads over social plans. She would commit them to events without asking, and he saw it as dismissing his preferences. But she later confessed that growing up isolated, she carried a deep fear of being forgotten or left out. Saying yes quickly wasn't disrespect—it was her way of protecting herself from feeling excluded again and of meeting a deep longing to belong.

A fourth couple had ongoing tension about home repairs. He dragged his feet on fixing things, and she assumed laziness. But he eventually admitted that years of being criticized for "not doing it right" had left him feeling inadequate. Avoiding repairs wasn't about neglect—it was about shielding himself from shame.

In each situation, what looked like rejection, disrespect, or lack of affection was actually a self-protective reflex. And once they uncovered the fears and wounds beneath the surface, forgiveness came easier—and the Crazy Cycle (or its cousin, the Loving-Friendship / Honorable Understanding Cycle) began to slow.

"It's so much easier to forgive," someone once said, "when you understand why your spouse did what they did."

Perspective doesn't erase pain. But it reframes it—and reframing dissolves resentment before it calcifies into bitterness. Once we see what's underneath the words or actions, we don't just let go of the offense—we may even find ourselves empathizing, appreciating, and drawing closer.

But I Have Proof: My Spouse Offends Me!

Yes, sometimes there are cruel, intentional words. She yells, "You don't love me!" He shouts back harshly, "Nobody could love you!" Or he says, "You never respect me," and she fires back with disdain, "Nobody could respect you!" Now they each feel justified. But what feels like proof is often just pain speaking—and pain, left unchecked, convinces us of lies about our spouse.

The truth is, once the Crazy Cycle starts, both spouses say and do things that feel hateful and scornful—not always from malice but from pain. Ironically, those hurtful reactions confirm each other's deepest fears: "I'm unloved by a man who hates me." "I'm disrespected by a woman who despises me."

It becomes a vicious feedback loop. Their reaction wounds us, so we assume it was intentional. We don't just feel offended—we stay offended. And when we've asked them to stop, and they haven't, we think, *They must not care. More proof. Case closed.*

Some couples live in this exhausting cycle for years.

A husband wrote, "From early on, heated arguments escalated into different versions of the Crazy Cycle. I've known she's crying out for something, probably love at her core—but I missed it. I defended, deflected, and finally attacked back. Eventually, I crossed lines—arguing in front of the kids, screaming, threatening to leave. It's painful to admit." Why? To force her to show him respect!

A wife shared, "I kept telling him what I needed—more time, more tenderness—but he shut down. That silence drove me crazy. I got louder, more critical, withheld affection. I told myself he was emotionally lazy, maybe incapable of love. The more I demanded, the more he withdrew. I got cold. We stopped talking. I told a friend, 'I think we've broken something we can't fix. He just doesn't care.'" Why? To force him to show her love?

Not every spouse withdraws or shouts. Some go into "courtroom mode," turning the argument into a battle of logic and facts, dissecting every detail without considering the heart behind the words. A husband confessed, "I wasn't going to tell her how I felt until she could articulate her position." For him, it wasn't about reconciliation—it was about winning the case.

Others avoid the conflict by deflecting with humor or sarcasm—making jokes, changing the subject, or using wit to dodge the discomfort. It lightens the moment temporarily, but it can leave the other person feeling minimized or mocked, as if their pain is a punch line rather than a priority.

In most marriages, what started the cycle wasn't cruelty—it was misunderstanding, self-protection, or emotional exhaustion. If we can recognize that—even now—we can begin to slow the spin and forgive more freely. Because so often, what we treat as proof of offense is really just the sound of two hurting hearts crying out to be understood. Even so, it can turn ugly and offensive.

Don't Confuse Frustration with Offense

There's an old saying: Marriages often don't collapse from one fatal blow but from a thousand paper cuts.

Some couples silently keep score—stockpiling small slights until every disagreement feels like proof that their spouse is selfish, neglectful, or hopelessly flawed. What began as normal human friction gets reinterpreted as rejection, disrespect, or even emotional abuse.

But not every hurt is an offense. Some are simply everyday frustrations that come with doing life as two imperfect people.

MARRIAGES OFTEN DON'T COLLAPSE FROM ONE FATAL BLOW BUT FROM A THOUSAND PAPER CUTS.

- Not every forgotten task is selfishness.
- Not every failure to listen carefully is a heart of indifference.
- Not every moment of inattentiveness is rejection.
- Not every negative look is hatred.
- Not every blunt comment is verbal assault.
- Not every act of withdrawal is abandonment.
- Not every expression of exasperation is a desire to leave the marriage.
- Not every disagreement is disrespect.
- Not every criticism is contempt.
- Not every lapse in affection is a lack of love.
- Not every defensive reaction is offensive.
- Not every harsh word is emotional abuse.
- Not every overlooked need is intentional neglect.
- Not every hurt is a sign of betrayal comparable to adultery.

Yes, these things hurt. But they aren't always moral failures or personal betrayals. Often they're rooted in fatigue, misunderstanding, distraction, or personality difference—not deliberate harm.

If we treat every disappointment like a deep wound, we'll begin to nurture bitterness instead of forgiving quickly.

One wise woman told me, "I realized I was walking around constantly offended—when really, I was just disappointed. He wasn't trying to hurt me. He was being himself. And I was keeping score."

Forgiveness becomes more difficult when we mislabel everyday tension as intentional mistreatment.

That's why Scripture warns us not to let anger fester: "Do not let the sun go down on your anger, and do not give the devil an opportunity" (Ephesians 4:26–27 NASB1995).

Satan doesn't need adultery to destroy a marriage. Bitterness will do just fine.

So when frustrations arise, the wise ask, "Was this truly an offense—or just a human moment I need to release?"

Forgiveness must often begin here—before the frustration becomes resentment, and resentment becomes contempt.

But sometimes "being themselves" does bring real pain, even if it's unintentional. A spouse with ADHD, for instance, may often forget tasks or follow through inconsistently. Even with effort, the struggle may not fully change. In those moments, Scripture calls us to bear with one another (Colossians 3:13), refusing to let disappointment harden into bitterness.

SATAN DOESN'T NEED ADULTERY TO DESTROY A MARRIAGE. BITTERNESS WILL DO JUST FINE.

After all, Jesus never grows bitter toward us, so unless we are without sin and free to cast the first stone (John 8:7), we have no grounds to harbor resentment toward our spouse. This is part of the "20 percent" I mentioned earlier: Some weaknesses won't vanish. Our call is not to demand perfection but to respond as Christ responds to us—with patience, grace, and endurance.

Forgiveness Becomes Easier When We Understand

The central theme of this chapter is that forgiveness often becomes possible the moment a spouse sees the deeper reason behind the other's behavior. Not justification. Not excuse. But understanding.

When spouses recognize that their conflict was less about cruelty and more about miscommunication, defensiveness, or fear, hearts begin to soften. Here are just a few real-life moments couples have shared:

"I used to think his silence meant he didn't care. But then I realized—it was his way of staying calm so we wouldn't spiral. That reframed everything."

"He didn't forget to check in because I didn't matter—he just doesn't track things like I do. I saw that it wasn't about neglect but wiring. That helped me let go."

"At first, I thought she was picking a fight—but I finally understood she just needed reassurance. Once I stopped seeing conflict and started seeing fear, I showed up differently."

"When she kept bringing up the same issue, I assumed she was nagging.

But I began to realize she was hoping I'd really hear her heart. That shifted how I listened."

Each of these realizations marked a turning point. The behavior hadn't changed, but their interpretation had. And that's what broke the Crazy Cycle and made forgiveness feel not only possible but natural.

Because when we begin to assume goodwill, understand defensiveness, and see our spouse's reactions as protective, not punitive—forgiveness stops being a battle. It becomes a response of love and respect. And if reframing could break the cycle for them, it can break it for you too—because forgiveness isn't about perfect behavior; it's about a new way of seeing.

Bitterness, Not Betrayal, Ends Most Marriages

But this is where the warning must be given. If we don't intentionally release those disappointments to the Lord, they begin to stack up. Left unchecked, those unaddressed frustrations ferment into bitterness—an inner poison that seeps into our words, tone, and even our prayers. That's why learning to bear with each other isn't just about surviving quirks—it's about guarding our hearts from the slow erosion not only of love and respect in the marriage (Ephesians 5:33) but of our love and reverence toward the Lord (v. 21).

Contrary to popular belief, most divorces don't begin with adultery or addiction. They begin with bitterness. When couples explain why they split, they rarely cite a dramatic betrayal. Instead, we hear the following: "We just grew apart." "We couldn't communicate anymore." "I didn't feel loved or respected." "We argued about everything." "We were more like roommates."

What's really underneath those statements? Often, years of unresolved hurt and buried resentment.

Many don't think of themselves as bitter. They say, "I'm just tired. I've tried everything." But if you dig deeper, what emerges is anger: "You didn't see me. You failed me. You never changed." That's not fatigue; that's resentment with a mask on, that's a wounded heart hardening into unforgiveness. And Hebrews 12:15 warns us, "See to it that no . . . bitter root grows up to cause trouble and defile many." This root grows slowly. It often begins with repeated disappointment. And left unattended, it poisons the marriage—and the person carrying it.

Most divorces occur not because of one destructive act but because of many small misunderstandings that were never healed by mutual understanding and grace. We allowed minor hurts to become major judgments. The apostle Paul gave us a better way: "Make allowance for each other's faults, and forgive anyone who offends you. Remember, the Lord forgave you, so you must forgive others" (Colossians 3:13 NLT).

In 1 Corinthians 7:10–11, Paul urged reconciliation—not dissolution—even in challenging marriages. He makes room for separation in some cases but leaves the door open for healing. The goal isn't to "win" the argument or tally the wrongs—it's to pursue peace, forgiveness, and restoration. Yes, some offenses are serious. But many are simply gray-area hurts that, with humility and forgiveness, can be overcome. Paul's counsel reminds us that in most marriages, there are no truly irreconcilable differences—not when forgiveness is practiced in the power, imitation, and command of Christ.

How Bitterness Opens the Door to Betrayal

May I offer a pastoral warning? If you've been faithfully enduring in your marriage but bitterness has begun to creep in—please be careful. Bitterness, even when "justified," is often the soil in which betrayal takes root.

Satan works subtly. He doesn't just tempt us to sin—he convinces us that we deserve better. That our spouse's failures give us permission to pull away emotionally, spiritually, even physically.

Bitterness begins with stockpiled offenses: "He never listens." "She never respects me." "I've tried everything, and nothing changes." That bitterness soon becomes entitlement: "I've been neglected. I deserve to be loved and respected by someone who truly gets me." And that opens the door to temptation. The fantasy of emotional escape becomes more attractive than the real work of restoration.

This is how the Enemy plays the long game: First, he plants bitterness. Then, bitterness justifies emotional distance. That emotional distance creates vulnerability. And finally, Satan and temptation walk in the door—and seem reasonable and deserved.

Hear again Paul's warning: "Be angry, and yet do not sin . . . and do not give the devil an opportunity" (Ephesians 4:26–27 NASB1995). He referenced this truth in 2 Corinthians 2:10–11: "What I have forgiven . . . I did so for your sakes . . . so that no advantage would be taken of us by Satan, for we are not ignorant of his schemes" (NASB). Unforgiveness doesn't just trap us emotionally—it creates a spiritual vulnerability. We become more open to an affair not necessarily because we are looking for one but because bitterness blinds us to our own weakness.

And here's the tragedy: The betrayal that now feels "justified" often didn't grow out of some massive sin by your spouse—it grew out of your own anger and unforgiving spirit. The devil didn't plant the affair. He planted and intensified the bitterness. And the betrayal followed.

UNFORGIVENESS DOESN'T JUST TRAP US EMOTIONALLY—IT CREATES A SPIRITUAL VULNERABILITY.

I have shared with many couples that when you give in to anger and an unforgiving spirit, you become meat in a pit bull's mouth. We grant Satan permission to clamp down, and once he has hold, he shakes until the marriage tears apart. The real danger isn't just the offense itself—it's what festers when forgiveness is withheld. That's why Paul urged us to forgive "so that no advantage would be taken of us by Satan" (2 Corinthians 2:11 NASB). Forgiveness isn't optional; it's protection.

When Bitterness Has Set In but You Haven't Given Up

Sometimes, despite all efforts to talk, pray, and try again, the tension lingers. You're still married. You still show up. But inside, a slow simmer of bitterness has taken root. You're not filing for divorce—you haven't thrown in the towel—but you no longer feel the same warmth toward your spouse.

This is a dangerous middle ground. Outwardly, the relationship looks intact. Inwardly, the heart is closing off. Hebrews 12:15 warns us to "see to it . . . that no root of bitterness springing up causes trouble, and by it many be defiled" (NASB1995). Once bitterness takes root, it doesn't just stay in one area—it spreads, coloring every interaction.

Bitterness often begins when you stop believing your spouse will ever change. You still share a bed, a table, a life—but not your heart. You rehearse past offenses and replay the same disappointments, each time feeling the hurt a little deeper. And slowly, your vision shifts: You no longer see what they do right, only what they do wrong.

But here's the hope: You don't have to stay there. The first step is not pretending the hurt isn't real, but identifying what's underneath it. Is the offense tied to a misunderstanding of intent? To a repeated pattern that may never fully change? To unhealed wounds from the past? When you name it, you can decide how to address it—or, in some cases, how to bear it without letting it poison your spirit (Colossians 3:13).

BITTERNESS OFTEN BEGINS WHEN YOU STOP BELIEVING YOUR SPOUSE WILL EVER CHANGE.

Choosing to forgive in this stage doesn't mean you approve of the hurt or stop addressing real problems. It means you refuse to let resentment dictate your tone, your words, and your heart posture. You act toward your spouse as Jesus acts toward you—showing grace in the face of imperfection, loving even when it's not reciprocated, honoring your vows not just with endurance but with intentional kindness.

Bitterness can be uprooted—but only if you're willing to do the deeper heart work before it hardens into contempt.

Why I Didn't Become Bitter

Over the years, I've walked with many people carrying deep wounds from their marriage or childhood. These conversations have often caused me to reflect on my own story—especially my relationship with my father.

He struggled with rage, used harsh words, was unfaithful to my mother, and never once visited me during my five years in military school. By any human measure, I had every right to grow bitter. I lacked the affirmation and love a child needs from their father.

And yet I didn't become bitter.

Why?

Because I came to a critical realization: Harboring bitterness would keep giving my father power over my heart—long after his actions had ended. The wounds were real. He used a verbal fire hose on my emotional flower bed. But clinging to those wounds would have enslaved me emotionally, spiritually, and relationally. I knew I had to forgive, not because he deserved it but because I needed freedom.

I made a choice—not an emotional one but a spiritual one—to surrender what I felt were my rights: the right to rehearse the wrongs, to resent him, to speak against him, or to retaliate in kind.

Over time, I began teaching this not just as a pastoral tool but as a personal practice of healing and obedience. I summarized it into four simple but bold acts of relinquishment: rehearse, resent, revile, retaliate.

When people came to me overwhelmed by unforgiveness, I would gently walk them through each one. Because it's often in naming what we feel entitled to that we begin to see the path toward peace.

And what I learned from God in that season has become a tool that continues to bring freedom to others.

The Four Bold Choices of Forgiveness

When we are wronged, it's easy to feel we have the right (justly so) to respond in kind. But forgiveness means making a different choice—a conscious, Spirit-empowered decision to release that right. Here are the four bold choices that lead us out of bitterness and into freedom:

1. Relinquish the Right to Rehearse the Offense

"Forgetting what lies behind and reaching forward . . ." (Philippians 3:13 NASB1995). Continually replaying the offense in our minds keeps us stuck in it.

We nurse old wounds, justify our resentment, and live emotionally anchored to the past. One wife wrote, "For nearly a decade, I kept replaying my husband's betrayal. But once I chose to stop rehearsing and focus on Christ's work in our lives, healing began." In my own story, I had to release the mental loops and focus on the calling God placed before me. He had begun a good work—and would finish it (Philippians 1:6). Fixating on the past would only slow me down. Forgiveness often starts here: choosing, moment by moment, to turn from replaying the hurt and instead rehearsing God's promises and purpose. Billy Graham modeled this. He rarely answered his harshest critics, once saying simply, "I just keep preaching the gospel and move on." He refused to waste energy rehearsing grievances or defending himself against attacks. Instead, he kept pressing forward on the mission Christ gave him.

And that's the call for us too: to move on. We cannot rewrite the past—but by God's grace, we can shape our future.

2. Relinquish the Right to Resent the Offender

"Let all bitterness and wrath and anger . . . be put away from you" (Ephesians 4:31 NASB1995). Resentment often feels like armor. It convinces us we're protecting ourselves. But it becomes a coffin, sealing us in, slowly eating us away. One husband admitted, "I carried resentment like a shield. I kept score and justified my coldness. But bitterness consumed me. My wife noticed. My kids noticed. I had to let it go." How tragic that what we perceive as protection actually entombs us.

Some fear that releasing resentment means pretending nothing happened. But forgiveness is not denial—it's surrender. At some point, you come to a crossroads and say, "Enough. I'm done carrying this."

For Paul, that's what "put away from you" meant: Let it be lifted off, removed. And many people have told me their breakthrough came in a single moment like this: "I was just done." They saw bitterness for what it truly is—poison. At the same time they heard Paul's command as God's own voice: "Put it away."

What once seemed impossible suddenly became not only realistic but necessary. The combination of the authority of God's Word and disgust at the fruit of resentment made the choice clear. And so, in one decisive act, they obeyed. Truly, Scripture is both simple and profound: "Let all bitterness . . . be put away from you."

3. Relinquish the Right to Revile the Offender

"When he was reviled, he did not revile in return" (1 Peter 2:23 ESV).

Reviling may feel justified in the moment—especially when we've been wounded repeatedly. We want to correct, prove a point, or just make our spouse feel what we've felt. But harsh words don't bring healing. They harden hearts.

One husband confessed, "When she questioned my loyalty, I shouted, broke things, even tried to 'scare' her into seeing my pain. I thought anger would work. It never did."

A wife shared, "For years I told myself I wouldn't be treated like a doormat. But in trying to stand up for myself, I became the aggressor. I was trying to stop his unloving habits while ignoring my disrespectful ones."

"But if I don't revile, they will keep wronging me!" That's the fear, isn't it? If I don't defend myself, I'll be walked on. If I don't strike back, I'll look weak. But reviling doesn't protect us—it only escalates the cycle.

Jesus Himself faced this exact temptation. "When he was reviled, he did not revile in return . . . but continued entrusting himself to him who judges justly" (1 Peter 2:23 ESV). He knew that reviling might feel satisfying in the moment, but it never produces righteousness (James 1:20). Instead, He trusted the Father to see, to judge, and to act in His time.

That doesn't mean you stay silent about sin or injustice. Scripture calls us to speak the truth in love (Ephesians 4:15) and set wise boundaries. But it does mean we refuse to fight fire with fire. Reviling doesn't stop sin; it fuels it. Respectful truth-telling, combined with trust in God's justice, breaks the cycle.

4. Relinquish the Right to Retaliate

"Not returning evil for evil or insult for insult, but giving a blessing instead" (1 Peter 3:9 NASB1995).

Forgiveness means refusing to "get even." Retaliation may feel justified—but it never heals. It only escalates.

A wife shared, "Letting him off the hook felt impossible. I wanted him to feel the pain he caused. But as we sat on the couch, we wept. We talked honestly. And letting go felt like freedom."

Another husband admitted, "I yelled. I shamed. I punched walls. I thought that would prove how much I cared. But it only pushed her further away."

Retaliation never convicts. It only hardens. Forgiveness, on the other hand, softens hearts—and sometimes, miraculously, restores what seemed lost.

But forgiveness does not mean overlooking evil. Scripture is clear: "'Vengeance is Mine, I will repay,' says the Lord" (Romans 12:19 NASB1995). And if something criminal or abusive has taken place, we do not "cover it up"—we turn to the proper authorities, whom God has established to enact justice (Romans 13:1–4). Forgiveness releases our own desire for revenge, but it does not shield sin from accountability.

Here's the truth: I cannot do to another what they did to me. If I repay offense with offense, I become the very thing I despise. I lose moral ground. I lose spiritual authority. Retaliation makes me the same as my offender. Forgiveness makes me more like Christ.

Let's Be Honest—We Can't Do This Alone

We forgive not because it feels easy but because it is commanded—and Christ has shown us how. Forgiveness is not denial. It's a decision to relinquish the right to rehearse the offense in our minds, resent the person in our hearts, revile them with our words, and retaliate with our actions. And when we make that choice, we are not becoming passive. We're exercising the strongest kind of spiritual authority: choosing forgiveness over vengeance both in obedience to God's command to forgive and in imitation of Jesus. As odd as this sounds, we must see this as an opportunity. But again, we need God's help.

"Apart from me you can do nothing" (John 15:5).

"It is God who works in you to will and to act" (Philippians 2:13).

None of us can forgive like this in our own strength. But Jesus never asked us to. He promised us the Holy Spirit—the Helper who would

FORGIVENESS IS NOT DENIAL.

empower what we cannot do alone (John 14:16–17, 26).

When forgiveness feels impossible, that's exactly when grace is most available. God doesn't expect perfection—He asks for surrender. And what feels unreachable in your strength becomes possible through His.

Carianne's story beautifully illustrates this truth after her husband's adultery:

> It is hard to explain the way my heart changed through this experience. I remain profoundly amazed that I have the ability to forgive something so unforgivable. I thought I would have to work so hard to pick up the pieces of my heart, but God just did it all. I was not even ready to let go of my anger and start to forgive, but God was already working.
>
> God gave me such compassion for my husband. I had a huge realization that we are all sinners and capable of anything if we take our eyes off of Christ. We are not above any sin, no matter how big. We all need a Savior, and I realized I needed to extend grace and forgiveness as God had done for me over and over. It changed me.
>
> God restored what I thought was dead. My husband didn't just come back to me—he came back to the Lord. He is a different man, and I am a different woman. We are not just back together—we are deeply in love, and we are in awe of what God has done.

Carianne didn't forgive because it was easy. She forgave because God moved her heart—even before she was ready. That's grace.

When you take the first step, God meets you there. When you choose obedience, He supplies the strength.

Seeing Your Spouse Through Christ's Eyes

Forgiveness flows more easily when we begin to see our spouse the way Christ does.

Ask yourself: Am I married to a Judas—or a Peter?

Peter failed Jesus. He denied Him. He acted out of fear and weakness—not hatred. But Jesus forgave him, restored him, and continued to trust him with ministry and mission.

Judas, by contrast, betrayed Jesus selfishly, willfully, and deceitfully.

Many spouses today treat their partner as if they are a Judas—beyond restoration—when in reality, they are a Peter: weak at times, but of goodwill, remorseful, repentant, and trying to grow.

Jesus saw Peter's heart through the failure. Can you?

Now to be clear: Some spouses have committed true betrayal—an affair, financial deceit, substance abuse. Forgiveness is still required, but rebuilding trust is a separate, equally biblical process.

This is where discernment matters. A forgiving spirit doesn't mean we ignore patterns of sin or reopen the door without wisdom. There must be repentance. And not just words.

As John the Baptist said: "Produce fruit in keeping with repentance" (Matthew 3:8).

Forgiveness frees your soul. But trust must be earned.

Rebuilding Trust After Betrayal: The TRUST Framework

Forgiveness is commanded, but trust must be rebuilt. The burden of proof is on the one who broke it. That's where the TRUST framework helps. I have used this to serve couples over the years. It is a practical tool for navigating serious betrayal without bitterness.

FORGIVENESS IS COMMANDED, BUT TRUST MUST BE REBUILT.

True repentance is never just words—it produces visible, reliable change. As Acts 26:20 states, "They should repent and turn to God and demonstrate their repentance by their deeds."

Here's what rebuilding trust requires:

T—Truthfulness

In the wake of betrayal, truth must be the starting place. Total honesty replaces secrecy. No more hiding. No more half-truths. No more protecting one's image at the cost of the other's healing. One man shared, "I told my wife everything—not just the affair, but the lies. That's when healing began." To the wounded spouse: You do not need every sordid detail to heal. Knowing what happened and why is often enough. The Enemy loves to hide in the details, sowing confusion and retraumatization. Ask God for clarity—not ammunition. Seek what brings understanding, not what feeds justification for an unforgiving spirit.

R—Remorse

True remorse runs deeper than regret. It's not just sorrow for the consequences—it's grief over the wound inflicted. One husband admitted, "At first, I was sorry I got caught. But when I saw her pain, I truly repented." To the betrayed: If your spouse demonstrates a consistent spirit of repentance—not defensiveness—there may come a time to soften. Lingering in mistrust after they've owned their sin may harden your heart unnecessarily. Be wise. But also remain open to the redemptive work of God. Remorse can be the soil where trust is slowly replanted.

U—Understanding

Healing begins when the one who wounded becomes willing to truly understand the pain they caused. This isn't about self-loathing—it's about insight and empathy. One husband said, "When I finally listened without defending myself, I saw how deeply I'd broken her trust." And to the wounded: If your spouse is listening well, validating your hurt, and not minimizing their failure, don't use their guilt as a weapon. Let humility be met with humility. Understanding doesn't erase pain, but it builds the bridge to restoration.

S—Safeguards

New boundaries must be put in place. Radical honesty. Shared passwords. Transparent calendars. Ongoing accountability. One couple reflected, "We created guardrails—no secrets, no private texts. It felt restrictive at first, but it brought peace." To the innocent spouse: These safeguards are not about control—they are about commitment. You are not overreacting to request transparency. And yet you don't need to become a detective. Pray this simple prayer: *Lord, reveal what I need to know.* Then release the rest. God is your defender. Let Him do what only He can.

T— Third Parties

Rebuilding trust almost always requires outside support. Pastors. Mentors. Christian counselors. Trusted friends. One husband shared, "A mentor couple walked with us. Their presence brought safety and wisdom." If you're the wounded spouse and feel hesitant to invite third-party guidance—especially when that guidance touches your part of the dynamic—please don't retreat. The path to healing often requires both humility and accountability. And if you are the one who broke trust, understand this: Your spouse's boundaries aren't punishment. They are protection. Trust cannot be demanded. It must be rebuilt slowly, with consistency, and without entitlement.

Bottom Line

Forgiveness frees the heart—but trust is what restores the relationship. Both are biblical. Both are needed. But they are not the same. One is granted. The other is earned. And with God's help, both are possible.

Checklist for Forgiving When Misunderstandings Trigger You

Philosopher Dallas Willard once said in effect that it is very difficult to offend a man or woman who walks in maturity and with character.[1] I like that. So true. I want to be that type of person.

Here's a practical filter for practicing that maturity when conflict arises—not when your spouse has betrayed you but when misunderstanding and disappointment have left you wounded.

Ask yourself:

- Is this really sin or just human weakness? Am I reacting to a moral offense or simply to something frustrating or disappointing?
- Was this pain personal or protective? Did my spouse react out of hostility or were they shielding themselves from feeling unloved or disrespected?
- Am I assuming goodwill? Does one moment define their entire heart, or could this be stress, fatigue, or fear?
- Could I be misinterpreting? Is it possible I've misunderstood their motive or misread their reaction?
- Can I see their wound? What fear or unhealed place might be behind their tone, withdrawal, or words?

Forgiveness becomes far easier when we stop interpreting everything through the lens of offense and start viewing it through the lens of grace. Not every negative interaction is a personal attack. Not every failure is malicious. Sometimes it's simply two imperfect people navigating life with different lenses, wounds, and needs.

When we look beyond the behavior and into the heart—our spouse's and our own—we position ourselves not just for healing but for Christlike transformation.

And in marriage, that changes everything.

Forgiveness Is the Door to Freedom

Forgiveness is not weakness. It is not excusing. It is not forgetting. It is Christlikeness under pressure.

It doesn't mean you approve of the hurt. It means you refuse to let the hurt own you anymore.

It doesn't mean you stop setting boundaries. It means you stop building walls around your heart.

It doesn't mean you ignore truth. It means you surrender the truth to the vengeance of the One who judges justly.

You forgive because you've been forgiven. You don't release them because they've repented perfectly.

A Prayer of Relinquishment: Letting Go of the Inner Rights That Keep You Bound

Lord Jesus,

You see what others don't. You know the hurt I've carried in silence. You've witnessed the thoughts I've rehearsed late into the night—the bitterness I've nurtured, the sharp words I've spoken in my mind, the subtle ways I've tried to even the score. But today—right here, right now—I lay it all down. In obedience to You, I surrender the rights I've been clinging to, the ones that have only deepened my wounds and delayed my healing.

I relinquish the right to rehearse the wrong. I will no longer loop their failures on repeat or keep reopening the wound with mental replay. I turn my eyes away from the past and toward the future You've called me into. "Forgetting what lies behind and reaching forward to what lies ahead . . ." (Philippians 3:13 NASB1995).

I relinquish the right to resent the one who hurt me. Bitterness may feel justified, but it has only drained me. It has soured my joy and hardened my heart. Today, I release it—not in weakness but in trust. "Let all bitterness and wrath and anger . . . be put away from you" (Ephesians 4:31 NASB1995).

I relinquish the right to revile with my words. I will not retaliate with my tongue or repeat the offense to others in the name of "processing." I will remain silent, sharing only with those who are part of the solution or in need of the truth. "When he was reviled, he did not revile in return" (1 Peter 2:23 ESV).

I relinquish the right to retaliate with my actions. I will not mirror the harm done to me, nor seek to punish, shame, or control. I surrender the gavel. You are the righteous Judge, not me. "Never take your own revenge . . . 'Vengeance is Mine, I will repay,' says the Lord" (Romans 12:19 NASB1995*).*

I entrust myself—and the one who hurt me—fully into Your hands. I cannot do this on my own. So, Holy Spirit, come. Meet me in the frailty of my heart. Melt what has hardened. Restore what has been broken. Let obedience lead where emotion cannot. Let my heart follow the decision I make today.

Jesus, You forgave me when I had no defense. You bore my shame and set me free. Now help me extend that same mercy—not because they deserve it but because You do. Not because it's easy but because You live in me. And I want to walk in the freedom that forgiveness brings.

In Your strong and healing name, amen.

TWELVE

OUR EMPOWERMENT: FREE AND STRONG WHEN I LIVE OUT "MY RESPONSE IS MY RESPONSIBILITY"

Liberating realization: As counterintuitive as it feels, inner strength and freedom grow when I embrace this: "My response is my responsibility."

I've taught this simple, powerful truth for decades—and it continues to transform hearts and marriages, starting with my own. I receive emails with just that phrase and little else: "Wow. My response is my responsibility." One couple wrote, "My wife, Tricia, and I have repeated that statement for fifteen years. It has never stopped shaping our marriage."

Why does this truth resonate so deeply with so many followers of Christ? Because it frees them.

It reclaims agency. It moves us from being reactors to responders. It grounds us not in our spouse's behavior but in our obedience to Christ.

Let me tell you about Josh and Emily. They loved Jesus—and they loved each other—but they were stuck, not in hatred or scandal, but in quiet patterns of blame, disappointment, and emotional distance.

Both longed for a better marriage, but neither realized how much they were waiting on the other to change. Then came a moment of clarity—one for Josh, one for Emily—that opened the door to something more profound than compromise: It opened the door to a new empowerment to influence and improve the relationship.

Josh's Story

Josh considered himself a "good guy." Faithful. Hardworking. A provider. But at home, when tension built, so did his defensiveness.

His thoughts ran in a loop: *If Emily didn't nag me so much, I wouldn't get so angry. If she respected me more, I'd be a better husband.*

It felt logical. Fair, even. When he shut down or snapped, he pointed to Emily's faults as justification. But deep down, bitterness was growing. He felt trapped—believing he couldn't win until she changed.

What Josh had never asked himself was *What does my reaction say about me?*

He lived under the quiet lie that Emily was the cause of his moods and responses. He didn't see that his reactions weren't caused by her—they were chosen by him.

Then one night, after yet another argument left them both drained and distant, Josh picked up a book on marriage. A single sentence hit like lightning: "Your spouse does not cause you to be the way you are—they reveal the way you are."

That was the shift.

Emily didn't control his emotions—he did. She didn't dictate his peace—he did. He had been waiting for her to change so he could be a better man, when the Spirit had been waiting on *him* to change, regardless of what Emily did.

That night, Josh stopped asking for a changed wife and began praying for a changed heart.

"My response is my responsibility," he whispered aloud.

It wasn't a declaration of guilt. It was a declaration of freedom. He didn't have to wait for Emily to behave better. He could obey Christ now.

- He couldn't control her actions, but he could control his own.
- He wasn't a victim of her moodiness—he was a steward of his mood.
- He didn't need her to be Christlike for him to be Christlike.

That changed everything.

Josh began walking a different path. Not perfectly but purposefully. He stopped expecting Emily to set the tone. He set boundaries with calm. He engaged without rage. He no longer excused unloving behavior with "Well, she pushed me." That self-justification and blame-placing not only evidenced lack of leadership but displeased Christ, who called him to lead with a loving demeanor.

And though he still felt the sting of conflict, he was no longer controlled by it. Emotions still rose, but they no longer ruled. The trigger points that had once pushed him into angry, mean-spirited reactions became places where he paused, prayed, and chose differently.

Over time, Emily noticed. And what softened her was Josh's Christlike response—calm, loving, steady. It convicted her far more than all his past anger, defensiveness, or blame ever had.

Emily's Story

Emily was warmhearted and sincere, but she often lived on an emotional roller coaster. Her peace rose and fell with Josh's attentiveness. When he was affectionate, she felt secure. When he was distant, she spiraled into accusations or quiet resentment. *If he would just love me better*, she thought, *I'd be more respectful.*

Some friends reinforced this view: She was the "loving one," while Josh was the unloving one who needed to change. She believed he didn't deserve respect because he wasn't as loving as she was, while she deserved respect because she was "the more loving one."

But over time, God's Word pierced that illusion. She realized she had been deceived—respect wasn't conditional on Josh's behavior. Scripture calls wives to respectful conduct *even with imperfect husbands* (1 Peter 3:1–2). And respect wasn't a reward; it was her responsibility before Christ. Her reverence for Jesus—not Josh's performance—was the standard (Ephesians 5:21).

And what broke Emily most wasn't Josh's failures but the recognition of her own self-righteousness, thinking she was superior and more deserving. She had excused her disrespect under the guise of "standing for love," but in reality, she was disobeying God's call and masking it with condescending judgment.

Her prayer shifted: *Lord, my response is my responsibility. Help me show Josh respect, not because he always earns it but because I honor You. Let my words and demeanor reflect reverence unto Christ—even when I must address hard things.*

That realization freed her. She was still affected by Josh's shortcomings, but she was no longer controlled by them. She could set boundaries without bitterness, speak truth without contempt, and respond firmly without becoming harsh.

And what surprised her most? When she stopped trying to change Josh through criticism and started honoring Christ through respect, Josh began to soften. What her angry words and complaints never accomplished, her steady reverence for Christ began to produce.

Emily discovered the paradox: By relinquishing her "right" to disrespect Josh, she found her freedom. Respecting Josh wasn't submission to his faults—it was submission to Jesus. And that changed everything.

Josh and Emily didn't fix their marriage overnight. But they stopped trying to fix *each other.*

They stopped blaming and started owning. And that changed everything.

From Within Me Come the Challenges

Everyone longs for freedom—freedom from being ruled by others and freedom to influence them with love, honor, and truth. That freedom begins here: *My response is my responsibility.*

Jesus makes this unmistakably clear in Mark 7: "What comes out of a person is what defiles them. For it is from within, out of a person's heart, that evil thoughts come" (Mark 7:20–23).

According to Jesus, sin doesn't come from our spouse's behavior—it comes from within us. And yet, in marriage, we often reverse this. We say:

"I wouldn't lose my temper if you didn't push me."

"I wouldn't be distant if you didn't disrespect me."

We justify our reactions by blaming their actions.

To drive this point home, let's look at how Jesus describes the source of sin in His list in Mark 7—and how we often twist it in marriage:

- Folly → "Yes, I exploded. But can you blame me? You constantly trigger me."
- Arrogance → "I'm the only smart one here. If I don't lead, nothing works."
- Slander → "I wouldn't talk badly about you if you treated me better."
- Envy → "Everyone praises you, but no one sees how much I carry."
- Lewdness → "You neglect me, so I'll chase the sensual thrill wherever I can get it."
- Deceit → "I hide things because you never support me."
- Malice → "You wounded me—now I want you to feel it too."
- Greed → "You never dream big. I want more, more of what I deserve."
- Adultery → "You don't love me—someone else made me feel seen."
- Murder (in the heart) → "I just want you gone. I hate you."
- Theft → "You control everything. I had to take something for myself."
- Sexual immorality → "You deprive me. I turned to porn for relief."

Each of these justifications sounds emotionally believable—but biblically, they're false. Jesus says sin flows not from what others do but from what's already in us. That doesn't mean your spouse's sin doesn't matter—it does. But it does mean their sin doesn't justify yours.

This isn't condemnation. It's liberation.

Because if sin comes from *within*, then change is possible—starting with *you*. You're not at the mercy of their attitude, tone, or failures. You're free to choose a Christlike response, and that's where real growth begins.

The Power of Emotional Punches

Let's acknowledge we all experience intense emotional pain from verbal hits or inaction.

- A pang of hurt when your spouse makes a sharp remark
- A jolt of fear when they raise their voice
- A stab of disappointment when they forget something important
- A flash of anger when they dismiss your concerns
- A wave of embarrassment when they criticize you publicly

BECAUSE IF SIN COMES FROM *WITHIN*, THEN CHANGE IS POSSIBLE—STARTING WITH *YOU*.

These are involuntary, emotional spikes—not sinful in themselves. The key is what comes *after* the emotional punch. The moment of emotion is not the danger—it's what you do with it. Do you surrender it to the Spirit? Or do you let it dictate your reaction?

You may feel the surge of anger, but you are not powerless to it. No one "makes" you yell. No one "forces" you to shut down. They may trigger the emotion—but only you can choose the reaction.

This is good news. Because it means you're not a victim of emotional reflexes. You are a steward of your responses. You can pause. You can pray. You can ask, *What is this moment revealing about me?* And in that space, you open the door to freedom, influence, and maturity.

The Freedom and Empowerment of My Response

Let's not just talk about responsibility—let's talk about what it frees you to do. Because if your response is your responsibility, then it's also your opportunity. You're not just accountable—you are empowered in Christ.

Freedom

First, no one controls your inner person. At our conferences, I often say, "Your spouse can hurt your feelings, even your body—but they cannot touch your spirit." That belongs to Christ. He has sealed you by His Spirit, and no one—not even someone who deeply disappoints or wounds you—can make you sin. You are free to respond in a way that honors God, regardless of how your spouse acts.

Second, you are freed from regret. One man told me, "The regret I used to feel after losing my temper was awful. But now, when I stay steady, I walk away with peace—and no shame." When you walk in the Spirit, your soul walks in peace. You may not be able to fix everything—but you'll have nothing to clean up from your own words or reactions.

Third, you're not a victim—you are a responder. A woman once said to me, "I used to feel stuck, like I had no choice. But now I see—I can't control him, but I can control me." That is not denial. That is real power. Victimhood says, "I'm trapped." But the Spirit of God says, "You are not helpless."

Fourth, you resist the false victim narrative. One woman shared, "Everyone told me to leave. But I wasn't telling them the whole story. When I admitted my part, things began to heal. I even confessed to my husband and children that I'd misrepresented him—and he wept." There is something sacred about truth-telling. Blame can feel like self-protection, but only truth brings restoration.

Fifth, you please God—even if no one else sees. One wife told me, "Sometimes when I stay calm, it feels invisible. Like being the adult doesn't matter." But she clung to this: "If when you do what is right and suffer for it you patiently endure it, this finds favor with God" (1 Peter 2:20 NASB1995). God sees. He rewards what others miss.

Empowerment

When you respond well, you reveal Christ. One husband told me, "Even when I was deeply hurt, no one could stop me from obeying God." His faithful, Spirit-led response became a quiet testimony—more powerful than any defense or argument.

You also break the Crazy Cycle when you don't react. Another man told me, "When I stopped taking the bait—refusing to escalate—the whole dynamic changed. It wasn't fair, but it worked." Remember, the Crazy Cycle spins when *both* partners contribute to it. You have the power to step off—and that alone can change everything. A wife may be disrespectful, but that doesn't "cause" a husband to be unloving. He is free to obey God's command to love regardless. A husband may be unloving, but that doesn't "cause" a wife to be disrespectful. She is free to obey God's command to respect regardless.

You also regain real influence. A woman wrote me, "Blaming never helped. But when I owned my reactions—even when I had to bite my tongue—my husband softened. Years of contempt never worked. Quiet strength did." That's the kind of strength Proverbs calls "noble." Respect—even when undeserved—does not enable sin but invites change.

And finally, you model strength for others. One mother told me, "My kids are learning more from how I respond in conflict than from anything I say." She started saying, "Watch how Mommy responds." That small sentence deepened her sense of responsibility—and her growth.

"My response is my responsibility" is not just a motto. It's a declaration of maturity, freedom, and obedience. You may not see fruit right away. But God sees. And His favor always follows faithfulness. And often, in time, your steadiness will bear the fruit of transformation—not only in you but perhaps even in the relationship you thought was beyond repair.

As in Parenting, So Too in Marriage

In parenting, we accept a basic truth: A child's disobedience doesn't *cause* a parent to be unloving—it *reveals* the parent's character in that moment. A wise parent stays calm, even when the child is acting out. Why? Because the parent is the adult in the room.

We don't question that standard. We understand that maturity means modeling patience and restraint, especially when it's hard.

But here's the disconnect: We rarely apply that same truth to marriage.

We tell ourselves, *My spouse's childish actions and reactions made me react this way.* But the truth is, your spouse doesn't cause you to be unloving or disrespectful. Their behavior simply reveals whether you choose to respond with love and respect—or not.

Just as God calls a parent to be the adult in the room, He calls you to be the adult in your marriage. That doesn't mean perfection. It means responsibility. It means owning your tone, your reactions, your posture—especially when things are tense.

Think about it: Few parents would say, "I had a meltdown and yelled at my child—but they need to get over it. They brought it on themselves." That would feel harsh, even immature. We expect more of ourselves as parents.

And yet how often do we say something similar about our spouse? "Yeah, I blew up, but they need to get over it. This is on them."

Why the double standard? Why do we extend grace, patience, and responsibility in parenting but excuse emotional outbursts in marriage?

The truth is, our reaction still belongs to us. And maturity in marriage calls for the same ownership we expect in parenting.

But I Can't Do This

You may be thinking, *This sounds right, but I can't do it. I don't have that kind of strength.* And you'd be absolutely right.

You're not supposed to be able to do this on your own. Responding like Christ—especially when wronged—is not a matter of willpower. It's a matter of surrender. Scripture never commands us to be 100 percent strong in ourselves. It says, "Be strong in the Lord and in the strength of His might" (Ephesians 6:10 NASB1995). Jesus was clear: "Apart from me you can do nothing" (John 15:5).

So you're not called to gut it out. You're called to abide—to let Christ live through you. You imitate Him not by trying harder but by depending more deeply. You don't carry the burden of change alone. You carry it with the One who carried the cross. "Come to me," Jesus invites, "all you who are weary and burdened, and I will give you rest" (Matthew 11:28). The apostle Paul echoed this when he said, "I labor, striving according to His power, which mightily works within me" (Colossians 1:29 NASB1995).

So if you're feeling weak, you're not disqualified—you're ready. You can't. But He can.

Seven Fears and Seven Counters to Those Fears

When people first hear "My response is my responsibility," a wave of honest fears often surfaces. Let's walk through those together and respond with the truth that sets us free.

Fear of Having to Be Perfect

"If I'm responsible for my response, then I have to be perfect—and that's overwhelming."

Counter: You're called not to perfection but to growth. Proverbs 24:16 says, "A righteous man falls seven times, and rises again" (NASB1995). We stumble. We learn. We rise again.

God's mercies are new every morning (Lamentations 3:22–23). This truth doesn't demand perfection—it empowers perseverance.

Fear of Never Being Allowed to Be Offended

"If I'm responsible for my response, does that mean I'm not allowed to feel hurt?"

Counter: Feeling hurt isn't wrong. Scripture acknowledges offense (Proverbs 18:19; 2 Corinthians 6:3). The issue isn't whether we're wounded—it's how we respond.

Taking responsibility doesn't deny the wound; it prevents the wound from controlling our behavior. You can acknowledge pain without surrendering to it by screaming.

Fear That God Will Punish Imperfect Responses

"If I react poorly, will God condemn or punish me?"

Counter: "There is now no condemnation for those who are in Christ Jesus" (Romans 8:1).

God may lovingly discipline us (Hebrews 12:6), but never in wrath. The fallout we sometimes feel is usually the natural result of relational strain—not divine punishment.

We must also learn to live under grace. Christ already bore the punishment for our sin on the cross. What remains is the Father's training hand, not His condemning fist. Some of us are too quick to label every consequence as "God getting back at me." That's not the gospel.

When we stumble, God's discipline is restorative—meant to put us back on track—not retributive. Punishment fell on Christ. Discipline falls on children He loves.

Fear of Being Falsely Judged

"If I take ownership, my spouse might weaponize it and call me a hypocrite when I fail."

Counter: Yes, people may twist your sincerity. Jesus said people would "falsely say all kinds of evil against you" (Matthew 5:11).

But their false accusation isn't proof of our hypocrisy. Regardless, owning your failure is maturity. If your spouse uses your words against you, remain humble. Apologize when necessary—but don't let their reaction define your integrity.

What may feel like weakness in front of your spouse shines as strength before your Savior, who will show His favor to you.

Fear That My Spouse Will Blame Me for Everything

"If I own my reactions, my spouse may never own theirs."

Counter: That's possible. But their refusal doesn't change your call. As

1 Peter 2:20 reminds us, "If when you do what is right and suffer for it you patiently endure it, this finds favor with God" (NASB1995).

God sees. God rewards. And your maturity may become the most compelling influence your spouse ever sees.

When you take ownership of your part, even if your spouse doesn't, you're not excusing their sin—you're entrusting justice to God and reflecting Jesus in the place it matters most: your own home.

Fear of Having No Healthy Boundaries

"If I take responsibility, does that mean I have to accept harmful treatment?"

Counter: Never! Saying, "My response is my responsibility" is not permission for others to mistreat you. Ephesians 5:11 says, "Have nothing to do with the fruitless deeds of darkness, but rather expose them."

Boundaries are Christlike when set with clarity, respect, and love—not retaliation. You can say "enough" without hatred and contempt. You can and must protect your well-being and the family's. Saying no to mistreatment is often the first step to saying yes to God's way. Saying no to mistreatment is not rejecting your spouse—it is choosing to honor Christ with how you live.

Fear of Suppressing Emotions

"Will taking responsibility cause me to bottle up real emotions?"

Counter: Controlling emotion is not denying it—it's directing it with wisdom. We're told to "[speak] the truth in love" (Ephesians 4:15) and "be angry, and yet do not sin" (Ephesians 4:26 NASB1995).

Emotional maturity isn't silence—it's stewardship. We reveal, but we don't revile. We express, but we don't explode. Truth seasoned with grace brings clarity and connection—not chaos.

Taking responsibility doesn't mean pretending everything is okay. It means trusting that *Christ in you* is enough to respond rightly—even when things aren't okay.

Following Christ in How We Respond

Permit me to speak plainly.

Some of you are truly suffering in your marriage. You may relate to my mother, who left my father for five years—not from rebellion but from emotional exhaustion and some fear. You've endured betrayal, abandonment, or persistent emotional harm. For you, the words of 1 Peter aren't just theological—they're survival. This is the path theologians call the imitation of Christ—following Jesus in how we respond to injustice.

But for many of us—and I include myself in this—our frustration isn't persecution. It's disappointment. Inconvenience. Irritation with a spouse who is imperfect but of goodwill. And yet we react as if we've been deeply wronged. We lash out, shut down, justify our outbursts, and say things like, "Well, if they hadn't done that, I wouldn't have acted this way."

Let's be honest: Most of us think we're in group one—the suffering saints. But we're actually in group two—the spiritually immature. And into our confusion, Peter speaks with clarity:

"To this you were called, because Christ also suffered for you, leaving you an example, that you should follow in his steps" (1 Peter 2:21).

Peter didn't just say, "Jesus suffered." He told us what Jesus did in that suffering (vv. 22–24):

- "He committed no sin, and no deceit was found in his mouth."
  - Jesus didn't sin with His words—even under pressure.
- "When they hurled insults at him, he did not retaliate."
  - He didn't strike back, even though He could have.
- "When he suffered, he made no threats."
  - He didn't try to control others through fear.
- "He entrusted himself to him who judges justly."
  - He didn't demand fairness—He trusted the Father.
- "He himself bore our sins."
  - He carried burdens that weren't His—out of love.

These aren't passive acts. They are powerful, Spirit-filled choices. And Peter said: "Follow Him."

"This finds favor with God" (1 Peter 2:20 NASB1995).

This doesn't mean you excuse sin or endure abuse. It means that even when wronged, your response is your responsibility—and your opportunity to look like Christ.

In marriage, this matters deeply.

Most of us aren't being persecuted. We're just upset that our spouse forgot to text when running late—again. Or that they missed a cue for appreciation—again. Or that we weren't heard the way we hoped—again.

And yet we unravel as if we've been slandered and possibly slain. We say:

- "Why should I be warm when he doesn't notice me?"
- "I shut down because she never respects my input."
- "I snapped because he made me feel small."
- "I yelled because she lipped off to me."

But Scripture never gives us a free pass to sin just because someone else did first.

The next time the tone is sharp, the appreciation is missing, or even the toothpaste is squeezed from the "wrong" end, pause. In the moment, those things can feel big—bigger than they really are—because they tap into deeper needs and expectations. The point isn't to equate minor annoyances with deep pain; it's to help us stop and say, "Hey, maybe my outrage is out of proportion here." That moment of perspective can be the difference between reacting in the flesh and responding in the Spirit.

Remember: You are not a victim. You are a follower. And your response is your responsibility.

A story I heard makes this point. Some women were told they'd receive fake facial scars before a job interview. Makeup artists applied the scars—but secretly removed them before the interviews. The women went in believing they were scarred, and afterward they reported high levels of discrimination, citing comments they thought proved bias. In reality, there were no scars at all.

The lesson? We see what we expect to see. And when we live as victims, we'll interpret everything as proof that we are.

Do You Agree with the Following Truths?

Take a moment. Breathe. Let these statements settle into your soul. They are not tests to pass—they are invitations to follow in His steps.

Responsibility and Ownership

- My response is my responsibility.
- My spouse does not cause me to be the way I am—they reveal the way I am.
- When I react unlovingly or disrespectfully, I am choosing that response.
- Blaming my sin on my spouse makes me a victim, not a steward of my own heart.

Freedom and Spiritual Agency

- I may be affected by my spouse's sin, but I am not controlled by it.
- I obey Christ not based on my spouse's behavior but because I'm free in Him.
- My spouse's actions don't determine my spiritual response—I do.
- I can't control outcomes in them, but I can choose obedience in me.

Boundaries and Wisdom

- Being faithful doesn't mean being passive or naive.
- I can set boundaries without being bitter or disrespectful.
- A Christlike response includes strength, clarity, and self-control.
- Grace doesn't erase accountability—it elevates how we express it.

Christlikeness and Influence

- I am never more Christlike than when I respond with love or respect in the face of failure.

- God's favor rests on me when I respond rightly—even when wronged.
- My example can influence my spouse far more than my correction.

Maybe you're feeling stirred right now—not by guilt but by longing. A longing to grow, to live from a deeper source, to be the kind of person who reflects Christ even when things are hard.

If so, let that desire rise. Don't wait for your spouse to change. Start with the one person you can influence—yourself.

From My Heart to Yours

There are moments in every marriage—maybe today—when you feel hurt, dismissed, or just plain tired. And in those moments, your response matters. Not just for your marriage but for your walk with Christ.

DON'T WAIT FOR YOUR SPOUSE TO CHANGE. START WITH THE ONE PERSON YOU CAN INFLUENCE—YOURSELF.

For years, when Sarah and I hit tension, I thought my defensiveness came from her words. But the truth hit me: It wasn't coming from her—it was coming from me. That realization was humbling but freeing. If the problem is only "out there," I'm stuck. But if it's also "in here," then by God's grace, I can change.

This is our human default: blame. Adam blamed Eve. Eve blamed the serpent. We've been dodging responsibility ever since. But if I don't own my response, I stay stuck—governed by someone else's behavior instead of guided by the Spirit of Christ.

The lie says, "If my spouse were easier, I'd be more godly." The truth says, "You can't make me hate you. You can't make me treat you with contempt. Only I can hand you that power." That's not pride—that's freedom in Christ.

Fairness isn't the standard of the gospel. "While we were still sinners,

Christ died for us" (Romans 5:8). So I can't excuse my flesh just because Sarah failed me. I must follow Jesus, whether or not she does.

Here's what I've learned to practice:

- **Pause before reacting:** "Is this Christ in me or just my flesh?"
- **Say it out loud:** "I feel frustrated, angry, or hurt, but I can still respond with love and respect."
- **Pray first:** "Lord, guide my tone and words."

I don't always get it right. But every time I choose Christ over blame, I grow stronger—and freer. This is empowerment. I am free to respond, not react. I am liberated. Even though it feels counterintuitive, inner strength grows when I embrace this truth: "My response is my responsibility."

At the end of the day, it comes down to this:

The victim says, "My response is their responsibility."

The victor says, "My response is my responsibility."

Which will be our testimony?

POSTSCRIPT

YOU'RE CLOSER THAN YOU THINK

We've now walked through three fundamental dimensions of a Christ-centered marriage:

The Upward: Deepening Faith
The Outward: Enhancing Skill
The Inward: Cultivating Wisdom

We began with our core beliefs—anchoring your heart in what matters most—your *value*, not assigned by your spouse but given by God Himself. You saw how your *intent* in marriage goes far beyond momentary happiness; it's about loving and reverencing Christ through how you love and respect each other. We zoomed out to eternity—to the truth that your faithfulness today carries weight forever. And we recalibrated your *worldview*, setting aside cultural scripts in favor of God's timeless wisdom. This is the foundation your marriage stands on—unshakable when storms hit.

From there, we stepped into effective interactions—the conversations, compromises, and crossroads that define your journey together. We talked about the need for *clarity*, not just talking more but truly understanding each other. About finding *harmony*, even when your personalities or plans differ. About humbly offering *acknowledgment*—that both of you have valid perspectives, especially in the gray areas. And about how to handle *tension*—those moments when a small frustration threatens to eclipse the bigger picture of goodwill and grace. These skills are not flashy, but they are sacred. They're how love and respect endure in the daily grind.

Finally, we moved toward inner competencies—into the heart-work that often determines whether your marriage heals or hardens. We've looked at *self-awareness*—how our defensive reactions can come across as offensive. In the end, we do ourselves no favors when our reactions misrepresent the true desires of our hearts. We explored *authenticity*, learning the difference between motivating with love and respect and manipulating through the opposite. We talked about *forgiveness*, not as a feeling but as a choice, rooted in Christ's example and especially vital when "offense" is due to honest misunderstandings. And we embraced *empowerment*—the life-changing truth that "my response is my responsibility." This is the real work of maturity. It's not easy. But it's the pathway to freedom.

So now what?

You don't need to be perfect. You don't need to fix everything by next week. You just need to keep walking in the light! As you step forward, perhaps choose one truth from the Upward, one skill from the Outward, and one attitude from the Inward to practice intentionally this week. Small steps compound over time.

KEEP WALKING IN THE LIGHT!

May these twelve biblical perspectives—the lightbulb moments in marriage—illuminate our paths and grow our marriages in ways beyond anything we ever dared imagine. The God who began this work in you is faithful to complete it. He wishes for you to experience success and satisfaction!

NOTE TO THE READER

Most of the stories in this book are factual—drawn from verbatim quotes people have written to me or from situations I know about firsthand. However, confidentiality is important, and I've taken care to edit emails and conversations for clarity and readability while preserving their heart and message.

Some of the stories are composites—crafted from recurring themes we've seen in thousands of testimonies over the years. While names and details have been deleted or changed to protect privacy, each one reflects the emotional and spiritual truths people have entrusted to us. These are real-to-life representations of what many couples have experienced.

If a story seems to be about you, know this: You are not alone—and you are deeply seen and deeply loved by the God who led you to these pages. He knows your challenges, your longings, your mistakes, and your hope. And He is for you.

This book is not written to shame, criticize, or diagnose. It is written to bring clarity—to turn on the light in places where frustration, confusion, or silence have crept in. My prayer is that what you find here will stir hope, not heaviness—encouragement, not defeat.

While many testimonies speak from the voice of a husband or wife, the principles apply to both. This book does not highlight one spouse's shortcomings over the other. Rather, it invites both to consider how their words, tone, and choices impact the spirit of the one they wish to love and respect unto Jesus.

It's also important to say this clearly: If you are in a harmful, abusive, or unsafe situation, this message is not asking you to remain silent or passive. Please seek safety, support, and wise counsel. You matter, and your safety matters.

Ultimately, this book is about more than marriage—it's about personal responsibility and spiritual maturity. These lightbulb moments are not just for resolving conflict—they're for realigning ourselves with Christ, who calls us to respond with love, respect, and wisdom, even when it's hard.

In His grace,
Emerson Eggerichs

ACKNOWLEDGMENTS

I am deeply grateful to the many readers who emailed me their stories of a light-bulb moment—your honesty and openness gave this book its heartbeat. My thanks also go to the leadership at HarperCollins for believing in this message, especially Damon Reiss and Caren Wolfe, whose support and encouragement helped bring these pages to life.

Most of all, I want to thank my wife, Sarah. From the very beginning of this project, she prayed daily for this book—for the words I would write, for the readers who would one day hold it in their hands, and for the marriages that would be touched by its message. But even more importantly, Sarah has faithfully prayed for me since 1973. Her steadfast love and respect, her unwavering faith, and her quiet intercession through the decades have been the greatest gifts of my life. Whatever fruit this book bears is inseparable from her prayers, her encouragement, and her partnership in ministry and marriage.

And finally, to my agent and daughter, Joy Eggerichs Reed—thank you for making this book possible. Your insight, persistence, and belief in this project carried it from idea to reality, and I could not have done this without you.

NOTES

Chapter 4

1. "There's No God; No One Directs Our Fate, Says Stephen Hawking in Final Book," *The Economic Times* (India), last updated October 18, 2018, https://economictimes.indiatimes.com/magazines/panache/theres-no-god-no-one-directs-our-fate-says-stephen-hawking-in-final-book/articleshow/66273272.cms.

Chapter 9

1. Submitted by Rose Mattix, Decatur, Illinois, *Reader's Digest.*

Chapter 11

1. Dallas Willard, *Renovation of the Heart: Putting On the Character of Christ* (NavPress, 2002).

ABOUT THE AUTHOR

Emerson Eggerichs, PhD, is an internationally known communication expert and author of the *New York Times* bestseller *Love & Respect.* Just as Dr. Eggerichs transformed millions of marital relationships with a biblical understanding of love and respect, he also turned these principles to one of the most important relationships of all in *Mother & Son: The Respect Effect.* As a communication expert, Eggerichs has also spoken to groups such as the NFL, NBA, PGA, US Navy SEALs, and members of Congress. He was the senior pastor of Trinity Church in East Lansing, Michigan, for almost twenty years. Eggerichs holds a PhD in child and family ecology from Michigan State University, a BA in biblical studies from Wheaton College, an MA in communications from Wheaton College Graduate School, and an MDiv from the University of Dubuque Theological Seminary. He and his wife, Sarah, have been married since 1973 and have three adult children.